OFFICIAL
PREPARATION MATERIAL

Cambridge English

Objective
Advanced

Student's Book
with answers

Felicity O'Dell   Annie Broadhead

Fourth Edition

Cambridge University Press
www.cambridge.org/elt

Cambridge English Language Assessment
www.cambridgeenglish.org

Information on this title: www.cambridge.org/9781107657557

First edition © Cambridge University Press 2002
Second edition © Cambridge University Press 2008
Third edition © Cambridge University Press 2012
Fourth edition © Cambridge University Press and UCLES 2014

First published 2002
Second edition 2008
Third edition 2012
Fourth edition 2014
4th printing 2015

Printed in Italy by L.E.G.O. S.p.A

A catalogue record for this publication is available from the British Library

ISBN 978-1-107-65755-7 Student's Book with answers with CD-ROM
ISBN 978-1-107-67438-7 Student's Book without answers with CD-ROM
ISBN 978-1-107-68145-3 Teacher's Book with Teacher's Resources CD-ROM
ISBN 978-1-107-64727-5 Class Audio CDs (2)
ISBN 978-1-107-68435-5 Workbook without answers with Audio CDs
ISBN 978 1-107-63202-8 Workbook with answers with Audio CDs
ISBN 978-1-107-69188-9 Student's Book Pack (Student's Book with answers with CD-ROM and Class Audios (2))
ISBN 978-1-107-63344-5 Interactive ebook: Student's Book with answers

Additional resources for this publication at www.cambridge.org/objectiveadvanced

Cover concept by Tim Elcock

Produced by Hart McLeod

Map of Objective Advanced Student's Book

TOPIC	EXAM PRACTICE	GRAMMAR	VOCABULARY
Unit 1 **Getting to know you** 10–13 People and places	Paper 4 Speaking: 1 Paper 3 Listening: 4	Conditionals	Describing people Collocations
Exam folder 1 14–15	Paper 1 Reading and Use of English: 1 Multiple-choice cloze		
Unit 2 **Living life to the full** 16–19 Hobbies and free time	Paper 2 Writing: 2 Paper 1 Reading and Use of English: 2	Dependent prepositions	Prepositional phrases
Writing folder 1 20–21	Informal and formal writing		
Unit 3 **In the public eye** 22–25 In the media	Paper 1 Reading and Use of English: 5	Wishes and regrets	Idioms (verb + *the* + object)
Exam folder 2 26–27	Paper 1 Reading and Use of English: 2 Open cloze		
Unit 4 **Acting on advice** 28–31 Giving advice	Paper 1 Reading and Use of English: 3	Modals and semi-modals (1)	Prefixes and suffixes
Writing folder 2 32–33	Formal writing		
Unit 5 **Dream jobs** 34–37 Jobs	Paper 2 Writing: 2 Paper 3 Listening: 2	Relative clauses	Connotation
Units 1–5 Revision 38–39			
Unit 6 **Connections** 40–43 Communications technology	Paper 1 Reading and Use of English: 6 and 8	Phrasal verbs (1)	Collocations with *have, do, make, take*
Exam folder 3 44–45	Paper 1 Reading and Use of English: 3 Word formation		
Unit 7 **A successful business** 46–49 Work and business	Paper 2 Writing: 2	Reason, result and purpose	Work and business collocations
Writing folder 3 50–51	Essays		
Unit 8 **Being inventive** 52–55 Inventions	Paper 4 Speaking	Modals and semi-modals (2)	Positive and negative adjectives
Exam folder 4 56–57	Paper 1 Reading and Use of English: 4 Key word transformation		

TOPIC	EXAM PRACTICE	GRAMMAR	VOCABULARY
Unit 9 **Urban living** 58–61 Modern cities	Paper 1 Reading and Use of English: 5 and 7	Future forms	Collocations to describe cities
Writing folder 4 62–63	Reports		
Unit 10 **You live and learn** 64–67 Further study	Paper 1 Reading and Use of English: 6 Paper 2 Writing Paper 4 Speaking: 2	Participle clauses	Word formation
Units 6–10 Revision 68–69			
Unit 11 **Fashion statements** 70–73 Fashion	Paper 3 Listening: 2 Paper 4 Speaking: 2	Reported speech	Fashion
Exam folder 5 74–75	Paper 1 Reading and Use of English: 5 Multiple choice		
Unit 12 **Making decisions** 76–79 Decisions	Paper 3 Listening: 2 Paper 4 Speaking: 3	-*ing* forms	Fixed phrases and collocations
Writing folder 5 80–81	Letters / emails		
Unit 13 **Colour** 82–85 Colours	Paper 3 Listening: 2	Past tenses and the present perfect	Noun and verb forms Adjective order
Exam folder 6 86–87	Paper 1 Reading and Use of English: 6 Cross-text multiple matching		
Unit 14 **Language** 88–91 Human communication	Paper 3 Listening: 3 Paper 3 Listening: 2 Paper 1 Reading and Use of English: 3 and 5	The passive	Word formation
Writing folder 6 92–93	Essays (2)		
Unit 15 **In my view ...** 94–97 Family life	Paper 1 Reading and Use of English: 5 Paper 4 Speaking: 3 Paper 3 Listening: 4	The infinitive	Expressing opinions
Units 11–15 Revision 98–99			
Unit 16 **Who we are** 100–103 The human body	Paper 1 Reading and Use of English: 5	Inversion	Idioms of the body
Exam folder 7 104–105	Paper 1 Reading and Use of English: 7 Gapped text		

Acknowledgements

The authors and publishers acknowledge the following sources of copyright material and are grateful for the permissions granted. While every effort has been made, it has not always been possible to identify the sources of all the material used, or to trace all copyright holders. If any omissions are brought to our notice, we will be happy to include the appropriate acknowledgements on reprinting.

The publisher has used its best endeavours to ensure that the URLs for external websites referred to in this book are correct and active at the time of going to press. However, the publisher has no responsibility for the websites and can make no guarantee that a site will remain live or that the content is or will remain appropriate.

Texts

Text on p. 18 adapted from 'Social Networking Tip: The Pros and Cons of Social Networking Sites' by JJC13, 2009. http://hubpages.com/hub/Pros-and-Cons-of-Social-Networking-Sites; CBS News for the text on p. 23 from 'Michelle Obama on love, family and politics' by Katie Couric, *CBS Evening News*, 18.06.09. Copyright © CBS News Archive; Cambridge University Press for the text on p. 27 adapted from *The Cambridge Encyclopedia of the English Language* by David Crystal. Copyright © 1995 Cambridge University Press; Art Markman for the text on p. 29 adapted from 'What is the best way to give advice?' by Art Markman, *Psychology Today*, 16.04.10. Reproduced by kind permission of Art Markman; NI Syndication Limited for the text on p. 37 adapted from 'Our young face watched by 1000 million eyes' *The Times*, 21.04.00; for the text on p. 45 adapted from 'Nowhere Man' by Sarah Sims *The Times* 11.03.00; for the text on p. 70 adapted from 'Talking clothes get our measure' by Paul Nuki, *The Sunday Times*, 22.03.99; for the text on p. 95 adapted from 'What these kids need is discipline' by Ann McFerran, *The Times*, 22.08.99. Copyright © NI Syndication Limited; Jennifer Beaumont and Alison MacDiarmid for the text on p. 38 adapted from 'Valuing New Zealand's marine environment' by Jennifer Beaumont and Alison MacDiarmid, NIWA. Reproduced by kind permission of Jennifer Beaumont and Alison MacDiarmid; MoneyWeek Limited for the text on p. 39 adapted from 'Catherine Cook: the brainwave that made me $10m by the age of 18' by Jodie Clarke, MoneyWeek, 26.09.08. www.moneyweek.com. Copyright © 2008 *MoneyWeek* Limited; Daily Mail for the text on pp. 42–43 adapted from 'Did we really believe in the joy of text?' by Craig Brown, *Daily Mail*, 1.4.10; for the text on p. 99 adapted from 'The $25,000 Levis' by David Gardner, *Daily Mail*, 16.05.01; for the text on p. 112 adapted from 'Men lie six times a day and twice as often as women, study finds,' *Daily Mail*, 14.09.09; for the text on p. 149 adapted from 'Binging on chocolate makes trousers too tight' by Paul Kendall, *Daily Mail*, 23.04.00. Copyright © Daily Mail; Crimson Business for the text on p. 46 adapted from 'Dominic McVey - The entrepreneurial whizz-kid talks to Startups.co.uk about his amazing rise to success' *Startups*, 11.08.04. Reproduced with permission; Patently Absurd! for the text on p. 52 from Patently Absurd! www.patentlyabsurd.org.uk. Reproduced with permission; Telegraph Media Group Limited for the text on p. 68 adapted from 'When the office is your best bet' by Tom Standage, *The Telegraph*, 01.10.96; for the text on p. 104 adapted from 'Look on the bright side' by Harry Wallop, *The Telegraph*, 05.07.03; for the text p. 129 adapted from 'Is honesty the best policy?' by Thea Jourdan, *The Telegraph*, 17.10.00. Copyright © Telegraph Media Group Limited; Desso for the text on p. 82 adapted from 'The psychology of color at retail' by Patricia Beks, Retail Customer Service, 20.03.09. Reproduced with permission; Van Gogh Gallery for the text on pp. 86–87 adapted from 'Vincent van Gogh: sunflowers, a brief understanding of sunflower paintings,' Van Gogh Gallery. Reproduced with permission; Listening exercise on p. 88 from 'Evolutionary factors of language' http://www.ling.lancs.ac.uk/monkey/the/linguistics/LECTURE4/4evo.htm reprinted with permission; Guardian News & Media Ltd for the text on p. 99 adapted from 'Why teenagers can't concentrate: too much grey matter' by Amelia Hill, *The Guardian*, 31.05.10; for the text on p. 128 adapted from 'Art's masters draw the queues' by Maev Kennedy, *The Guardian*, 09.02.01; for the text on p. 151 adapted from 'Beaten by a tomato, but I still loved the world and it loved me' by David Munk, *The Guardian*, 23.04.01; for the text on p. 156 adapted from 'Sucker for soccer: Octopus predicts World Cup finalist' by Mark Tran, *The Guardian*, 07.07.10. Copyright © Guardian News & Media Ltd 2001, 2010; Random House Group and Bill Bryson for the listening exercise and text on p. 101 extract from *A Short History of Nearly Everything* by Bill Bryson. Copyright © 2004 by Bill Bryson. Reprinted by permission of Bill Bryson and Random House Group. All rights reserved; James Berardinelli for the text on p. 107 adapted from 'Casablanca, a film review' by James Berardinelli, *Reel Reviews*. Reproduced with kind permission by James Berardinelli; TechMediaNetwork Inc. for the text on p. 113 adapted from 'Difficult to Deceive?' by Denise Show, *Live Science*, 31.05.13. Copyright © TechMediaNetwork, Inc 2013; Text A on p. 125 adapted from 'Food is of Key Importance in a Sustainable Society' by Lena Strålsjö, *Sustainability Journal*, January 2009; Hwei Li Chang for text B on p. 125 adapted from *Food in Chinese Culture: Anthropological and Historical Perspectives*, edited by K.C. Chang, published by Yale University Press, 1977. Reprinted with kind permission of Hwei Li Chang; David Hayden for text C on p. 125 adapted from 'The Importance of Food Science,' FarmingAmerica.org, 18.11.10. Reproduced with kind permission of David Hayden; Text D on p. 125 adapted from 'The Importance of Securing Global Food Supply,' European Crop Protection Association, 26.04.12. Reproduced with permission of The Henry Jackson Society; The River Group for the listening exercise on p. 130 from 'Treasure Island,' *Flightbookers, Travelling and Freestyle Magazine*, Autumn 2000. Reproduced with permission; Summersdale for the text on pp. 130–131 extracts from *Running a Hotel on the Roof of the World* by Alec Le Sueur, published by Summersdale. Reproduced with permission; Climatadata.info for the graph on p. 136 'Comparison of temperature estimates'. www.climatedate.info. Reproduced with permission; New Scientist for the text on p. 136 adapted from 'What's the weather' *New Scientist*, 16.09.00. Copyright © 2000 Reed Business Information UK. All rights reserved. Distributed by Tribune Media Services.

Photos

p. 10: wavebreakmedia/Shutterstock; p. 10-11: Rex Features/Blend Images; p. 11: bikeriderlondon/Shutterstock; p. 12: PT Images/Shutterstock; p. 13 (a): Hemera/Thinkstock; (b): Paul Miles/Axiom Photographic/Newscom; (C): © Charles O. Cecil/Alamy; (d): © Ian M Butterfield (Tunisia)/Alamy; (e): © Jack Sullivan/Alamy; p. 16 (L): Axiom Photographic/Design Pics/SuperStock; (R): Rex Features/Image Source; p. 19 (L): Beyond/SuperStock; (R): poco_bw/Fotolia; p. 22: © Keith Erskine/Alamy; p. 23: Rex Features/Pete Souza; p. 24: Jupiterimages/Thinkstock; p. 26: Rex Features; p. 28 (students): Rex Features/David Oxberry/Mood Board; (flight attendant): © Antonio Saba/Corbis; (weight training): Stockbyte/Thinkstock; (confused man): © MBI/Alamy; p. 31: Syda Productions/Shutterstock; p. 34 (T): Hero Images/Getty Images; (C): Cusp/SuperStock; (B): Rex Features/Caiaimage; p. 35: wilar/Shutterstock; p. 37: Rex Features/Caiaimage; p. 38: age fotostock/SuperStock; p. 39: Christopher Futcher/Thinkstock; p. 40 (L): Rex Features/Courtesy Everett Collection; (R): Neil Farrin/The Image Bank/Getty Images; p. 41 (L): Hubert Moal/AWL Images/Getty Images; (R): Dean Drobot/Shutterstock; p. 43 (T): JEROME FAVRE/EPA/Newscom; (C): Rex Features/Sipa Press; (B): Fancy Collection/SuperStock; p. 46: Rex Features; p. 47: Monkey Business Images/Shutterstock; p. 48: AVAVA/Shutterstock; p. 49 (T): iStockphoto.com/craftvision; (C): © John McKenna/Alamy; (B): withGod/Shutterstock; p. 53 (dishwasher): part/Shutterstock; (wifi): amasterphotographer/Shutterstock; (bread): Sergey Peterman/Shutterstock; (biro): Lipik/Shutterstock; (video recorder): You Touch Pix of EuToch/Shutterstock; (mouse): iStockPhoto.com/Jonas_; (personal stereo): Wasan Srisawat/Shutterstock; (toaster): Les Scholz/Shutterstock; (wristwatch): Ozaiachin/Shutterstock; (ring-pull can): Olinchuk/Shutterstock; p. 43 (a): Chuck Rausin/Shutterstock; (b): scyther5/Shutterstock; (c): Maxx-Studio/Shutterstock;
(d): ericlefrancais/Shutterstock; (e): Neamov/Shutterstock; (f): CHROMORANGE/M. Weber/picture alliance/Newscom; p. 58 (T): Nils Z/Shutterstock; (B): leoks/Shutterstock; p. 58 (C) & p. 59 (T): leungchopan/Shutterstock; p. 60 (Kuala Lumpur): © Steve Thomas/Alamy; (Dubai): Shahid Ali Khan/Shutterstock; (Delhi): CatchaSnap/Shutterstock; (Bangkok): Gavin Hellier/Robert Harding/Newscom; p. 61: Andre Kohls/imagebrok/imagebroker.net/SuperStock; p. 64: Monkey Business Images/Shutterstock; p. 65 (L): wavebreakmedia/Shutterstock; (R): © Chris Pearsall/Alamy; p. 69: Rex Features/Sipa Press; p. 73 (a): Valeriy Lebedev/Shutterstock; (b): Monkey Business Images/Shutterstock; (c): Rex Features/Sipa Press; p. 75: Christopher Artell/Geisler-Fotop/picture alliance/Newscom; p. 76 (dice): Pertusinas/Shutterstock; (signs): Rtimages/Shutterstock; (man at fork): Blend Images/SuperStock; p. 77: keko64/Shutterstock; p. 78: Adam Gregor/Shutterstock; p. 80: © Lee Martin/Alamy; p. 83 (both images): Robyn Mackenzie/Shutterstock; p. 85 (T): MARCELODLT/Shutterstock; (C): hxdbzxy/Shutterstock; (B): ariadna de raadt/Shutterstock; p. 86: Zadorozhnyi Viktor/Shutterstock; p. 88 (L): michaeljung/Shutterstock; (baby and book): Chepko Danil Vitalevich/Shutterstock; (baby and tablet): victorsaboya/Shutterstock; p. 94 (a): Rex Features/Paul Brown; (b): Rex Features/Image Source; (c): Rex Features/Leah Warkentin/Design Pics Inc.; (d): Jupiterimages/Thinkstock; p. 95: © Design Pics Inc./Alamy; p. 97: © J Marshall - Tribaleye Images/Alamy; p. 98: Rex Features/Monkey Business Images; p. 99: Image Courtesy of The Advertising Archives; p. 100–101 (cells): Rex Features/DEA PICTURE LIBRARY/UIG; p. 101 (microscope a): Tetra Images Tetra Images/Newscom; (microscope b): Science and Society/SuperStock; p. 103: © Golden Pixels LLC/Alamy; p. 104: Krzysztof Kostrubiec/Shutterstock; p. 106: Courtesy of Base Backpackers; p. 107 (Casablanca): Warner Bros/Ronald Grant Archive; p. 109 (a): Ronald Grant Archive; (b): LucasFilm/Ronald Grant Archive; (c): Rex Features/c.Dreamworks/Everett; (d): MOSFILM/THE KOBAL COLLECTION; p. 110: TWENTIETH CENTURY-FOX FILM CORPORATION/THE KOBAL COLLECTION; p. 112 (L): Tony Anderson/The Image Bank/Getty Images; (C): Jiang Jin/SuperStock; (R): © Picture Partners/Alamy; p. 113: Blaj Gabriel/Shutterstock; p. 115: Photobank gallery/Shutterstock; p. 116: Rex Features/Courtesy Everett Collection; p. 118: ginosphotos/iStock/Thinkstock/Getty Images; p. 119: Diego Cervo/Shutterstock; p. 121: iStockPhoto.com/MychkoAlezander; p. 124 (yin-yang): Sarun T/Shutterstock; (woman eating hamburger): © Peet Simard/Corbis; (people in desert): © Jason Florio/Corbis; (lettuce): © Cephas Picture Library/Alamy; p. 127: Chris Hondros/Getty Images; p. 128: © Emely/Corbis; p. 21 (L): frantisekhojdysz/Shutterstock; (C): Pete Niesen/Shutterstock; (R): Ron Chapple/The Image Bank/Getty Images; p. 131 (T): China Tourism Press/The Image Bank/Getty Images; (B): © Roger Cracknell 14/Asia/Alamy; p. 132: Manamana/Shutterstock; p. 133 (L): irakite/Thinkstock; (R): SGM Stock Connection USA/Newscom; p. 136: Jacqueline Larma/AP/Press Association Images; p. 137 (T): Rex Features/James D. Morgan; (C): Rex Features/KPA/Zuma; (B): Rex Features/KPA/Zuma; p. 138 (T & B): Clover/SuperStock; p. 139: © Hinrich Baesemann/dpa/Corbis; p. 144: © i love images/Alamy; p. 145: Vladru/Shutterstock; p. 146 (a): Jakub Cejpek/Shutterstock; (b): Glow Images/SuperStock; (c): Monkey Business/Fotolia; p. 147 (T): Rex Features/Blend Images; (C): Monkey Business Images/Shutterstock; (B): Vitalii Nesterchuk/Shutterstock; p. 148 (T): © geogphoto/Alamy; (B): © Chris Batson/Alamy; p. 149: Digital Vision/Photodisc/Thinkstock/Getty Images; p. 150 (T): Jonathan Hayward/The Canadian Press/Press Association Images; (B): © STRINGER/BANGLADESH/Reuters/Corbis; p. 154 (violinist): Ryan McVay/Thinkstock; (dolphins): David Schrader/Thinkstock; (classroom): © Andrew Fox/Alamy; (researcher): Biosphoto/SuperStock; p. 155: Mary Evans Picture Library; p. 156: Rex Features/Sipa Press; p. 159: iStockPhoto.com/skynesher; p. 160 (L): © Peter Horree/Alamy; (R): © Patrick Batchelder/Alamy; p. 161 (L): Mark Williamson/Photolibrary/Getty Images; (R): © Universal Images Group Limited/Alamy.

Illustrations by Paul Williams/Sylvie Poggio

Picture research by the Bill Smith Group, Inc

Recordings by Leon Chambers at The Soundhouse Ltd Recording Studios

Content of Cambridge English: Advanced

Cambridge English: Advanced, also known as Certificate in Advanced English (CAE) consists of four papers. It is not necessary to pass all four papers in order to pass the examination. There are three passing grades: A, B, C. As well as being told your grade, you will also be given a statement of your results which shows a graphical profile of your performance on each paper.

Extended certification

Cambridge English: Advanced is set at Level C1 of the Common European Framework of Reference for Languages (CEFR). Extended certification can give you additional credit for the language skills you demonstrate in the exam. It works in two ways.

- If you perform particularly well, you can get credit at a higher level on the CEFR. If you get grade A in the exam, you receive a certificate indicating that you are at C2 level.
- You can also receive credit for your English language skills, even if you do not achieve a passing grade. So if you do not get enough marks for a grade C in the exam, you can still be awarded a certificate showing performance at level B2 if you show this level of ability in the exam.

Results	CEFR Level
Grade A	C2
Grades B and C	C1
B2 level	B2

Paper 1 Reading and Use of English 1 hour 30 minutes

There are eight parts to this paper and they are always in the same order. Parts 1–4 contain texts with accompanying grammar and vocabulary tasks. Parts 5–8 contain a range of texts and accompanying reading comprehension tasks. The texts used are from newspapers, magazines, journals, books, leaflets, brochures, etc.

Part	Task Type	Number of Questions	Task Format	Objective Exam Folder
1	Multiple-choice cloze	8	A text with eight gaps, each with four options. This mainly tests vocabulary: idioms, collocations, fixed phrases, etc.	1 (14–15)
2	Open cloze	8	A text with eight gaps which must be filled with one word each.	2 (26–27)
3	Word formation	8	A text with eight gaps. Each gap corresponds to a word. The stems of the missing words are given and must be changed to form the missing word.	3 (44–45)
4	Key word transformation	6	Six questions, each with a gapped sentence which must be completed in three to six words, including a given key word.	4 (56–57)
5	Multiple choice	6	A reading text followed by multiple-choice questions.	5 (74–75)
6	Cross-text multiple matching	4	Four short texts, followed by multiple-matching questions. You must read across texts to match a prompt to elements in the texts.	6 (86–87)
7	Gapped text	6	A text with missing paragraphs. You must use the missing extracts to complete the text.	7 (104–105)
8	Multiple matching	10	A text (or several short texts) with multiple-matching questions.	8 (116–117)

Paper 2 Writing 1 hour 30 minutes

There are two parts to this paper. Part 1 is compulsory and you have to answer it in 220–260 words. In Part 2 there is a choice of tasks. You must write an answer of 220–260 words to one of these tasks.

Part	Task Type	Number of Tasks	Task Format	Objective Writing Folder
1	essay	1	You have to write an essay based on two points in given information. You need to decide which of the two points is more important, and to explain why.	**2** Formal writing (32–33) **3** Essays (50–51) **6** Essays (2) (92–93) **9** Persuasive writing (140–141) **10** The Writing Paper: general guidance (152–15**3**)
2	report review letter / email proposal	Choose 1 from a choice of tasks.	You are given a choice of tasks which specify the type of text you have to write, your purpose for writing and the person or people you have to write for.	**1** Formal and informal writing (20–21) **2** Formal writing (32–33) **4** Reports (62–63) **5** Letters / emails (80–81) **7** Reviews (110–111) **8** Proposals (122–123) **9** Persuasive writing (140–141) **10** The Writing Paper: general guidance (152–153)

Paper 3 Listening approximately 40 minutes

There are four parts to this paper. All the recordings are heard twice. The recordings are set in a variety of situations. In some parts you hear just one speaker; in others more than one speaker.

Part	Task Type	Number of Questions	Task Format	Objective Exam Folder
1	Multiple choice	6	You hear three short extracts and have to answer two multiple-choice questions on each. Each question has three options, A, B and C.	**9** (134–135)
2	Sentence completion	8	You hear a recording and have to write a word or short phrase to complete sentences.	**9** (134–135)
3	Multiple choice	6	You hear a recording and have to answer multiple-choice questions with four options.	**9** (134–135)
4	Multiple matching	10	You hear five short extracts. There are two matching tasks focusing on the gist and the main points of what is said, the attitude of the speakers and the context in which they are speaking, etc.	**9** (134–135)

Paper 4 Speaking 15 minutes

There are four parts to this paper. There are usually two of you taking the examination together and two examiners. This paper tests your grammar and vocabulary, interactive communication, pronunciation and how you link your ideas.

Part	Task Type	Time	Task Format	Objective Exam Folder
1	Three-way conversation between two students and one of the examiners	2 minutes	The examiner asks you both some questions about yourself and your interests and experiences.	**10** (146–147)
2	Individual 'long turn' with brief response from partner	4 minutes	You are each given some visual and written prompts and the examiner will ask you to talk about these for about a minute. You are asked to give a short response after your partner has finished their 'long turn'.	**10** (146–147)
3	Collaborative task	4 minutes	You are given some spoken instructions and written stimuli for a discussion or decision-making task and you discuss these prompts with your partner.	**10** (146–147)
4	Three-way interaction between students and one of the examiners	5 minutes	The examiner asks you and your partner questions relating to topics arising from Part 3.	**10** (146–147)

1 Getting to know you

Speaking

1 Work with a partner and discuss this question. Do you find it easy to get to know other people?

2 Decide which five of these questions would be useful to ask if you wanted to get to know someone. Give reasons by discussing what you think the answers would reveal.

1 What would be your ideal way to spend a weekend?
2 Do you prefer to work or study on your own, or with other people?
3 How important is it for you to keep up with the news?
4 Would you ever do an extreme sport, such as bungee jumping?
5 Which is your favourite meal of the day? Why?
6 Do you make detailed plans for your future, or do you just wait and see what happens?
7 What's the first thing you notice about people when you meet them for the first time?
8 What's the furthest you've ever been from home?

3 Work with a different partner. Ask and answer the five questions you chose. Discuss what you think the answers revealed.

4 Look at the photos. What is your first impression of each person?

🔽 Exam spot

In Part 1 of Paper 4 (the Speaking test), you have about two minutes to answer questions about yourselves (where you come from, your leisure activities, etc.). Use a range of grammar and vocabulary, as well as clear pronunciation.

In Part 2, you need to compare, describe and express opinions about two photos from a set of three. Phrases such as *You could say …*, *She seems …* and *I'd describe her as …* are useful for this.

Vocabulary

1 Complete these sentences with words from the box. There may be more than one possible answer.

> conscientious narrow-minded courageous
> unconventional competent down-to-earth
> outgoing decisive knowledgeable
> persuasive

1 She seems very *conscientious* and is obviously putting a lot of effort into her new job.
2 With two years' experience in the classroom, I'd say he's a very *competent / knowledgeable* teacher.
3 I think she'd make a great team leader because she's a *decisive* sort of person, whereas I find it hard to make up my mind.
4 It was a *courageous* decision to resign in protest at the company's pollution record.
5 I'd describe her as a *down-to-earth* sort of person with no pretensions.
6 One of his daughters is *outgoing* , while the other one is really shy – how strange!
7 To my mind, he has a very *unconventional* way of dressing – it's very creative.
8 You could say they display the typical, *narrow-minded* attitudes of small communities.
9 She gave a very *persuasive* speech about the need for more funding.
10 If she's an international lawyer, then she needs to be very *competent* in her job.

2 🔊 **1 01** Listen and check your answers. Mark the stress on each word in the box (e.g. conscientious).

3 Work in pairs. Use the adjectives from exercise 1 to talk about the people in the photos.

3 Work with a partner. How could you rephrase these sentences using structures from the table?

1 Should you have any problems, I will be available to help. *if you have any problems*

2 Had it not been for Jane, the manager would have got the wrong impression of me. *if it weren't for / had not been for Jane*

3 I'll keep my real opinion to myself if it makes the situation easier.

Conditionals

1 Look at these examples of conditional sentences. What are the grammatical differences? Which one seems more 'real'?

If she's an international lawyer, then she needs to be very knowledgeable in her job.

What would be your ideal way to spend a weekend?

2 Complete the table about the four basic types of conditional.

Type	Tense – *if* clause	Tense – main clause	Use for ...
zero	present simple or continuous	present simple or continuous	*common stable events*
first	*present simple*	*continuous (will)*	*possible future*
second	past simple or continuous	*would could should might*	hypothetical situations
third	*past perfect*	*would have* + past participle	*hypothetical past situations*

4 Complete the sentences using words from the box.

| given if so unless otherwise provided |

1 He might be lonely. ___*If so*___ , I suggest he joins a sports club.

2 Let's take a taxi to the party, ___*otherwise*___ we'll be late.

3 ___*Given*___ he increase in social-networking, it's easier to keep in touch with people.

4 I won't go ___*unless*___ you come with me.

5 ___*provided*___ that you follow this advice, you'll do well in your new college.

 Corpus spot

Be careful with *given* and *provided*. The *Cambridge English Corpus* shows exam candidates often mistake these.

*The tour wasn't as pleasant as we thought it would be, **given** that the coach broke down on the way.*

NOT ~~The tour wasn't as pleasant as we thought it would be, provided that the coach broke down on the way.~~

G→ page 162

Culture shock

Posted by Joy: Today 10.12 am

Today marks exactly one year since I came to London! When I made the decision to leave Singapore, it was incredibly exciting. Soon, though, I had to face the challenge of experiencing a different way of life. It hasn't always been easy, living on (literally) the other side of the world. I guess I shouldn't be surprised that people who have grown up in different places have different ways of behaving, thinking and expressing themselves.

Before I set off on my adventure, I had certain images of English people: polite, serious people, always drinking tea, obsessed with the weather … These things aren't exactly false, but they're only the tip of the iceberg. I soon realised that people's behaviour wasn't always consistent with my preconceptions.

Let's start with the things I love. London is a big, bustling, cosmopolitan city. So, in that respect, things weren't totally new for me. There are lots of things to do all year round and I can go to museums, musicals and plays whenever I want. Also, because of where London is, I can easily just pop over to Paris or Brussels for a weekend getaway.

But after going through the 'tourist phase' of finding everything completely new and exciting, more and more things started to surprise me. I discovered the 'iceberg' hidden under the water and started to gain some insight into British culture. For example, some of the TV programmes and newspapers were a bit of a shock. Sometimes it seems that, in the media, anything goes. The English sense of humour is really interesting, too. A lot of the time, it's really self-deprecating humour. Sometimes it can be quite obvious and crude (and not at all polite). At other times, you don't really know if they're being sarcastic or being serious. It took me a while to get used to that, and read between the lines. But it helped to watch a lot of chat shows and comedies (English people love watching TV – in fact, that's what a lot of their conversation and cultural references are about). In fact these programmes are a rich source of information about the British and the British way of life.

All this got me thinking about culture – not just in England, but everywhere. It's like a kind of social glue, it holds society together. We learn about the culture of our own society in a very natural way as we grow up – it's the 'dos' and 'don'ts' about how we treat people, what is acceptable behaviour.

The aspects of culture you can see are based on those values and beliefs that you can't. It will take a long time to understand those deeply held values and beliefs, because you have to notice them slowly and work them out.

My advice to anyone going to a new country is this: don't be afraid to try out new things. That's the whole point of going and how you gain experience. But before you go, check out good websites for information about the place and get a good guidebook. When you're there, explore it as much as you can – get out and make friends with 'real' people! You'll find that the more you do, the more you'll gain confidence.

Reading

1 Work with a partner and discuss these questions.

1 Have you ever visited or lived in a foreign country? If so, what cultural differences did you notice?

2 What might a visitor to your country perceive to be the biggest cultural difference?

3 What is *culture shock*, do you think? Have you ever experienced this?

2 Read Joy's blog about living in London.

1 Why does she compare culture to an *iceberg*?

2 What is her final piece of advice to people going to live in another culture?

3 Work in small groups and discuss these questions.

1 What are the dangers of making general statements about national characteristics?

2 What generalisations are made about people from your country? Do you agree with them?

Vocabulary

↘ Vocabulary spot

It is important to know which words collocate (commonly go together). A good dictionary will tell you this. When you see or hear good examples of new collocations, make a note of them.

1 **The phrase *tip of the iceberg* is made from two nouns. Look at these other collocations from the blog. What types of word are they made from?**

  1 culture shock

  2 make a decision

  3 incredibly exciting

  4 acceptable behaviour

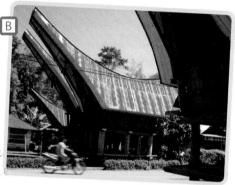

2 **Look at Joy's blog again. Find more collocations.** *gain insight / gain experience / gain confidence*

  1 three different words that collocate with *gain*

  2 three expressions using *way* or *ways* *sense of humor*

  3 two phrases with *humour* *self-deprecating humour*

  4 two nouns that follow *made* or *make*

  5 a phrase that collocates with *values* and *beliefs*

3 **Work with a partner. Discuss whether some personality types are more likely to suffer from culture shock than others.**

Listening

↘ Exam spot

In Part 4 of Paper 3 (the Listening test), you listen to five short monologues. There are two multiple-matching tasks with eight options each. You need to match the correct five.

1 🔊 **1 02 You will hear five short extracts in which speakers are talking about meeting new people. Listen and match each speaker with a photo (A–E).**

2 **Listen again. Match a speaker with a topic (A–H).**

Speaker 1
Speaker 2
Speaker 3
Speaker 4
Speaker 5

  A Testing friendships
  B Exchanging money
  C No way to get to know a lady
  D Sharing a passion
  E Business and pleasure
  F Strangers are not so strange
  G Friends for life
  H Sharing the environment

3 **Which speakers did you find most interesting? Why?**

Exam folder 1

Paper 1 Part 1

Multiple-choice cloze

In Part 1 of the Reading and Use of English test, you choose one word from a set of four (A, B, C or D) to fill a gap. The focus is on vocabulary, so you have to think about the meaning of the word and whether it collocates with another in the text. Sometimes, you have to check the word fits the grammatical context of the sentence and the text as a whole.

Below are some examples of the types of words that are tested in this part of the paper.

Collocations

All that was left for breakfast was some .... bread and tea.

A stale   **B** rotten   **C** sour   **D** rancid

The correct answer is A. We say *stale* bread, *rotten* fruit/vegetables/meat, *sour* milk and *rancid* butter.

Fixed expressions

I .... sight of an old friend when I went to the bank yesterday.

A saw   **B** caught   **C** set   **D** gained

The correct answer is B. The expression is *to catch sight of someone/something*.

Phrasal verbs

He intends to .... up a computer business with his brother.

A put   **B** lay   **C** get   **D** set

The correct answer is D – *to set up* means to establish a company/business.

Connecting words

He decided to go, ... his family begged him not to.

A although   **B** despite   **C** otherwise   **D** if

The correct answer is A. *Despite* would require the construction *despite his family begging him not to* or *despite the fact that his family begged him not to*. *Otherwise* means 'or else' and *if* does not make sense here.

Meaning

Emma fell down and .... her knee.

A skimmed   **B** grazed   **C** rubbed   **D** scrubbed

The correct answer is B. *Graze* means to break the surface of the skin by rubbing against something rough. *Skim* means to move quickly just above (a surface) without, or only occasionally, touching it. *Rub* means to press or be pressed against (something) with a circular or up-and-down repeated movement. *Scrub* means to rub something hard in order to clean it.

1 **For questions 1–8, read the text below and decide which answer (A, B, C or D) best fits each gap. There is an example at the beginning (0).**

Social-networking sites and personality

Social-networking sites are a great way to keep in touch with people and **(0)** .... *B* .... new friends. However, by using them, we also unintentionally **(1)** .... a lot about our personalities. These sites are increasingly being studied by psychologists to gain **(2)** ... *sight* .... into people's personalities.

After years of **(3)** ... *research* .... into how relationships in real life are formed, psychologists are finding that social-networking sites provide a rich **(4)** .... of useful data. It's possible to study **(5)** ... *complex* .... social-networks and communication patterns in new ways.

We no longer have to rely **(6)** .... on people reporting how they feel about each other. Messages and images on these sites act as open-ended stimuli that people react to in ways **(7)** .... with their personalities. Psychologists have found enough **(8)** .... to be able to confirm that extroverts post more messages and photos on social-networking sites than introverts. For example, introverts tend to read messages, but not respond to them.

EXAM ADVICE

- Read the title of the text – this will help you predict the main topic.
- Always read the whole text first, to understand the gist.
- Look carefully at the sentence where the gap is. Also, look carefully at the sentences before and after the gap.
- Make sure that the word you choose makes sense in the context of the text as a whole.
- Consider each alternative carefully, dismissing those which do not fit.
- Finally, read through what you have written, and see if it sounds right.

0	**A** build	**B** make	**C** cause	**D** design
1	**A** reveal	**B** give	**C** deliver	**D** exhibit
2	**A** vision	**B** insight	**C** intuition	**D** comprehension
3	**A** exploration	**B** testing	**C** trial	**D** research
4	**A** origin	**B** source	**C** heart	**D** core
5	**A** immense	**B** excessive	**C** complex	**D** incalculable
6	**A** solely	**B** merely	**C** barely	**D** uniquely
7	**A** constant	**B** reliable	**C** consistent	**D** stable
8	**A** assurance	**B** evidence	**C** basis	**D** foundation

Speaking

1 Work with a partner. Discuss these questions.

1 Do you like doing or learning new things or travelling to new places? Why? Why not?
2 To what extent does living your life to the full mean not being afraid to try new things?
3 What do you think of the idea of not watching TV, videos, etc. for a month and limiting your use of your phone and the internet to a maximum of an hour a day?
4 Describe four things you'd love to do (e.g. travel, write a novel, try a new sport).

2 Read the email. Then discuss these questions.

1 Who is Ms Bryant, and why is Amanda writing to her?
2 Is the email written in formal or informal language? Why?

Dear Ms Bryant,

Thank you for your email in which you confirm my place on the tennis coaching course starting 5th July.

I apologise for the delay in replying, but I have been sitting my final exams in Sports Psychology at university. As soon as my results are available, I will forward them to you. I am sure I will be able to **draw on the knowledge** that I have acquired at university during my course. *put into practice*

I am delighted that I have been assigned to the group *what I've* specialising in coaching 11–18-year-olds, as this is the *teams* age range I am particularly interested in. I believe in the importance of encouraging participation in sports especially for teenagers because this is a period in their lives when they **opt for** what I consider to be life choices. If a person engages in sport as a young person, they are more likely to continue to lead a healthy life in adulthood.

I wonder if I could ask a couple of questions. Is breakfast included in the fee we pay for campus accommodation?

Can I assume that as you have asked me to bring two tennis rackets and my sports kit, I will be provided with any extra equipment necessary for the course, such as a tennis ball cannon?

I very much look forward to taking part in the course.

Yours sincerely,

Amanda Forester

Writing

 Exam spot

In Part 2 of Paper 2 (the Writing test), you may be asked to write an email or a letter. It should be neutral or formal in style. Read the situation carefully and decide who you are writing to and why. Make sure you are consistent in your style of writing and that your purpose is clear.

1 **Read Amanda's email again.**

   1 It begins with *Dear Ms Bryant* and ends with *Yours sincerely, ...* . What other beginnings and endings can formal emails have?

   2 What do you notice about the type of vocabulary used? Give examples.

   3 Are contractions used? Why? Why not?

   4 What are the differences between formal and informal writing?

   5 Write a sentence summarising each paragraph.

2 **Read a friend's message. What is the problem with her letter?**

> As you know, I'm studying hotel management and as part of the course, we have to work in a hotel. I've got to write to the hotel where I'll be working to introduce myself. Could you have a look at what I've written so far? It's only the start of the letter. How can I change it to make it more formal?
>
> ---
>
> Dear Tom,
> I'm coming to your hotel for the month of August. It's part of my Management course at Branston College. My course is great fun and I've done lots of stuff on receptionist duties, customer care and some finance. I like customer care best and hope that I'll be able to learn a lot more about that at your hotel. I've worked in a restaurant before as a waitress but only as a holiday job when I was at school.

3 **Put the words in order to make sample phrases that could be used to make the message more formal.**

   1 Management / part / my / course ... / of / As

   2 subjects / as ... / course / such / covers / The

   3 Customer care / area / particularly / me. / is / that / interests / an

   4 be / to / my / of ... / I / hope / able / understanding / develop / to

   5 have / experience / some / waitress. / working / of / a / I / as

4 **You have found a summer job at a hotel. Write to the hotel, introducing yourself. Write 220–260 words.**

   • refer to your studies and experience
   • explain what you hope to learn from the job
   • ask questions about the hotel or your work

Dependent prepositions

1 **Look at these extracts. Then, underline more examples of dependent prepositions in Amanda's email.**

Thank you for your email in which you ...
I apologise for the delay in replying ...

2 **Complete the sentences with the missing prepositions.**

   1 Drawing ....on.... personal experience, I think it's much better to do a range of different sports instead of trying to perfect just one.

   2 Are the classes included ....in.... the cost of gym membership?

   3 Many people opt ....for.... adventure holidays these days because they want to get the most out of their free time.

   4 I'm looking forward ....to.... eating at the Mongolian restaurant because I've never eaten Mongolian food before.

   5 Max has completed the upper intermediate Russian course and has been assigned ....to.... the advanced class.

   6 I definitely believe ....in.... living life to the full.

   7 In her spare time, Jessica engages ....in.... volunteer work.

   8 We were provided ....with.... all the materials we needed on the painting course.

   9 When I've completed my business degree, I'm going to specialise ....in.... marketing.

   10 I won't be able to take part ....in.... the play because I'm going to be on holiday for most of August.

 Corpus spot

Be careful not to choose the wrong prepositions. The *Cambridge English Corpus* shows that exam candidates often do this.

*I saw a video that reminded me **of** old memories.*

NOT ~~I saw a video that reminded me for old memories.~~

Correct the mistakes in these sentences.
1 She is recovering of a bad illness.
2 I'm doing research in children's behaviour.
3 I like reading, so I have very good background knowledge on history and geography.
4 I wish I could travel back to time.
5 We put a lot of effort to organising the party.
6 I have the pleasure in inviting you to our presentation in July.

G → page 162

Reading

1 Read the article quickly. How does the internet help us live life to the full? How does it prevent us?

2 Complete gaps 1–16 with a preposition.

3 Work with a partner and discuss these questions.

   1 Think about how you use the internet. Which points in the article do you agree with most?

   2 In what ways does the internet help you live your life to the full?

Does the internet help us live life to the full?

I'm a great fan of the internet and all that it can offer. However, I feel I should reflect (1) __on__ the pros and cons of using it so much. I'd like to consider whether it really is helping people live their lives to the full or not.

Pros

Firstly, getting information on any subject is fast and easy. A simple online search provides us (2) __with__ information, teaches us about the world in general, or can help us plan a holiday. Secondly, many people choose to engage (3) __in__ a range of activities online because they want to let their friends and family know about all the exciting things that they are doing. And this appeals (4) __to__ people who want to live their life to the full and don't have enough time to write emails or letters to everyone in their circle of friends. Now, we can send messages or photos to hundreds of friends around the world in no time at all. This next point is tricky, but I choose to include it (5) __in__ the pros – it's online shopping. You can buy almost anything online as businesses increasingly opt (6) __for__ the internet as a means of promoting their products and services (7) __to__ the public. Some people blame the internet (8) __on__ the increase in the number of people getting into debt, but I'm not sure this is true.

Cons

There is serious concern about the increase (9) __in__ the amount of time people spend on their own in front of a screen. We should beware (10) __of__ letting time slip by without face-to-face contact with friends. People who devote an excessive amount of time (11) __to__ using their computer may risk feeling lonely and isolated. For some people, the internet has made it more difficult to tell the difference (12) __between__ work and leisure time. People can contact us at any time and any place. Not all employers comply (13) __with__ the terms of their employees' contracts, and expect them to be available to answer emails after normal working hours. Unfortunately, the internet has become associated (14) __with__ working more and having less free time. Although we are aware of this, it is almost impossible to shield ambitious employees completely (15) __from__ this negative aspect of the internet.

Knowing the pros and cons of the internet allows us to make better decisions about how to spend our time. And although I admit that those who campaign (16) __for__ a better work-life balance have a valid point, in my opinion, the internet helps us live our lives to the full more than it prevents it.

Exam spot

In Part 2 of Paper 1 (the Reading and Use of English test), you may have to complete a gap with a dependent preposition. Remember to look at the words immediately before and after the gap. Also, read the whole sentence containing the gap and the surrounding sentences to make sure you understand the meaning of the text.

Vocabulary

Vocabulary spot

Look at the prepositional phrases in these sentences.
- *This appeals to people who want to live their life **to the full**.*
- *We can send a message or photos to hundreds of friends around the world **in no time at all**.*

These phrases, which begin with a preposition, add extra information to the main part of the sentence. Prepositional phrases are often fixed, so you can learn them as one 'chunk'.

1 Complete these prepositional phrases. What do they mean? Use the context to help you.

by	by	at	for	in	on

1 I've started eating more healthily, and this __in__ turn has given me more energy to do exercise.

2 __By__ and large, it's been easy to adapt to my new lifestyle.

3 Everyone started talking all __at__ once.

4 Our plans to go on holiday are __on__ hold until we've saved up more money.

5 I found out __by__ chance that she's moved to Argentina.

6 Haven't you heard? He's gone to live abroad __for__ good.

Listening

1 Look at the photos of two students, Yolanda and Martin. Do you think they both live life to the full? What do you think are the typical hobbies and future hopes of young people like this?

2 **1▪03** Work in pairs. One of you listen to Yolanda and the other to Martin. Make notes on these questions.

    1 Where are you from?
    2 What languages have you studied?

3 **1▪04** Now listen to the next part and make notes on what Yolanda and Martin say about these topics.

    1 hobbies
    2 future hopes
    3 live or work abroad permanently?
    4 earliest memories of school

4 Do you have anything in common with either Yolanda or Martin?

Speaking

1 What do you think makes someone a good communicator?

2 In the recording, we heard Yolanda and Martin develop their answers by giving extra information. Work with a partner and discuss ways of developing the answers to these questions.

    1 What do you enjoy about where you live?
    2 Why are you studying English?
    3 What interesting things have you done lately?
    4 What are your plans for the future?

3 Work in groups of three.

- Student A, ask the questions in exercise 2 and another three general questions of your own. Make a note of whether or not the other students develop their answers with a main idea and extra information.
- Students B and C, develop your answers as fully as possible and make them interesting. Try to use a range of structures (e.g. present, past and future forms) and vocabulary.

4 Apart from a range of structures and vocabulary, what other features are important when speaking?

Yolanda

Martin

Writing folder 1

Formal and informal writing

1 **Work with a partner. Look at email extracts A–D. Answer the questions for each email.**

   1 Is it informal or formal?
   2 Who wrote it?
   3 Who was it written to and why?

2 **There are many set phrases which we can use in formal or neutral writing. Decide what the purpose is for each of these phrases, and whether they are formal or informal.**

   1 It was wonderful to read all your latest news. *referring back to a previous letter (informal)*
   2 With reference to your letter dated July 9th …
   3 I'm really sorry I've taken so long to get back to you but …
   4 We apologise for the delay in replying to your letter of October 9.
   5 Thanks for writing and telling me all about your plans for the summer holidays.
   6 I am extremely grateful for the advice you gave me concerning …
   7 It's really kind of you to invite me to the wedding and I'd love to come.
   8 Please do not hesitate to contact me should you need further information.

3 **Now think of two phrases, one informal and one formal, for each of these categories.**

- refusing an invitation
- congratulating
- giving your opinion
- giving advice

A Then for the last week, I'll have a holiday and I'm going to spend it in Prague. I've got a friend who went there last year and she said it's great – a beautiful city, really friendly people and lots to do. What could be better after my holiday job? I'll tell you all about it when I get back.

B

File Edit View Insert Format Tools Message Help

I apologise for the delay in replying to your email of October 6. However, I am pleased to confirm that you have been accepted on Module A503. You will receive an Information Pack, giving details of the course and your accommodation, within the next ten days.

C Email

Thanks for your email with all your latest news. It's a real shame you missed the party – it was great. You know that guy who goes to the sports club on Saturdays? Well, he was there – gorgeous or what! I got talking to him and he's just as nice as he looks. I hope you're feeling better now and …

D

Thank you for your application. Your film club membership is being processed. If you have already paid your membership fee, a receipt will be sent to you within 24 hours.

4 Here are some more examples of phrases from formal writing. Complete the words.

1 I w*ould* be g*rateful* if you c*ould* send me f*urther* information about …
2 Please could you a*cknowledge* r*eceipt* of this letter.
3 Please find my CV a*ttached* to this email.
4 I w*ould* very much a*ppreciate* an early r*esponse* to my letter.
5 I look f*orward* to h*earing* from you at your e*arliest* c*onvenience*

Corpus spot

The *Cambridge English Corpus* shows that advanced students often have problems with appropriate language. Formal writing often requires you to be firm, while remaining diplomatic.

Grade these sentences, which exam candidates have written, in accordance with the key. Then discuss ways in which you could improve some of them.

> ✓ firm and tactful
> ? might be OK but could be improved
> ✗ likely to antagonise the reader and needs to be improved

1 I must admit the level of service didn't live up to my expectations, so after a few days I became totally disinterested.
2 People may not be aware that breakfast is the main meal of the day and therefore they are stupid.
3 But the worst thing was your canteen. The food there was awful and disgusting, it could hardly be eaten.
4 Unfortunately, I was not quite satisfied with my job and the conditions of my employment were not appropriate.
5 I hope you treat this seriously and I want a refund for your overpriced tour.
6 As a resident of this town, I feel that some suggestions can help to avoid the problems mentioned above.
7 I am very grateful for your reply and for all your help.
8 I would be happy if you could ask your kids to be quieter.

---

5 Read this task carefully. Underline the most important points.

> **You have seen this notice in an international magazine.**
>
> We are running a series of articles on the importance of living life to the full.
>
> Readers are invited to write **a letter** to the magazine giving their opinions on this topic. We would like to hear why you think it is important to live life to the full, how best to achieve this aim and what in your opinion prevents some people from living life to the full.

6 Now start planning your letter with a partner. Discuss these points.

- content – What main points will you include?
- language – Which phrases are most appropriate?
- organisation – How can you organise the content into different paragraphs?
- connecting words – How will you link clauses, sentences and paragraphs?
- style
- the opening and closing of the letter

7 Write a first draft of the letter in 220–260 words. Then, exchange first drafts with another pair of students and check through it, using the information in the Exam advice box.

EXAM ADVICE

The purpose of your writing should be clear and it should have a positive effect on the reader. This is what the examiners are looking for. When you check through your writing, use the following checklist.

Have you …
- checked for errors?
- used language naturally?
- used a good range of vocabulary?
- checked the spelling?
- used a range of grammatical structures?
- fully completed the task?
- used a range of linkers?
- used an appropriate and consistent style?
- made sure no important information is left out?

3 In the public eye

Speaking

1 **Look at the magazine covers. Work with a partner and discuss these questions.**

1 What would you expect to read about in these magazines?
2 Which magazines or TV programmes do you know where famous people are interviewed? Do you like reading or watching interviews?
3 What sort of people make good guests on TV chat shows?
4 Why do you think famous people appear on chat shows or give interviews to magazines?
5 Who would you most like to interview? How would you approach the interview to encourage the person to give full and honest answers?

Reading

1 **Work with a partner. You are going to read an interview with Michelle Obama. What questions do you think will be asked?**

2 **Read the interview to check your ideas.**

3 **Choose the best answer for these questions.**

1 What did Michelle like about Barack as a friend?
   A He had a light-hearted attitude.
   B He talked a lot about his upbringing.
   C He laughed at her jokes.
2 How did she feel at first when he asked her out?
   A confused because it was unexpected
   B unsure whether it was the right thing to do
   C thrilled and accepted immediately
3 Where did they go on their first 'date'?
   A to a training session in a church
   B to a business seminar
   C to a talk by a lawyer
4 What impressed her when they first went out?
   A Barack gave his time to community projects.
   B He was an adaptable person.
   C He could explain complex ideas to ordinary people.

4 **Work in pairs and discuss these questions.**

1 Why does Michelle say *you don't want people to get caught up in emotion*?
2 What does she say about a leader of the US and the US people?

5 **Work with a new partner and discuss the questions.**

1 What do you think it's like to be the partner or spouse of a famous person?
2 What did you think of the way Michelle answered the interviewer's questions?
3 What other questions would you have asked if you had been the interviewer?

'Change isn't emotion. It's real work and organisation and strategy.'

Let me ask you about when you first met your husband. Before you were married, the two of you worked at a law firm together in Chicago. And I read when he first asked you out, you said, 'No, thank you,' not wanting to mix business with pleasure.

Right.

But then he invited you somewhere. And your view of him changed dramatically. Why was that? And what happened?

Well, we were friends from the start, because I was his advisor. And my job was to welcome him to the firm. I took him out to lunch. And immediately I liked him because he didn't take himself too seriously but he was very bright, had a very interesting background, just a good guy to talk to. You know, you could laugh easily with him. So I was, like, this is a friend.

But then he asked me out on a date. And I thought, 'Well, my advisee. Hmm, I don't think that looks right.' But he invited me to go to one of the churches because he had been a community organiser and worked on the far South Side with a group of churches. And he took me to a training session that he was giving. And there were mostly single-parent mothers, mostly African Americans on the South Side.

And in this training, he was talking about concepts like the world as it is and the world as it should be and how the job of ordinary people is to try to narrow the gap between those two ideas. And to see him transform himself from the guy who was a summer associate in a law firm with a suit and then to come into this church basement with folks who were like me, who grew up like me, who were challenged and struggling in ways that I never would, and to be able to take off that suit and tie and become a whole 'nother person and connect with people in the same way he had connected with folks in that firm, you don't see someone who can make that transition and do it comfortably and feel comfortable in his own skin and to touch people's hearts in the way that he did, because people connected with his message. And I knew then and there that there's something different about this guy. Because you see people who can live well in corporate America. They can wear that uniform well. They can't make the transition and vice versa. Barack lived comfortably in those two worlds.

And it was impressive. And his message was moving. I mean, it touched me.

It made me think differently about what I am doing with my life. And how am I adding to the notion of getting us to the world as it should be? Am I doing it in my law firm? You know? So he made me think in ways that I hadn't before.

And you were smitten after that?

I thought ... I could hang out with this guy. I was impressed. I really was.

You've seen the crowds, the way they embrace your husband. Some commentators have used the word 'messianic'. Do you ever wish that the whole thing, the whole movement, wasn't so over the top for some voters?

Barack and I talk about this all the time. We talked about it before the decision to run, because ... when you're really trying to make serious change, you don't want people to get caught up in emotion because change isn't emotion. It's real work and organisation and strategy – that's just the truth of it. I mean, you pull people in with inspiration, but then you have to roll up your sleeves and you've got to make sacrifices and you have got to have structure.

And you've gotta, you know, you have to have support and you have to have interests to move things forward. So we do think about that all the time.

I mean, that's one of the reasons why we try to laugh at ourselves to sort of keep all this excitement to a reasonable level. That's why I teased Barack about putting away the socks and, you know, making sure he's putting away the butter. It's not that, you know, I'm trying to ...

... emasculate him?

Exactly. The point is that Barack, like any leader, is human. And, you know, our challenge in this country isn't finding the next person who's gonna deliver us from our own evil. Because our challenges are us. The challenge that this country faces is how are we as individuals in this society gonna change? What are we gonna do differently?

Wishes and regrets

1 Look at this question from the interview. Then complete gaps 1–7 with the correct form of the verbs in brackets.

Do you ever wish that the whole thing wasn't so over the top?

1 Do you wish you ....*had met*.... (meet) me earlier?

2 I wish I .... (have) more time to spend with my family but I haven't.

3 I wish .... (inform) you of our decision.

4 If only that .... (be) true!

5 If only the photographers .... (give) us a bit more privacy.

6 I wish you .... (ask) such personal questions. I'm finding it embarrassing.

7 If only I .... (know) what it would be like before I started this job!

2 Look at this conversation and change *would rather* to *would prefer*. Make any other necessary changes.

A: Would you rather watch an interview with someone, or read it in a magazine?

B: Well, I think I'd rather see the person, because when they're asked an awkward question, you can see if they'd rather not answer it.

A: I don't like it when people ask awkward questions. For example, why did this interviewer ask about Michelle Obama's personal life?

B: You mean you'd rather she'd focused more on questions about politics?

3 Write the correct form of *start*.

1 It's time for us .... the interview.

2 It's time we .... the interview.

4 Complete this blog extract.

> Many people wish that magazines **(1)** .... (have) more in-depth interviews with real people. They always seem to focus on the same things – skeletons in the cupboard or a celebrity's love life. They would rather **(2)** .... (read) about people's beliefs, aims and ambitions. According to some, it is high time magazines **(3)** .... (wake up) to the fact that the general public has had enough of media invasion into people's privacy. If only I **(4)** .... (be born) with the necessary talent and expertise, I would start a magazine for the company where I work. It really is time for me **(5)** .... (do) something instead of complaining about other magazines.

5 Work with a partner and discuss your own wishes or regrets, and things you'd like to change.

G → page 163

Listening

1 **1 05** Listen to an interview with David Burns, a soap-opera actor. Tick the topics he mentions.

- school life
- hobbies
- a person who helped him
- fans
- his working relationship with a director
- his marriage
- his relationship with his parents
- his daughter
- his future acting roles

2 Listen again for expressions 1–10 below and mark them according to the key.

> ✓ = I know the meaning.
> ? = I'm not sure about the meaning.
> ✗ = I don't understand and can't guess the meaning from context.

1 the public eye   **6** playing villains

2 a bully   **7** an edgy person

3 snapped   **8** it can turn nasty

4 downward spiral   **9** obsessed

5 a tough upbringing   **10** hog the limelight

3 Find out the meaning of the phrases you marked **?** and **✗** from other students, your teacher, or a dictionary.

4 Work with a partner and discuss these questions.

1 How has David Burns had a troubled past?

2 Do you think childhood experiences affect people in later life?

Vocabulary

1 **Work with a partner and match verbs 1–6 with nouns a–f.**

1	to face	a	the issue
2	to address	b	the record straight
3	to fit	c	the difference
4	to put	d	the music
5	to tell	e	the best of both worlds
6	to have	f	the description

2 **Complete this article with the correct form of fixed phrases from exercise 1.**

Hollywood – truth and lies

One of the biggest names in Hollywood has written her biography in order to address some of the rumours about her teenage years. Her biography is extremely well written and includes more than enough detail to (1) .... If you read it, you will discover a different person from the one portrayed recently in the newspapers.

One recent tabloid article, supposedly (2) .... of her bad behaviour, said that she had run away from home at the age of 15 after making her parents angry. The article said she had lived on the streets for six months until she finally went home (3) .... However, as the biography makes clear, stories like these are greatly exaggerated. In fact, according to the film star's new book, many tabloids find it difficult (4) .... between fact and fiction.

3 **Which method of finding out the meaning of phrases do you prefer and why?**

- guessing
- looking them up in a dictionary
- asking classmates
- asking the teacher for an English paraphrase
- asking the teacher for a sentence using the phrase
- asking the teacher for a translation into your language

4 **Another form for fixed phrases is: prepositional phrase + *the* + noun. For example, *to be in the dark* (= to know nothing about something). Match phrases 1–5 to definitions a–e.**

1 to be over the hill
2 to be on the spot
3 to be in the running
4 to be up to the mark
5 to be under the weather

a to have a reasonable chance
b to feel ill
c to be considered too old
d to be as good as the usual standard
e to be at a place where an event is happening

Speaking

1 **Work with a partner and think of a famous person you both know. Role-play an interview.**

1 First, decide who you are going to play: the interviewer or the interviewee. Prepare some questions and answers, perhaps focusing on the interviewee's regrets and wishes. In the interview, you must not say who the famous person is because other students are going to guess.

2 Role-play the interview for the class. Can the other students guess who the famous person is?

3 As a class, decide which interviews you liked and why. Who do you think would make good interviewers?

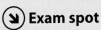

Exam folder 2

Paper 1 Part 2

Open cloze

In Part 2 of the Reading and Use of English test, you must complete a text by writing missing words in eight gaps. You can use only one word for each gap. The main focus is on grammar, so you have to think about structure and meaning to fill the gaps. Check whether the word fits the grammatical context of the sentence and the meaning of the text as a whole.

1 **Read these sentences and decide what kind of word might fit the gap (e.g. a verb, a preposition, etc.).**

1 Most celebrities love publicity. In ....._other_..... words, they like to be at the centre of attention.
2 Living in the city means we can enjoy many cultural events as well ...._as_........ take advantage of first-class sports facilities.
3 The cold, grey morning was far from welcoming and Janis pulled her coat tightly ....~~_around_~~.... _around / round_ her before she went outside.
4 Some people believe the only way to learn a language is to go to the country where it is spoken, ..._whereas_..... others recommend learning the basics at home first.
5 Our teacher used to give us a vocabulary test ...._every_....... single day of the week.
6 It was a period ....~~_____~~.... _which / that_ produced a true flourishing of the arts.
7 Jack was not sure ...._whether_..... he should answer the question or not.
8 Each classroom has ...._its_....... own display area, computer workstation and quiet corner.
9 Anne hadn't set ....~~_____~~.... _out_ to cause such a disturbance among her colleagues.
10 The problem ......~~_____~~_is_..... that John rarely meets deadlines.

2 **Now complete the sentences.**

3 **Work with a partner. Choose eight suitable words to gap in this text. As you do this, look back at exercise 1 and think about the type of words the exam is likely to test in this task.**

Dealing with press intrusion

Many famous people find themselves in the public eye as soon as they step out of their front door.

However, most celebrities have their own way of dealing with the paparazzi. One strategy can be to adopt a reserved personality. Some actors in particular say that this helps them ignore the photographers. Another strategy is to take on a victim mentality and simply to accept that there is nothing that can be done about the unwanted attention, so it is pointless getting upset about it. It should be seen as a part of the job.

However, some people who are related to famous people – members of the celebrity's family – may well have problems with having attention from the press. It may take years for them to get used to it. If they have a group of photographers following them around when they are trying to carry on with their normal daily life, it can be hard to block it out and pretend it is not happening.

4 Work with a different partner and compare the words you chose to gap. Discuss which words work best and why.

5 Work with a partner.

   1 Discuss what you understand by the title of the text below. What do you think you might read about?

   2 Give some examples of *jargon* and discuss when they might be useful and when they might cause problems.

   3 Read the whole text without filling in any of the gaps. Then discuss the main ideas it contains.

Jargon – the upside

The reality is that **(0)** ..... *everyone* ..... uses jargon. It is an essential part of the network of occupations and free-time activities which **(1)** .....m..k..s..... up society. All jobs have an element of jargon, which workers learn as **(2)** .....they..... develop their expertise. All hobbies require mastery of a specific jargon. What's more, each society grouping has **(3)** .....has its..... own jargon. And this phenomenon turns **(4)** .....out..... to be universal – and valuable. It is the jargon element which, in a job, can promote economy and precision of expression, and this helps make life easier **(5)** .....for..... the workers.

When we have learned to use it well, jargon is something we can readily take pleasure in, **(6)** .....which..... the subject is motorcycling, baseball or computers. It can add pace, variety and humour to speech. We enjoy the showing off which stems **(7)** .....from..... a fluent use of terminology, and we enjoy the in-jokes which a shared linguistic experience permits. In fact, we are often quick to criticise anyone who tries to be part of our group without **(8)** .....being..... prepared to take on its jargon.

6 Go through the text and decide which type of word could fit each gap. Check the sentences before and after the gap if you need clues.

7 Now think of the word which best fits each gap. Use only one word in each gap.

> **EXAM ADVICE**
>
> ● Remember, you must write only one word in each gap.
> ● You are never required to write a contraction (*it's*, *don't*, etc.). If you think the answer is a contraction, it must be wrong, so think again.
> ● Decide what type of word fits the gap (a preposition, a pronoun, etc.).
> ● Try to justify your answer grammatically by referring to the text.
> ● Check your spelling. Your spelling must be correct to get a mark.
> ● Try reading the sentence to yourself to check if it sounds right.
> ● Always write something. You never know – you might be lucky even if you are not sure of the answer!

4 Acting on advice

Listening

1 Have you ever been in situations like the ones in the photos? What happened? What problems did you have?

2 🔊1 06 Listen to someone giving instructions. In what situation would you expect to hear them?

3 Look at these examples from the listening. Which grammatical structures are used?

　1 Come into the room quietly.
　2 Can you look for your candidate number on the desk and sit there?

4 Listen again and note down similar examples that are used to give instructions. Which structure sounds more direct? Which structures sound more polite?

5 Work with a partner and discuss these questions.

　1 Think of situations where you were given instructions. What were they? Who gave them? Were they strict or polite? How did you feel about being given them?
　2 Think of situations where you gave instructions. What were they? Were you strict or polite? How did you feel about giving them? Were they followed?

Reading

1 Work with a partner and discuss these questions.

1 When did you last ask for (or give) advice?

2 How do you feel about asking for or giving advice?

3 What advice would you give to someone who wanted to improve their reading skills in English?

2 Work with a partner. Tick the topics that you would expect to read about in an article called 'What is the best way to give advice?'

1 an introduction to the topic of giving advice

2 an evaluation of different types of advice

3 a recommendation for the best way to give advice

4 an evaluation of the best sort of person to give advice

5 a calculation of how often people follow advice

6 an explanation of the possible consequences of giving the wrong type of advice

7 an explanation of why some people do not follow advice

3 Read the article and tick the topics in exercise 2 which are mentioned.

4 Discuss these questions.

1 Explain in your own words the difference between these two types of advice: *information* and *decision-making techniques.*

2 How much information are you given about the people who took part in the studies and what they had to do?

3 According to the article, what type of advice is best? Do you agree?

4 Have you ever felt that you lost a bit of independence when you followed someone's advice?

5 Do you think that, if you've made a decision about a situation in the past, it could help you make other decisions about the same or similar situations? Can you think of any examples?

What is the best way to give advice?

A lot of our daily conversations involve giving and getting advice. For example, you might be talking about new movies, and a friend recommends that you should go and see a particular one. Another friend wants to go to a Tex-Mex restaurant, and you recommend that they avoid one that just opened. Later, you mention that you are thinking about joining a new gym, and a friend points out that a new gym nearby offers free personal trainers some afternoons.

Are these kinds of advice effective? A paper by Reeshad Dalal and Silvia Bonaccio in a 2010 issue of *Organizational Behavior and Human Decision Processes* looked at several different kinds of advice that people give. They distinguished between four types of advice.

- **Advice for** is a recommendation to choose a particular option.

- **Advice against** is a recommendation to avoid a particular option.

- **Information** supplies a piece of information that the decision-maker might not know about.

- **Decision-making techniques** suggest how to go about making the choice, but do not make a specific recommendation. (For example, if you have a friend who wants to see a good movie, you might recommend a website that summarises movie reviews. You aren't recommending a particular movie, but you are suggesting a technique that allows your friend to make a decision.)

In the studies, college students had to imagine making a particular decision. They were given a variety of advice and they were asked how satisfying and useful the advice was for making the decision.

In general, people found all of the types of advice to be useful to some degree. However, **information** was the most useful kind of advice across the studies. That is, people found it most helpful when people told them something that they might not have known about already.

There are a few reasons why information is more valuable to people than other kinds of advice. First, when someone makes a recommendation for or against a particular option, a decision-maker may feel like they have lost a bit of their independence in making their choice. When the advice comes in the form of information, though, the decision-maker still feels like they have some autonomy. Second, information helps people to make decisions later, in similar situations. Finally, getting information makes people feel more confident in the decision they ultimately make. The information provides reasons for or against a particular option. There is a great deal of evidence that people feel better about decisions when they are able to give a reason for making the choice.

Modals and semi-modals (1)

1 Modals (e.g. *could*) and semi-modals (e.g. *need to*) tell us something about the attitude of the speaker. In these sentences, the modals are used for giving instructions and advice. What is the meaning behind each one?

1 You **might** want to try this website.
2 **Could** I ask for silence now?
3 You **must** make a decision before Monday.

2 Modal verbs can have other meanings. Match the modal verbs below to the meanings from the box.

> ability   negative certainty   making an offer instruction   permission   request theoretical possibility

1 **Can** this camera take panoramic shots?
2 **Could** I get you something to drink?
3 That **can't** be the answer. It doesn't fit.
4 **Would** you help me with this question?
5 You **should** go through the statistics while I phone the new customers.
6 The school **might** take 1,000 pupils.
7 You **can** park here, but only if you buy a ticket.

3 Work with a partner. Discuss the difference in use between the words in bold in each pair.

1 a I **could** get into the house by climbing through the window.
  b I **was able to** get into the house by climbing through the window.
2 a She **may** get here by 10 if she catches the 8.30 train.
  b **May** I use the office photocopier to make a copy of my passport?
3 a She **might** get here on time if she leaves work early.
  b **Might** I make a suggestion?
4 a I **must** remember to email Joanna.
  b We **have to** write 5,000 words for our project.
5 a You **need to** make three copies of this.
  b You **didn't need to** switch the TV off.
6 a You **needn't have** posted it; I could have picked it up later.
  b You **don't need to** show any ID to get in.

G → page 163

4 Prepare some instructions or advice.

1 Choose one of the situations below, or a situation of your own.
  • choosing a new phone
  • installing new software
  • following a healthy diet
  • making a study plan
  • staying calm when you're feeling stressed
  • learning new vocabulary
2 Think about who you are giving advice to, and how you want to sound. Use appropriate language (e.g. imperatives or modal verbs).

5 Modal verbs can also be used to speculate about things. Look at the pictures and discuss what happened to the people, what they are doing or what they might have done.

The man in picture A could have fallen into a river.

Listening

1 **When you phone a company, you often hear a set of instructions telling you what to do next. Discuss these questions.**

   1 How do you feel about hearing recorded instructions over the phone?

   2 Does it provide efficient customer service?

   3 Do you prefer speaking to real people? Why? / Why not?

2 **1 07 Listen to the instructions. What should you do in situations 1–6?**

Phoning your mobile-phone provider

   1 you want to top up the credit on your phone

   2 you want to change your tariff

Phoning a dentist

   3 you want to make an appointment for a check up

   4 you want to prove your identity or address

Phoning a bank

   5 you need to give your security code

   6 you want to check your balance

Vocabulary

⤵ Vocabulary spot

A prefix is a letter or group of letters added to the beginning of a word to make a new word.

A suffix is a letter or group of letters added to the end of a word to make a new word. Suffixes fall into two categories:

- those connected with the grammatical form of the word, for example, *-ly* (for an adverb) as in *carefully*, or *-ation* (for a noun) as in *recommendation*.
- those connected with meaning, for example, *-less* (meaning 'without') as in *careless*.

1 **Match the prefixes (*dis-*, *non-*, etc.) with the words. Sometimes there is more than one possible answer.**

dis- non- il- mis- im- un- in- ir-	appear avoidable lead logical mature accessible polite rational regular continue sensitive personal smoker literate trust conventional justified conclusive

2 **Complete these rules with *il-*, *im-*, or *ir-*.**

   1 We often use ....*im*.... before words beginning with *m* and *p*.

   2 We often use ....*il*.... before words beginning with *l*.

   3 We often use ....*ir*.... before words beginning with *r*.

⤵ Exam spot

In Part 3 of Paper 1 (the Reading and Use of English test), there is one short text with a total of eight gaps. You need to fill in the gaps with the correct form of the word given. This often means you have to add a prefix or suffix to the given word.

3 **Match the words to the suffixes. Sometimes there is more than one possible answer and you may have to change the spelling.**

photocopy count judge time efficient explore rude speech employ dramatise frequent argue aware recommend deceit care point respect tend rely	-able -ation -ency -ful -ly -less -ment -ness

Writing folder 2

Formal writing

> Written English tends to be more formal than spoken English. You will probably have to write neutral or formal English in the Writing test.

1 **These sentences have a similar meaning, but what is the difference?**

   1 Give us a ring soon.
   2 We look forward to hearing from you at your earliest convenience.

2 **Here are some of the types of writing that you may need to do in the Writing test. Tick the types of writing that you have already done in your own language.**

   1 an essay for a teacher
   2 a letter of complaint (e.g. to a newspaper)
   3 a proposal (e.g. for a town council on how public transportation could be improved)
   4 a report (e.g. for your manager)
   5 a review (e.g. for a newsletter)

3 **Work with a partner and discuss these pieces of advice relating to formal writing. If necessary, modify the pieces of advice to make them more appropriate.**

   1 Avoid verb contractions.
   2 Avoid phrasal verbs.
   3 Never use slang or colloquial expressions.
   4 Keep to formal layout conventions.
   5 It is particularly important in formal writing to make the structure of what you are saying totally clear.
   6 Use connecting words and phrases to help clarify the structure of your writing.

4 **It is important to choose words and phrases appropriate to the style you are writing in. Rewrite the sentences below, written by exam candidates, using language more appropriate for a formal style.**

   1 Moreover, we are content with your staff. Having kind and helpful personnel is important – people expect this kind of stuff.
   2 Lastly, I would like to say that the discount seems a bit smaller than the ten per cent originally promised.
   3 I am writing this letter to your newspaper because I think you guys made a mistake the other day.
   4 Interviewees' responses depended on how old they were, whether they were male or female, their occupation and educational background.
   5 And some more things, I would like to make a few suggestions, which I hope you can take into consideration.

5 Complete the paragraphs with connecting words from the boxes.

secondly   moreover   finally   firstly

The people present raised a number of objections to the plan for the club's yearly programme proposed by the committee. **(1)** ...., they felt that the proposed programme did not contain enough to attract new members. **(2)** .... they considered that there were not enough meetings geared towards younger members. **(3)** .... several people made the point that the events suggested were not varied enough. **(4)** .... it was suggested that some new young members be co-opted onto the committee and a new programme be proposed as soon as possible.

so that   however   consequently   although

Having been employed as an accountant for five years in a small printing company, I have gained considerable experience and **(5)** .... I very much enjoy my work, I would now like to work for larger organisation. **(6)** .... I can take on a role with more responsibility, I would like to apply for the job of management accountant that you are advertising on your website. I have taken eight of the Institute of Accountants' exams and have received very good grades (see attached CV). **(7)** ...., I still have another six exams to take before I can become a member of the Institute of Accountants. **(8)** ...., it is very important to me that I am able to continue my programme of studies in my new job.

after that   finally   because   especially   then   firstly   when   gradually

If you have only a couple of hours to spend in the countryside near our city, **(9)** .... this is the most valuable way to spend them.
(10) ...., starting from the city centre, walk out of town along the river. You will see the last blocks of flats **(11)** .... you have been walking for about two kilometres.
(12) .... you will move into a more natural area where there are cottages and gardens where vegetables are grown. You will probably see some very colourful boats along the way.
(13) .... you will be completely out of the town and will be able to enjoy magnificent views over the local countryside. Keep an eye open **(14)** .... for bird life and for flowers **(15)** .... both are particularly rich in this area. **(16)** .... you will come to an attractive place near the river where you can enjoy lunch or a drink before catching a bus back to the city.

6 You have seen this notice in your college newsletter.

We would like to improve the information for new students on our college website. At present, the website has lots of factual information about courses. We would like to include more advice for new students. We would appreciate your views on topics such as study skills, living in a new city, dealing with finances and making new friends. Please write to the website director, explaining what sort of advice new students might find useful.

Write your letter in 220–260 words in an appropriate style.

5 Dream jobs

Speaking

1 Work with a partner. Discuss these questions.

1 What would be your dream job? Why?
2 Some people say there is no such thing as a 'dream job' because every job turns out to have advantages and disadvantages. What do you think?

2 Read extracts A–C from blogs by people who got their dream jobs? What do you think each job is?

3 A recent survey asked people what their dream job would be. Being a pilot was the most popular choice and being an artist was the least popular. Rank the jobs in the box.

> Formula 1 driver   pilot   actor   doctor   writer   musician
> singer   journalist   photographer   artist   sports trainer

4 Check your answers on page 160.

A Before I applied, I hadn't realised that getting on the course would be so hard: 500 people applied, 275 were selected for further screening, 70 got on the course and 45 graduated! The training is physically and psychologically tough but it's worth it when you're finally working 30,000 feet above the ground.

B Even before I went to university, I knew what I wanted to specialise in. Now, as I prepare to go into the operating theatre, I feel honoured to be doing such work. Last week, I did a valve repair on a five-year-old girl's heart and I can't describe to you how good I felt when I saw her walking around the ward after only a couple of days. I can't believe I still get such a thrill from things like that. I was sure it would wear off after a few years.

C It would have been unreasonable to expect the job to be easy, and it hasn't been. There have been days when I've barely managed to write more than 500 words. I thought I'd get periods when it was hard, because I was lacking inspiration. But it turns out I'm so worried about financial insecurity, that sometimes I can't work effectively.

Reading

1 Read the article on page 35 quickly. Is the writer for or against trying to find a 'dream job'?

> ⤵ **Exam spot**
>
> A good reading skill is to scan a paragraph and to summarise the main idea expressed. This skill is especially useful for Paper 1 (Parts 7 and 8 of Reading and Use of English).

2 Choose the best summary of each paragraph.

Paragraph 1
A Luck plays an important part in finding your dream job.
B You need the right sort of personality to find your dream job.
C Doing your dream job never feels like hard work.

Paragraph 2
A Science graduates stand a better chance of finding their dream job than other graduates.
B It has become increasingly difficult to find a dream job over the last decade.
C What you studied at university shouldn't determine what kind of job you look for.

Paragraph 3
A Avoid comparing yourself to your contemporaries.
B It's advisable to choose a job with good financial rewards.
C Make sure you meet your future boss before you accept a job.

3 Write two sentences to summarise the two main ideas in the fourth paragraph.

4 The fifth paragraph summarises the key ideas from the whole text. Make notes of the key ideas.

A really determined person will always succeed

[1] The majority of people think that their dream job is too hard to achieve, too competitive and believe that it is all a matter of luck. All this is true actually, but why should that stop anyone from trying to get the job they really want? A really determined person will always succeed and, in many ways, needs other people to give up trying so that he or she can succeed.

[2] Many job seekers feel limited by the choices they made at college or university. They may think that because they studied marketing, all they can ever do is work in marketing. All the evidence shows that, in fact, employers are less interested in acquired knowledge than the ability to think and learn. It is also very difficult to predict the needs of society. For example, if a person chose to study dentistry because there was a lack of dentists when they were in high school, that may not be the case when they graduate. The needs of employers and the economy can change very quickly, and often unexpectedly. Research from the Higher Education Careers Services Unit found that in 2006–2007, twice as many psychology graduates as civil engineers were out of work. Four years later, after the crash of the construction industry in the UK, more civil engineering graduates than psychologists were unemployed.

[3] Of course, if it is a very tough time economically, it is hard to find employment straight after university, but it is by no means impossible. It might take several months longer to find a job after graduating, but there is work out there. My chosen career has always been competitive, but I never thought about the other people going for the same jobs. It may be human nature to compare your progress to your peers, but perhaps the best advice would be to try not to. Be focused on what you want and how you are going to get it. After all, it may appear that a friend who has a really well-paid job is doing well, but how do you know what their job is actually like? They may be working 12-hour days, have an unreasonable boss, or be stressed out trying to meet unrealistic targets.

[4] Have a plan in place, even if it is a sketchy one. Have both short-term and long-term aims. In my final year at university, my short-term aims were to gain experience at a local newspaper. My long-term aim was always to get a job at a national paper. It sounds easy for me to say it now, but I always thought that with really hard work, dedication, a willingness to put myself out and a bit of luck, I could get my dream job. It is also essential to be completely dedicated to the business you want to get into. Know as much as possible about it, then you can feel part of it and understand how it works.

[5] A really key piece of advice is never get downhearted by rejection, because there will probably be a lot. You can achieve your dream job, whatever it is. You must never give up. Be prepared to work hard and for long hours without necessarily climbing up the career ladder. There is a lot to be said for learning your 'trade' from the bottom up. At the start, there will probably be little money, but it will be worth it in the end. The best jobs are not supposed to be easy – that is what makes them challenging. And if you like a challenge, just keep your head down and go for it.

Writing

1 **1 08 Listen to friends talking about a job advert.**

   1 What's the job title and where is the job?
   2 What are the salary and other benefits?

2 **Write a letter of application for the job.**

   1 Plan a letter of application, paying attention to the organisation of ideas. Then write a first draft of the application.
   2 With a partner, read each other's first draft and then give feedback on clarity of purpose, paragraphing, and use of formal vocabulary.
   3 Write the final draft in 220–260 words.

⊗ Exam spot

You may be asked to write a formal letter in the Writing test.
- Use an appropriate greeting and ending.
- Make sure that the style is consistent and the purpose is clear.
- Consider the effect the letter will have on the reader.

Vocabulary

> ## ⊙ Vocabulary spot
>
> Connotation is the feeling or mood suggested by a particular word. For example, in the recording, you heard *an abundance of wildlife*. The word *abundance* has a positive connotation, suggesting it's a good thing to have so much wildlife. If you said an area was *swarming with insects*, *swarming* has a negative connotation, suggesting you didn't like the fact that there were so many insects.

1 **When applying for a job, it is important to present yourself in positive terms. Make these sentences more positive.**

My only experience is of working in sales.
I have specialised in working in sales.

1 I did a first-aid course and I think I've got the certificate somewhere.
2 I speak English, more or less.
3 Thank you for inviting me to an interview. I might be able to attend one soon.
4 I don't mind working shifts.
5 I am an adequate communicator.

2 **Work with a partner. Choose the best options in these sentences from a job advert.**

1 We are looking for *a wise / an experienced* individual …
2 … who is able to work under pressure and face *challenges / problems*.
3 You will be responsible for our *new / novel* sales team.
4 We can offer the successful candidate *an aggressive / a competitive* salary …
5 … and *flexible / easy-going* working times.

3 **In academic situations, people often use the more formal version of a word (e.g. *collaborate* instead of *work with*). What is the more formal equivalent of 1–10?**

> funds   delayed   repeat   in addition
> therefore   exceed (the word limit)
> out of order   eliminate
> install (a computer program)
> my predecessor

1 rule out
2 to be over
3 money
4 the person who had the job before me
5 so
6 load
7 late
8 do again
9 doesn't work
10 and

4 **Choose the most appropriate words to complete this formal letter.**

Dear Sir or Madam,

I am writing (1) *about / in response to* your advertisement for a sales assistant, which (2) *appeared / I saw* on Jobline yesterday.

I am (3) *attaching / giving* you a copy of my curriculum vitae, which (4) *provides / gives* details of my qualifications and experience. As you will see, I worked in a (5) *business like yours / similar business* last summer, which I (6) *liked a lot / enjoyed enormously*.

I (7) *am available / can come* for an interview at any time (8) *convenient to / good for* you.

Yours faithfully,

J. Perkins

Relative clauses

1 **Explain the difference in meaning between these sentences. Which contains a defining relative clause? Which has a non-defining relative clause?**

1 I am writing in response to your advert, which appeared on Jobline yesterday.
2 I am writing in response to your advert which appeared on Jobline yesterday.

2 **Write sentences from these prompts, two with defining relative clauses and two with non-defining relative clauses.**

1 The company – gave job to – person – show determination
2 The applicant – graduated Bologna University – has a degree in biology
3 Head office – New York – employs 2,000 people
4 The manager – interviewed me – kind and helpful

3 **Explain the omission of the relative pronoun in this sentence.**
This is the job I like best.

4 If the relative pronoun is not necessary in any of these sentences, cross it out.

1 I worked in a building **which** had no air conditioning.
2 The clothes **that** she wore to the office were very scruffy.
3 The place **where** she works has a gym for staff.
4 The place **that** I worked in last summer was great.
5 He has an inspirational quality **which** defies analysis.
6 Her colleagues are also the people **that** she socialises with.

5 Which sentence in each pair is more formal?

1 **a** This is the man to whom I was talking.
   b This is the man I was talking to.
2 **a** The beach was very far from the hotel that I was staying in.
   b The beach was very far from the hotel in which I was staying.

Corpus spot

The *Cambridge English Corpus* shows that exam candidates often make mistakes with relative pronouns and prepositions, or sometimes leave them out completely.

*I am writing to recommend the one-month business course **on which** I was sent recently.*

NOT ~~I am writing to recommend the one-month business course where I was sent on recently.~~

Correct these sentences.
1 This is the area of research which he is working.
2 Here are some new statistics you can have confidence.
3 This is a theory for that there is little support.
4 Is this the person who you spoke?
5 Unfortunately, the conference what you enrolled on has been cancelled.

 page 164

Listening

1 Work with a partner. Discuss these questions.

1 How do you feel about dangerous sports like Formula One?
2 Some people say sportspeople are paid too much because it's not a 'proper' job. Do you agree? Why? Why not?
3 How do you think fame and money can affect someone?

2 You are going to listen to an interview with Cesar deMatos, a successful Formula 1 driver. What words do you think might complete these sentences?

1 Cesar says it is his .... who was responsible for him taking up Formula 1 racing.
2 Cesar's mother does not like facing a .... whenever she goes out.
3 Cesar's father believes that because Cesar is a .... person, he will be a winner.
4 In Australia, Cesar was in .... place when his car developed mechanical problems.
5 Cesar remembers the time when his father did not have enough money for ....
6 According to the interviewer, there are many .... who would love to get Cesar to sign a contract with them.
7 The next thing he wants to buy is a ...., even though he may be criticised for it.
8 Cesar differs from his old friends in that he has swapped ....

3 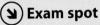 Listen and complete the sentences with a word or short phrase. How close were your predictions?

Exam spot

In Part 2 of Paper 3 (the Listening test), you will be asked to complete gapped sentences. When you have written your answers, read the whole sentence again to make sure that it makes sense and is grammatically correct. Check your spelling too.

4 Work in groups and discuss the things in your life you have been successful at, or can do well.

Topic review

1 Work with a partner. Discuss these questions.

1 How would you describe your personality?
2 If you went to stay with a family from another country, what would you take them as a gift from your country?
3 Why do you think some people don't live their lives to the full?
4 If you could have three wishes, what would they be?
5 How would you cope if you were famous and constantly in the public eye?
6 What would be your dream job?

Grammar

2 Complete this blog. Sometimes more than one answer is possible.

I wish I (1) .... stay here forever; it's perfect! For a start, there are so many different sports to choose from and then there are great treks that we can go on too. I wish I (2) .... wasted so much money on holidays in the past where I just lazed on the beach all day. This is what I call living life to the full! I'd rather (3) .... up at dawn and hike into the mountains than lie in bed till midday. If only this type of holiday (4) .... possible for more people ... I mean it's quite expensive. Having said that, it's definitely worth saving up for. Perhaps it's just personal choice, the sort of holiday people opt for. But I do think it's time some friends of mine (5) .... more carefully about what they're doing in their free time. A lot of them seem to spend most of their time online instead of getting out into the real world. Supposing you (6) .... a friend like that – what would you advise them to do?

Vocabulary

3 Read the text and decide which word best fits each gap.

This work placement has (0) _B_ me the opportunity to work on an environmental project in New Zealand. The aim of the project is to (1) .... the issue of coastal management. Coastal environments throughout the world are threatened by human activity as we increasingly (2) .... in activities such as coastal construction and shipping. (3) .... in the threats associated with shipping are the introduction of non-native species and pollution from fuel and oil spills. In order to minimise the impact of such threats, it is important that coastal managers are (4) .... with data on the distribution of costal species. This is particularly important for vulnerable or rare species or habitats. Some of this vital data collection had to be put on (5) .... until more funding was made available and more people recruited. (6) .... on this data, scientists will be able to identify which native species and habitats will be affected by the invasion of alien species. There has been no previous attempt to map, and in (7) .... , estimate the value of New Zealand's marine environment in a consistent or comprehensive way to enable effective management. By and (8) .... , it is thought that this project will go a long way to supporting coastal management.

0	A proposed	B offered	C enabled	D presented
1	A deal	B focus	C refer	D address
2	A involve	B engage	C allow	D practise
3	A Comprised	B Integrated	C Included	D Contained
4	A given	B passed	C delivered	D provided
5	A track	B duty	C hold	D balance
6	A Drawing	B Extracting	C Deriving	D Obtaining
7	A full	B turn	C brief	D general
8	A far	B chance	C large	D way

4 Choose the correct collocations.

1 The group *came through / came to* a decision only after hours of discussion.

2 People who are willing to *take in / take on* a challenge usually find their dream job.

3 Working on a research project was a *truly / totally* new experience for me.

4 I *set up / set off* on a trip of a lifetime, hoping to challenge myself physically and mentally.

5 It was *completely / incredibly* interesting talking to Marsha about her pilot training.

6 I didn't really understand what culture *surprise / shock* was until I came to live in this remote hillside village.

5 Choose the correct form of the word in brackets to complete these sentences. Each new word should be formed with either a prefix or a suffix.

1 It was thought that the lawyer had .... the jury into believing the accused had been in trouble with the police on a previous occasion. (LEAD)

2 This type of .... material is particularly suitable for outdoor wear. (WATER)

3 The manager's good .... can be put down to his years of experience. (JUDGE)

4 Andrew has a .... to leave things until the last minute. (TEND)

5 The .... of the department is measured in number of sales. (EFFICIENT)

6 Her claim for compensation was .... because she had no evidence to support it. (JUSTIFY)

7 There's no need to be so .... Don't you think you should apologise? (POLITE)

6 Work with a partner. How would you express these words/phrases in a more formal way?

1 she got a reply
2 at a time that is good for you
3 I'm looking forward to
4 but
5 a job like that
6 I'm writing about the advert in ...
7 I'm always on time
8 I'd like the chance to

7 Read this article about two successful young entrepreneurs. Fill each gap with a suitable word.

The brainwave that made me $10m when I was 18

Founded **(0)** ....*by*............ Catherine and David Cook, MeetMe.com became an overnight success in the social-networking world. In just a few years, it rose **(1)** .... become one of the most popular sites for teens, getting more than one million hits every day. It's an achievement all the more remarkable **(2)** .... you consider its two creators were only 18 and 19 respectively.

Catherine and David were looking at their school yearbook – the annual compendium of photos and memories **(3)** .... is a feature of most US high schools – when they came **(4)** .... a picture of a girl they both knew. 'This looks nothing **(5)** .... her,' said David. Catherine agreed. Wouldn't it, they wondered, be much better to do this online, and let people post their own photos?

The pair were lucky. Their older brother, Geoff, was already an established internet entrepreneur who had built **(6)** .... two successful websites. In 2002, he had sold them **(7)** .... nearly $10m. And he immediately saw the potential of Catherine and David's idea.

The Cooks' parents thought the idea was crazy, **(8)** .... Geoff wasn't put off. He offered $250,000 to get the project off the ground.

6 Connections

Speaking

1 **Work with a partner. Discuss these questions.**

  1 Look at the photos. How has telephone technology changed over the years?

  2 List as many things as possible that you can use your phone for.

  3 Compare your list with a partner.

2 **1·10 Listen to this anecdote.**

  1 Why did the woman want revenge?

  2 How did she take revenge?

  3 What message do you think the man might have left on the woman's voicemail when he realised what she'd done?

Phrasal verbs (1)

1 **1·11 You are going to hear six answerphone messages. For each, make notes on these points.**

  • For

  • From

  • Number

  • Message

2 **Listen to the phone messages again.**

  1 Note any phrasal verbs you hear.

  2 Match a phrasal verb to the definitions below.

> when your voice cannot be clearly heard
> connect a caller with someone else
> wait   end a phone call
> achieve a phone connection
> lose a phone connection

3 **Choose the correct options.**

  1 You have to stop using your mobile phone if *your battery runs out / you run out your battery*.

  2 Sometimes it is difficult to *get back / get through* to distant or remote places on a mobile phone.

  3 If you can't hear someone, you may ask *to speak them up / them to speak up*.

  4 You ring a large business and the receptionist there will *put through you / put you through* to the person you want to speak to.

  5 You ring a friend but he wants you to wait a moment while he answers the door. He says, '*Hang on a moment / Hang a moment on*'.

  6 You are talking to your dad. After a few minutes he says, 'I'd better *pass over you / pass you over* to your mum now.'

G → page 165

Speaking

1 **Practise using phrasal verbs in phone dialogues. Work with a partner. Take it in turns to be A and B. Choose the best response to what A says.**

A says:

a I can't hear you very well. ..*2*...

b Can I speak to the Finance department, please?

c We're going to have to stop talking soon. My battery's running out.

d Well, I guess I'd better go. It's getting late.

e Hang on a moment. I'll just turn the TV off.

f Did you manage to get through to the bank?

g I hate to say goodbye to you, darling.

h What's happening? I think we're breaking up.

i I think we've only got a few seconds left. We're going to be cut off in a moment.

j Do you want to come round to my house this evening?

B says:

1 I'll just put you through.

2 OK, I'll try to speak up.

3 Yes, we're going through a tunnel. I'll ring back in a few minutes.

4 No problem.

5 That'd be great. I'll check with my parents and call you back.

6 Would you like me to call you back?

7 No, don't ring off now – there's something I've got to tell you first.

8 OK, bye then. Thanks for ringing.

9 Me too. Shall we hang up?

10 Yes, but they put me on hold for 20 minutes.

Vocabulary

1 **Do these phrases collocate with *have*, *do*, *make*, or *take*? Sometimes there may be more than one possible answer.**

a phone call	a bath	a cake	a chance	a go
a mistake	a party	a photo	a shower
an effort	an excuse	dinner	fun	hold of
part in	the cooking	someone a favour
your best	someone seriously	an exam
a course	someone's word for it	work	sure

 Corpus spot

Be careful with collocations with *have*, *make*, *do* and *take*. The *Cambridge English Corpus* shows exam candidates often make mistakes with these.

Correct the mistakes that exam candidates have made in these sentences.

1 This report will describe the one-month business English course I recently had.

2 In Italy you can have a driving test only when you have reached the age of 18.

3 It's very sensible to take a light breakfast such as yoghurt, cereal, bread, coffee, etc.

4 There are some jobs mainly made by men, but in my opinion, this will change in the future.

5 We can visit museums, make some pictures, and visit clubs without going far from our workplace.

6 I hope that this information will help you to do a decision.

7 If clients are annoyed, they will not make business with us. It is therefore vital to add more phone lines.

8 Therefore, it would be a good idea to do some changes.

9 I am writing this letter to correct some mistakes you have done in your article.

Reading

⮯ Exam spot

Doing well in the Reading test – particularly Parts 6 and 8 – means being able to skim (read a text quickly to get a general impression of it) and to scan (look over a text quickly to find specific information).

1 Take one minute to skim the article. Then answer these questions.

    1 Which statement best summarises the article?

      A The writer feels that the best way to communicate is to talk to someone directly.

      B The writer is making the point that phone technology has changed very rapidly.

      C The writer believes that progress in phone technology has made communication simpler.

    2 Which word best describes the writing: *historical, satirical, sociological* or *futuristic*?

2 Now scan the article to answer these questions. Try to answer them all in one minute.

    1 What does the writer think now seems 'unimaginably primitive'?

    2 What does the writer say sometimes led to repetitive strain injury?

    3 What is there said to be in the town of Sutton Coldfield?

    4 What is described as one of 'the great breakthroughs of the age'?

    5 What was discovered 'out of the blue'?

    6 What do the initials 'PFC' stand for?

3 Underline the phrasal verbs in the article. Can you replace any of them with a more formal word or phrase?

4 Look at the highlighted verbs. What nouns do they collocate with?

5 Look at the photos. Work in small groups and discuss these questions.

    1 What do you think the writer of the article would think about the things that these photos represent?

    2 How often do you use the things shown and how do you use them?

    3 In what ways have they influenced how people live nowadays? Try to think of positive and negative consequences.

The Immobile Phone

Nowadays, it's hard for the young to imagine, but many years ago, people used to 'text' on their 'mobile telephones'. Historians tell us that it was a very long process which now seems incredibly primitive.

First of all, you needed to find your 'mobile phone'. This in itself could take some time. You should remember that these were the days before telephones were attached to the wall, so the chances of losing them were very high. Once you found your phone, you had to use your fingers to type a message into a tiny window. The messages often came out wrong, because everyone's fingers were bigger than the keys, and even when they came out right it was hard to work out what they meant, as it became traditional to leave out all the vowels in order to save time. You would then send, or 'snd', your message, or 'msg' to your reader.

But – and this is what seems so strange – you had absolutely no way of knowing whether the text had reached its destination, or whether the recipient had read it. Only if the recipient texted back – a process which would also take time – did you know whether your original message got through. This process, of course, became longer and even more drawn out if any form of 'conversation', texting to and fro, was required. In fact, some people needed to 'text' for such lengthy periods that they developed a form of repetitive strain injury.

Then came the invention of a telephone that allowed people to speak and be spoken to. Suddenly, conversations could take place between two people without any need for the tedious process of type, send, wait, read, type, send, and so on. It goes without saying that 'texting' soon turned into a thing of the past, though today you can sometimes still see people doing it in old movies and period dramas, and there is even a Museum of Texting in the town of Sutton Coldfield, in which performers dress up as old-fashioned teenagers in period costume ('jeans', 'T-shirts' and 'trainers') and 'text' one another.

After the invention of the 'speaking' mobile phone, people started to long for a phone that would be impossible to lose. Thankfully, someone came up with the bright idea of inventing a telephone with a wire linking it to the wall, so that it always remained in the same place.

'The invention of the *Immobile Phone* was one of the great breakthroughs of the age,' says a leading historian. 'For the first time, people could speak on the telephone without worrying about losing it, or its battery running down.' Another veteran of the period recalls the sense of freedom people felt at the invention of the Immobile Phone.

'You should remember that, before the Immobile Phone, people felt chained to their mobile. They were unable to leave their home or office without it, and felt the need to carry it with them even when they were shopping, or going for a walk.

'You even saw people walking around with them on their heads. The Immobile Phone changed all that, and gave the opportunity, for the very first time, to relax and switch off.'

Yet, there was still room to make more progress. Was it possible to come up with a way of talking to other people that did not involve talking into a machine? Some of the greatest scientists of their day set their minds to coming up with a solution.

And then – out of the blue – came the discovery of face-to-face conversation. 'It was extraordinary,' remembers someone who was there at the time. 'The human race was suddenly given this marvellous gift of talking to one another without needing to use a machine or a gadget.

'The world suddenly seemed so fresh. We had become so used to texting, and then to talking through mobiles, and then to talking through Immobiles, that we had no idea just how exciting it would be to talk to each other face-to-face. And there was no cost involved, no batteries, no problem with reception – it was all great!'

Since then, PFC, or 'phone-free conversation' has taken off all over the world. It seemed a bit strange at first, but now people are completely used to talking 'face to face', and they wouldn't have it any other way.

Exam folder 3

Paper 1 Part 3

Word formation

In Part 3 of the Reading and Use of English test, you are given a text. Most of the lines contain one gap. At the end of the line is a word in capitals. You have to form a word from the same root as the word in capitals to fit the gap in that line.

Some of the greatest .... of   SCIENCE
their day set their minds to coming
up with a solution.

It is clear from the context that the gap has to be filled by a noun (i.e. science, sciences, scientist or scientists). In this case, it is also clear that the noun required is a person noun in the plural. The answer is, therefore, scientists.

1   Read the text below. Each gap needs to be filled by a word beginning with the letters provided. What type of word is needed to fill each gap (a noun, a verb, etc.)?

2   Now decide which words you think fill each gap.

The development of mobile phones has a
(1) surpris........................... long history. In 1916, there were tests of mobile phones on some
(2) milita........................... trains and in 1926 public trains between Hamburg and Berlin offered a telephone service to first-class **(3) travel**........................... The mobile phone first appeared in **(4) liter**........................... in 1931. This was in a children's book called *The 35th of May or Conrad's Ride to the South Seas*. In the story, the author **(5) descri**........................... a situation that would have seemed quite fantastical at the time: 'A gentleman who rode along the sidewalk in front of them, **(6) sudde**........................... stepped off the conveyor belt, pulled a phone out of his pocket, **(7) enter**........................... a number into it and said: 'Gertrude, I'll be an hour late for lunch because I want to go to the laboratory.' Conveyor belt sidewalks are so far only to be found in some large airports but that type of phone **(8) convers**........................... can be heard every day in every city in the world.

3   In the exam, you may need to add a prefix to the root word. Add a negative prefix to each of these words.

Verbs	Adjectives	Nouns
wrap	safe	appearance
ice	loyal	security
tie	sane	comfort
engage	comfortable	balance
understand	responsible	mobility

⬇ Corpus spot

Take care when using negative prefixes. The *Cambridge English Corpus* shows that exam candidates often make mistakes with these.

*They were very **impolite** and unfriendly.*

NOT ~~They were very **unpolite** and unfriendly.~~

Correct these sentences written by exam candidates.
1 I am writing to express my unsatisfaction with the hotel.
2 The whole tour was dissatisfactory.
3 Your service was unadequate and should be improved.
4 It was unorganised from the beginning.
5 The food was good, and it was unexpensive.

4   List as many words as you can based on these words.

lawful, unlawful, lawyer, lawlessness ...

1 law
2 hope
3 act
4 press
5 centre
6 head
7 office
8 broad

5   Here is some more of the article on the history of mobile phone technology from exercise 1. Use the word given in capitals at the end of some of the lines to form a word that fits in the gap in the same line.

The first **(0)** .....*completely*..... automated mobile phone system for vehicles came   **COMPLETE**
into **(1)** .... in Sweden in the 1950s. This allowed calls to be made and   **BE**
received in a car. Calls which were made from the car were direct dial whereas
(2) .... calls required an operator to determine which base station the   **COME**
car was **(3)** .... closest to. Several different companies   **CURRENT**
(4) .... in producing the different pieces of equipment that were   **PART**
necessary to provide this service, the switchboards and the handsets, for
example. During the1960s and 1970s, technology **(5)** .... advanced and   **STEADY**
there were substantial improvements in the **(6)** .... of these early car   **RELY**
phones. The system that was developed was popular with customers and went
on to enjoy not **(7)** .... commercial success. Drivers continued to use   **CONSIDER**
the network until the early 1980s when it closed to make way for the
(8) .... of new technologies.   **INTRODUCE**

6   Now complete the text below.

Nine years ago, Philip Fletcher was a **(1)** .... married man with three   **HAPPY**
children. He had a responsible job as a highly **(2)** .... chemical worker.   **SKILL**
Then an accident changed his life beyond **(3)** .... He was plunged into a   **RECOGNISE**
surreal and totally **(4)** .... world when the accident left him with a serious **FAMILIAR**
head **(5)** .... This resulted in him being unable to remember anything   **INJURE**
of the previous 15 years. In the accident a metal pole fell from a considerable
height onto his head. Fletcher survived only thanks to his safety helmet. He was
taken to hospital but was **(6)** .... after only four hours. He seemed fine,   **CHARGE**
apart from his memory loss, and everyone expected his memory would gradually
return. **(7)** ...., it never did. For a number of years it was   **FORTUNE**
(8) .... very difficult for Fletcher and his family, and his breakthrough   **PSYCHOLOGY**
only came once he learned to accept his own limitations. Only then was he able
to start rebuilding his life.

Speaking

1 Work in groups. Discuss these questions.

1 Would you prefer to work as a company employee or as a freelancer? Why?
2 What do you think would be the advantages and disadvantages of setting up a business while still a teenager?
3 If you could run any business of your own, what would it be and why?

Reading

1 Take two minutes to skim the article below and answer the questions. Ignore the gaps for now.

1 How old was McVey when he started his business?
2 What kind of business did he have?
3 Who were his first customers?
4 How did his age help him?

2 Now read the article again and fill the gaps.

A successful young entrepreneur

At the age of just 13, Dominic McVey became known to the public when he started importing collapsible scooters from the US, making him a reported £5 million. Now a young adult, McVey is attempting to find other profitable gaps in the market, (1) .... varying success.

How did you first (2) .... up with the idea for importing the scooters?

I had been looking round the internet and was looking for a credit-card website, but I spelled it wrong and I accidentally came across a website which was manufacturing scooters. I really wanted (3) .... but I couldn't afford it and (4) .... could my parents, so I emailed the company and said 'I think you should send me a scooter, I would sell loads over here.'

They said no, but (5) .... you buy five, we'll give you one free. So, as I really wanted one for free, I saved up to buy five, (6) .... I did by organising under-18s discos, buying stocks and shares and selling mini disc players in Japan.

So I got five over, and got one for free, which I was really happy with, but then I thought I should sell the other five, which I (7) .... within a week, to family and friends. The next week I sold ten, and it just went on from there.

I never really saw the potential until the product landed on my doorstep, and I guess I had to take some action. I looked at business (8) .... a very childish and naïve way. This was probably the best way at the time because it meant I wasn't overwhelmed by problems.

I was very, very competitive. The press really liked me and everyone liked the product.

What really shone through to me was that I could see everyone in London going to work on one. I thought everyone needed one in the boot of the car just in (9) .... they got stuck in traffic and I really drove that message home.

I used to go up to the centre of London and hand out fliers; I'd shoot off on my scooter during my lunch break from school. I sold (10) .... lot to city executives as toys, and people then began to commute on (11) ....

Did you find your age was a problem in terms (12) .... being taken seriously?

People often didn't realise my age – a lot of the business I did was over the phone or on the internet. I was very good with computers at the time and had friends who were great with IT, so I had excellent presentations.

Whenever I did meet companies, even if I thought I couldn't get any business out of them, I asked them a million and one questions about how they (13) .... business. They loved telling me because they felt like the older brother telling the kid (14) .... to do.

3 Now answer these multiple-choice questions.

1 McVey found out about these scooters
   A through a credit-card website.
   B as a result of making a mistake.
   C thanks to his parents.
   D in an email he received.

2 His scooters were unusual because they
   A could move easily through traffic.
   B could be folded up small.
   C came from the US.
   D were relatively cheap.

3 McVey characterises himself when his business
   was beginning as
   A being overwhelmed by problems.
   B having a great deal of energy.
   C being keenly aware of business opportunities.
   D having a simple attitude.

4 What does McVey say about his age when he
   started his business?
   A He pretended to be older than he was in order
      to be taken seriously.
   B The nature of the business meant that his age
      was not a disadvantage.
   C Because of his age, older friends often gave
      business presentations on his behalf.
   D He was happy at that age to take advice from
      his older brothers.

Vocabulary

**1 Match words from A with words from B to make
collocations relating to work and business.**

A │ do   a gap   make   take   stocks   competitive
  │ daily   overwhelmed   stuck

B │ by problems   in the market   a profit
  │ business   action   commute   and shares
  │ in traffic   prices

**2 Now use a collocation from exercise 1 to complete
each sentence. You will need to change some verb
forms.**

1 It's been a pleasure .... with you.
2 My .... takes me about 20 minutes as
   long as I manage to avoid the rush hour. But if I
   get ...., it can take me an hour.
3 Suzie's stylish kitchen implements for left-
   handed people found .... and her
   business soon began to ....
4 My grandmother made quite a lot of money by
   buying and selling ....
5 There's no point just letting yourself feel
   .... – it's time you .... to
   improve the situation.
6 Jack has been very successful in business
   because he works for a city centre restaurant
   offering good food at ....

**3 Use the words given in capitals to form a word that
fits in the gaps.**

1 When you work in an office, you really
   appreciate that feeling of .... at the
   beginning of the weekend. (FREE)
2 None of Paul's business ventures have turned out
   to be very .... (PROFIT)
3 Our company sells a .... of teas.
   (VARY)
4 Our prices are lower than those of any of our
   .... (COMPETE)
5 Be careful what you say when you meet the
   boss – it's quite an .... situation.
   (EXPLODE)
6 I'm really fed up with his ....
   behaviour. (CHILD)

Reason, result and purpose

1 Read about Marta and her business success. Look at the highlighted phrases. Which one signals:

1 a result?
2 a purpose?
3 a reason?

Marta Bailey is one of the most influential figures in the retail industry. It's true that her former boss had a profound influence on her, but more importantly perhaps, she has worked hard for years *in order to get* the considerable financial rewards she has now. Recently, her increased sales *could be said to be a consequence of* an improved marketing campaign. Her interest in retail may be so strong *because of* a childhood passion for playing shops. It may also have its roots in her ancestry, as both her grandfathers were shopkeepers.

2 Read the next part. Choose the correct options.

Marta's sister had opened her own outlet, **(1)** *as / so* it was no wonder she also went into a career in sales. **(2)** *Because / Because of* her teachers also encouraged her, she had a lot of early support. **(3)** *Having / She had* a Saturday supermarket job while she was still at school had a considerable effect on her later approach to selling. Studying for an MBA was **(4)** *so / so that* influential that it brought about a complete change in her attitude to business. She started a mail-order service **(5)** *so as to / so* gain a wider customer base. Many potential customers had complained that, **(6)** *for / because of* work commitments, they could not get to her shop during opening hours. **(7)** *As a result of / With the result that* this new service, her sales tripled. Marta has had a wide range of influences and experiences, **(8)** *as a result of / with the result that* she has managed to be so successful in business.

◉ Corpus spot

Be careful with *because of* – the *Cambridge English Corpus* shows that exam candidates often make mistakes with this.

*A person cannot tell her nationality **because of** her excellent pronunciation.*

NOT *A person cannot tell her nationality **for** her excellent pronunciation.*

*I am not so happy with the tour **for** several reasons.*

NOT *I am not so happy with the tour **because of** several reasons.*

3 Discuss the reasons for and the results of 'success'.

1 Think of someone who is successful (a business person, actor, sportsperson, or family member).
2 Decide why that person became successful and what happened to them. Think about language of result, reason and purpose that you can use.
3 Work with a partner. Describe your person.
4 Why do people become successful? What happens when they achieve success?

G → page 166

Writing

1 Read a report written by 17-year-olds who took part in a supermarket work-experience programme. Is it generally positive or negative?

Work-experience programme
Ten students took part in this year's work-experience programme. We were all employed in the main branch of the supermarket and experienced various jobs; during one month, we spent a week each as checkout cashier, shelf stacker, office junior and kitchen hand.

Usefulness of the programme
Firstly, we learned about life behind the scenes in a large supermarket. None of us had experience of shop work and we found it more demanding than expected. Secondly, we enjoyed learning about the supermarket business. We had two days' induction and this taught us a lot. Thirdly, we benefited from the experience thanks to the way it highlighted the importance of dealing with the public. Finally, we feel that we gained confidence as a result of the opportunities we were offered. Consequently, we now feel better prepared for the 'real world'.

Drawbacks to the programme
At times, we felt as if we were being exploited. We worked as hard as the regular staff but only received a quarter of their wages. Nor were we allowed discounts on supermarket products. We enjoyed the experience, although we felt it might have been better to have the opportunity to work in the places we want to work in one day ourselves, for example, in the health service or in hotels for pupils who plan to become doctors or hotel staff.

Conclusion
In conclusion, we recommend continuing with this programme. However, based on our experience, we would include a wider variety of opportunities in a range of organisations.

2 Now discuss these questions.

1 Are the headings for each paragraph of the report appropriate?

2 Which words and expressions are used to link ideas within the text?

3 What language relating to reason and result does the writer use?

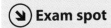 **Exam spot**

Looking at examples of good writing (writing which is well set out in terms of organisation and uses a good range of vocabulary and structures) can provide you with models to base your own writing on for Part 2 of the Writing test.

Listening and Speaking

1 Look at the photos. Which jobs are shown?

2 🔊 1.12 Listen to eight people talking about their jobs.

1 Which job is each person talking about? How do you know?

2 What does each person like and dislike about their job?

3 Why is the speaker doing each job?

3 Work with a partner. Choose the three jobs which you think are most valuable, and the three least valuable. Give reasons.

> airline pilot   astronomer   car mechanic
> chef   computer programmer   dentist
> English teacher   footballer   lawyer
> newsreader   plastic surgeon   plumber   poet
> politician   pop singer   refuse collector
> soldier   stockbroker   vet   waiter

4 Now work with a different partner. Compare your decisions.

5 Below are some job perks, a benefit you are given as part of a job, along with money. Add at least four more.

> being your own boss   pension   company car
> opportunity for creativity   flexitime
> opportunity to travel

6 Conduct a survey.

1 Choose one perk from exercise 5 and prepare two or three questions to conduct a survey on people's attitude to this aspect of work.

2 Ask your questions to other students. Make notes on the answers you receive.

3 Present your findings to the class.

4 Discuss how you would present your findings in the form of a report. What headings would you use? What kind of language would be appropriate?

Writing folder 3

Essays

In Part 1 of the Writing test, you have to write an essay.

1 **Look at this example of the kind of essay you will be asked to write and answer the questions.**

  1 How many words do you have to write?
  2 What is the topic you have to write about?
  3 How do the bullet points relate to the opinions in inverted commas?
  4 How many of the bullet points do you have to write about?
  5 What two things do you have to do with the bullet points you write about?
  6 What must you do if you use the opinions in inverted commas?

Your class has listened to a radio discussion about the impact of technology on employment opportunities. You have made the notes below.

Impact of technology on employment opportunities:

- fewer jobs

- more interesting work for people

- constant need to improve skills

Some opinions expressed in the discussion:

'Machines cause unemployment because they do jobs people would have done in the past.'

'People are free to do more interesting tasks.'

'No one will be doing the same job all their life any more.'

Write an **essay** discussing **two** of the ways in which technology has an impact on employment opportunities. You should **explain which way you think is more significant** and **provide reasons** to support your opinion.

You may, if you wish, make use of the opinions expressed in the discussion, but you should use your own words as far as possible.

Write your answer in 220–260 words in an appropriate style.

2 **Look at the sample answer to the essay.**

  1 How many paragraphs has the writer used?
  2 What is the purpose of each paragraph?

The impact of technology on employment opportunities

<u>Ever since</u> the start of the Industrial Revolution, people have argued about how technology will affect employment opportunities. Some people see the impact as largely negative for the workforce <u>while others</u> consider the changes to be predominantly positive.

<u>The former group of people</u> believe that technology means that there will inevitably be a decrease in the number and types of job available <u>as</u> automation and the use of robots slowly but surely take over tasks that people previously earned their living from. <u>These prophets</u> <u>of doom</u> believe that it will become much harder for people to find employment and, <u>as a result</u>, they will have no choice but to accept lower wages and poorer working conditions.

<u>On the other hand</u>, some people see the impact of technology in a more optimistic light. They view the future as a golden age <u>when</u> more people will be able to enjoy jobs which offer much more variety and are far more intellectually stimulating <u>because</u> the dull monotonous jobs will have been automated. They also argue that advanced technology will enable people to travel and work almost wherever they like in the world.

<u>Although</u> I appreciate that technology takes some jobs away from people, <u>my opinion is that</u> jobs are now more varied and so more interesting <u>than ever before</u>.

3 In extended writing, we link ideas to produce coherent and logical language. What is the purpose of each underlined phrase in the essay (e.g. to add information, explain a reason or time relationship, make a contrast, to refer back to something mentioned previously)?

4 Make a plan for the following essay by making notes on points 1–3 and completing the table below.

1 Which two bullet points will you write about?
2 Style: formal/informal?
3 Length?

Your class has listened to a panel discussion about the reasons for learning English in the modern world.

Reasons for learning English:
• increased work opportunities
• helpful for study
• useful when travelling

Some opinions expressed in the discussion:
'Knowing English allows you to do business all over the world.'
'Lots of academic books and articles are written in English.'
'Wherever you go on holiday you can get by if you speak English.'

Write an **essay** discussing **two** of the reasons for learning English in the modern world. You should **explain which reason you think is more important** and **provide reasons** to support your opinion.

You may, if you wish, make use of the opinions expressed in the discussion, but you should use your own words as far as possible.

Introduction	
Discussion of first bullet point	
Discussion of second bullet point	
Explanation of which bullet point is more important	

Brainstorming vocabulary

When planning the main body of your essay, write down the main points you want to include. When you do this, it is a good idea to brainstorm vocabulary and key phrases connected with the topic. For example, if you have an essay title which requires you to discuss the impact of advertising, you could make vocabulary notes like the following.

Vocabulary – advertising

1 Techniques: catchy slogan/jingle, celebrity endorsement, eye-catching packaging

2 Positive impact: raise awareness of product, encourage healthy competition between rival companies, creative/entertaining/stimulating

3 Negative impact: make false claims, raise unrealistic expectations, intrusive, create materialism, create false needs

5 Make notes on vocabulary and key phrases you might use in the essay in exercise 4.

Tips for essay writing

6 Look at the list of tips for essay writing. Add two more tips of your own.

- Highlight the key words in the question.
- List the points you want to include.
- Plan carefully.
- Give examples or reasons for your views.
- Link ideas.
- Present a balanced argument.
- Use formal/neutral vocabulary.
- Use a range of grammatical structures.

7 Write an essay for the task in exercise 4 in 220–260 words. Use the advice for brainstorming vocabulary and organising your essay.

8 Being inventive

Speaking and Reading

1 Work with a partner and discuss the photos on page 53.

1 Put the inventions in order, according to the year in which they were created. There is one invention for each decade of the 20th century.
2 Which inventions do you think are the most or the least important? Which do you use most frequently?

2 Work with a partner. Read about some more inventions below and discuss these questions.

1 Which do you think are the best? Which are the most ridiculous or ill-conceived?
2 Why do you think the inventors thought each might be successful?
3 Why do you think each invention failed to catch on? Suggest ways in which each might be changed to make them more successful.

3 Answer these questions about the vocabulary used in the texts.

1 What do you think these words mean? In each case, the context should give you some clues.

> courting   contours   suction pad
> treadmill   mop   pivotable

2 What is the significance of *mini-* in *minibus*? Give more examples of nouns which use this prefix.
3 What is the significance of *-able* (in *pivotable*) and *-less* (in *endless*)? Give more examples of adjectives which use these suffixes.
4 Find these words in the texts and suggest opposites.

> common   flexible   inner   drives
> mess up   stowed

CRAZY INVENTIONS

This glove is for courting couples who wish to maintain contact while holding hands. It has a common palm section, but two separate sets of fingers. Couples have the intimacy of direct contact, while still keeping their fingers warm.

This ladder enables spiders to climb out of the bath. It comprises a thin, flexible, latex rubber strip which follows the inner contours of the bath. A suction pad is attached to the top edge of the bath. Thus, spiders don't have to be removed before you run your bath.

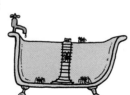

This is the horse-powered minibus. The horse walks along a treadmill in the middle of the bus. This drives the wheels via a gearbox. A thermometer under the horse's collar is connected to the dashboard. The driver can signal to the horse using a handle, which brings a mop into contact with the horse. The mop signals to the horse to slow down or move faster.

This umbrella can be worn on the head. The frame is designed so as not to mess up the wearer's hair. This brilliant invention means hands are free for carrying shopping or pushing a pram.

This is a portable seat which you wear on a belt. The seat cushion is pivotable between a stowed position and a seating position in which it hangs down so that you can sit on it. Never again does the wearer need to sit on a hard or cold seat.

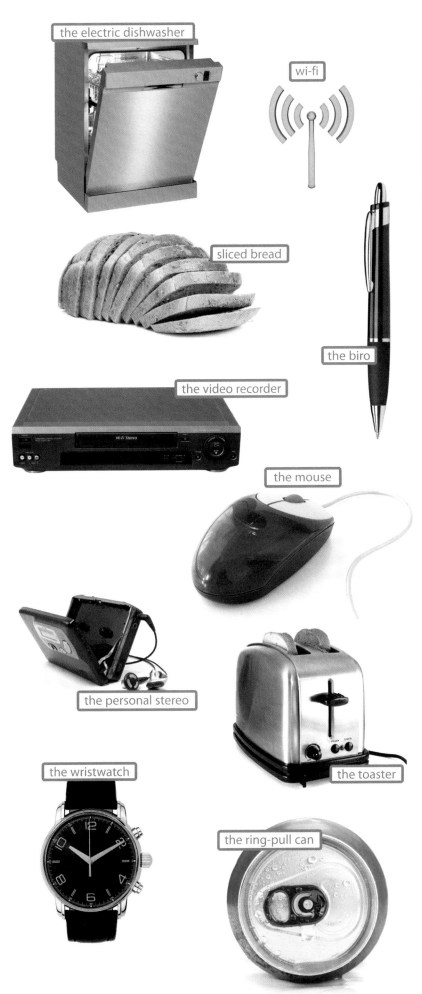

the electric dishwasher

wi-fi

sliced bread

the biro

the video recorder

the mouse

the personal stereo

the toaster

the wristwatch

the ring-pull can

Vocabulary

1 **Choose the best adjective in each sentence.**

1 This digital camera takes *inspired / engrossing / breathtaking* pictures.

2 I saw her grandmother in town wearing a *pointless / trivial / hideous* hat.

3 This is a wonderfully *absorbing / ingenious / stunning* device for crushing garlic without having to peel it first.

4 This idea is so *hackneyed / worthless / hideous* – there's nothing original about it at all.

5 Erika was wearing a really *invaluable / stunning / inspired* scarlet dress and jacket.

6 I find films with gratuitous violence utterly *trivial / impractical / appalling*.

7 Although the basic idea is *ridiculous / hideous / trivial*, and it clearly won't catch on, the design is *delightful / invaluable / engrossing* and the materials are first class.

2 **Work with a partner. Look at these adjectives and decide which could be used to describe the inventions you read about. Think about whether they usually have a positive or a negative connotation.**

absorbing	breathtaking	brilliant
delightful	imaginative	engrossing
appalling	hackneyed	hideous
worthless	impractical	ingenious
inspired	invaluable	pointless
cutting-edge	innovative	ridiculous
stunning	trivial	

3 **Now write sentences using five of these adjectives to describe your own favourite or least favourite inventions.**

Listening

1 🔊 **1.13** Listen to four people discussing things they could not live without. What do they say about these objects?

2 Listen again. Were these adjectives used with a positive or negative connotation?

> brilliant stunning inspired
> ingenious indispensable vain
> extraordinary hideous

Modals and semi-modals (2)

1 Underline the modal verbs in the speech bubbles. Then decide what each speaker is doing.

> Someone really ought to invent a machine to do the ironing for you!

1 Giving advice or suggesting something would be a good idea?

> This key ring bleeps when you whistle – that should help you next time you lose your keys.

2 Suggesting something is likely, or making a recommendation?

> You must get yourself a smart phone – everyone else has one.

3 Talking about an obligation or giving advice?

> My hairdryer's missing – my flatmate must have borrowed it again.

4 Making a deduction or expressing annoyance?

> You should have kept the instructions for the camera!

5 Expressing disapproval or praise?

> He submitted his request for a patent ages ago – he must be going to hear from the department soon.

6 Talking about probability or about necessity?

> You shouldn't have pressed that button.

7 Saying the person did or didn't do something wrong?

> The design has been approved and we should be starting production next week.

8 Expressing possibility, probability or certainty?

> Even when he was still at school, he would spend hours in the shed designing weird and wonderful inventions.

9 Talking about something that happened frequently or rarely?

> You will accept this design, or else!

10 How much choice does the speaker feel the person has about accepting the design?

> We must light a fire somehow but no one's brought any matches – what shall we do?

11 With the use of *shall*, is the speaker asking for predictions or suggestions?

2 Work with a partner. Complete these sentences using modals from the box. Sometimes, there is more than one possible answer.

must   mustn't   must have   ought to   shall
should   shouldn't   shouldn't have
should have   will   would   wouldn't

1 All pupils .... wear uniform at all times in school and on their way to and from school.

2 We're going to be doing a lot of walking, so I think you .... bring strong outdoor shoes.

3 I wonder where they can be. They .... got here by now. They .... missed their train.

4 After school we used to go to the shop on the corner where everyone .... buy sweets.

5 You .... smoke in the petrol station!

6 He's always late for work. He .... catch an earlier train.

7 .... you take this man to be your lawful wedded husband?

8 Jo looked very upset. You .... criticised her in public like that.

 Corpus spot

Be careful with *should, could* and *would*. The *Cambridge English Corpus* shows that exam candidates often make mistakes with these words.

If you have a problem, I **would** *be grateful if you could phone me.*

NOT *If you have a problem, I* **should** *be grateful if you could phone me.*

Choose the best option in these sentences written by exam candidates.

1 First of all, it *should / would* be advisable to select a better hotel than the Hotel Royal.

2 The company *should / would* hire an extra bus for the day trip to Stratford-upon-Avon.

3 I *could / would* also like to mention that the room is very small.

4 It *should / would* be a good idea if we invited your brother next time.

5 I think we *would / should* talk about this matter in a future meeting.

6 We *could / would* organise a party and have food from all around the world.

 G → page 166

Speaking

 Exam spot

It is useful to use exclamations (as well as other words such as *Yes, Right* and *Mm*) to indicate that you are listening when someone is telling you something. They can be said with different intonation in order to convey different reactions.

1 Match the exclamations (1–14) with language functions from the box.

expressing agreement
expressing admiration
expressing surprise or disbelief
expressing sympathy

1 Absolutely!
2 Fantastic!
3 That's interesting.
4 Oh dear!
5 Surely not?
6 That's terrible!
7 Brilliant!
8 What a coincidence!
9 Me too!
10 Poor you!
11 No, really?
12 What a surprise!
13 What a shame.
14 You're joking!

2 Look at these statements. Which exclamations do you think would be appropriate responses?

1 I've been offered a fantastic job at a software company in California but if I take it, I have to go for at least three years.

2 I've failed my driving test. Again.

3 I got a brilliant new mobile phone yesterday and someone stole it from my bag on the bus this morning!

4 They said I'll have to have an operation.

5 I've got some free tickets for the concert. Would you like them?

6 I'm sure the government will hold on to power at the next election.

7 I'm going to buy a new car.

8 I don't think I'm going to be able to afford a new computer now.

3 1 **14** Listen to ten sentences. Respond in an appropriate way, using intonation to show surprise, enthusiasm, etc.

4 Work with a partner. Take turns to tell each other about an interesting experience you recently had. When listening, use appropriate exclamations.

Exam folder 4

Paper 1 Part 4

Key word transformation

Part 4 of the Reading and Use of English test is a key word transformation task. This tests your knowledge of both vocabulary and grammar in that you have to make a sentence with the same meaning as another sentence and using a word that you are given.

There are six items, each consisting of one complete sentence, one given word and a sentence with a gap in the middle.

- You have to complete the second sentence using the word given.
- You cannot change the word given in any way.
- The second sentence must be as close as possible in meaning to the first sentence.
- You must use between three and six words, to complete the second sentence.

> I was about to leave school when I saw George.
> POINT
> I was _on the point of leaving school_ when I saw George.

In this example, you need to know the phrase *to be on the point of* and you need to know that *of* must be followed by a noun or *-ing* form.

1 Complete the sentences using the word given.

1 Sam's invention impressed his tutor.
MADE
Sam's invention .... his tutor.

2 He would only speak English with the visitors.
INSISTED
He .... English with the visitors.

3 The price of petrol went up a lot last month.
SHARP
There was a .... the price of petrol last month.

4 I saw the postman for a second as he passed by.
SIGHT
I .... the postman for a second as he passed by.

2 Why are these answers incorrect? Correct them.

1 Each new generation is told the secret recipe.
DOWN
The secret recipe *is handed down* each new generation.

2 I hadn't expected the present at all.
CAME
The present *comes as a complete surprise* to me.

3 The child's mother became very emotional when he was found.
OVERCOME
The child's mother *was overcome for emotion* when he was found.

4 Could you possibly help me with this suitcase?
HAND
Could you possibly *help my hand* with this suitcase?

Fixed phrases and collocations

In this part of the Reading and Use of English test, it will help if you know a wide range of collocations and fixed phrases (e.g. blissfully happy, which means extremely happy or to be at a loose end, which means to have nothing in particular to do).

3 Match phrases 1–6 with their equivalent phrases a–f.

1 He pointed out to me
2 I was shocked
3 I couldn't see him anywhere
4 He'll feel much better
5 I had no idea
6 He lost his job

a There was no sign of him
b He drew my attention to
c I was unaware
d He was made redundant
e It came as a complete surprise to me
f It'll do him good

Adjectives/verbs/nouns + prepositions

When you learn an adjective, verb or noun, make sure you also learn any prepositions that need to come after it.

4 Complete these sentences with a preposition.

1 She said that she always takes pride .... her work.
2 He's proud .... his daughter's achievements.
3 I was prevented .... entering the competition because of my age.
4 They specialise .... designing apps for educational purposes.
5 I agree that you could trust him .... your life.
6 He asked if there had been a huge increase .... the number of students going to university.

The transformation will also require you to think about grammar. For example, passives, conditionals, reported speech, etc.

5 Complete these sentences with three to six words, including the word given.

1 Unless we get the 8 o'clock train, we will miss lunch.
MEAN
If we don't get the 8 o'clock train, ... lunch.

2 They say Italian football players earn more than others.
HIGHEST
Italian football players are .... salaries.

3 'I'm sorry I forgot to email you the details earlier,' said the tour operator.
FOR
The tour operator .... emailing the details earlier.

4 I don't think the advice your accountant gave you was very good.
SHOULD
Your accountant .... better advice.

Practice

6 Complete the second sentence so that it has a similar meaning to the first sentence, using the word given. Do not change the word given. You must use between three and six words, including the word given.

1 Some people have to provide a medical certificate when they apply for a US visa.
REQUIRED
A medical certificate .... a US visa.

2 People say the island has a lot of natural resources.
RICH
The island .... natural resources.

3 Gina complains all the time.
NOTHING
Gina .... complain.

4 The candidate answered the questions honestly.
HONEST
The candidate .... the questions.

5 The tennis court was so wet, the match was cancelled.
BEEN
If the tennis court hadn't been so wet, the match .... off.

6 Regardless of the fact that you're my friend, I agree with your argument.
SIDE
I'd be .... you weren't my friend.

7 Sam said that there was no way he was prepared to help me.
FLATLY
Sam .... hand.

8 Could you get some milk as you're coming home?
WAY
Would you mind .... home?

9 Urban living

Speaking and Reading

1 Work with a partner. Discuss these questions.

  1 Look at the photos. What do you think it would be like to live in each of these places?

  2 What do you think are the good and bad points of where you live?

  3 What are the most memorable cities you have visited? Why are they memorable?

  4 What would be the perfect city to live in? List five characteristics that you and your partner agree on.

2 Read the article. Which sentence sums up each paragraph?

  a The question we face today.

  b How cities of the future can become good places to live.

  c The ideal combination of past and present.

  d How times have changed.

  e The consequences of poor or no planning.

  f Cities also need modernity.

  g The romantic attractions of the past.

  h Where the opportunities lie.

3 Read the article again and make notes on these questions.

  1 How do you think pre-automobile cities differ from later cities?

  2 Why does the writer say the cities have much to offer, yet leave much to be desired?

  3 List the ten things the writer mentions about the ideal city.

  4 Why does the writer say the scale of mega-cities can have de-humanising effects?

  5 In what ways is Asia particularly attractive for city planners?

  6 What change in China does the writer highlight?

  7 What three points does the writer make in paragraph 7 about the lessons of the past for future cities?

  8 What four factors are necessary to achieve the kind of future city he hopes for?

4 Work in pairs and compare your notes.

⬇ Vocabulary spot

Prefixes can help you understand unfamiliar words. For example, in this text you would find a knowledge of prefixes useful in understanding words such as: pre-automobile (*pre* = before); mega-city (*mega* = extremely large); de-humanisation (*de* = away from) and over-building (*over* = too much).

THE PERFECT CITY

1   What is your favourite city? Most people tend to choose somewhere rich in history like Cairo or St Petersburg. Usually, we go for places built in pre-automobile times with narrow streets and a vivid sense of times past.

2   But when we live in a city – or even when we visit it as a tourist – we need it to be more than just a reminder of a romantic past. We want it also to have the energy of a modern, prosperous mega-city such as New York, Rio de Janeiro or Shanghai, each with its unique, exhilarating atmosphere. However, for many people, the hustle and bustle of these cities also leave something to be desired.

3   What we really want is a city that has everything. It needs to have a sense of the past but it should also offer modern amenities alongside all the social, cultural and other opportunities that we now enjoy. We want it also to have some physical features to give it its own unique character – an attractive harbour, perhaps, or views of mountains. And, on top of all that, we want a well-managed city that is clean and does not have congested streets. That's quite a challenge for urban planners.

4   But perhaps it is unrealistic to expect so much. Cities today are so large that many people fear that this means de-humanisation. We want to avoid over-building, but how can this be done while still providing facilities for a rapidly growing population? Will it be possible to retain the qualities we value in the great cities of the past in a modern, vibrant mega-city?

5   The most exciting developments in architecture these days are to be found in Asia where cities are developing at an unprecedented speed. Urban planners in various cities have come up with some outstanding ways of dealing with the challenges they face, designing innovative solutions that should certainly make life better.

6   My father, who spent his life as an urban planner in London, told me about his first visit to China nearly 40 years ago. He said he would never forget his first sight of a Chinese city. There was not a skyscraper to be seen, and there were few cars. There were no motorways or underground railways. Now, the cities he visited then have altered almost beyond recognition, and are some of the biggest cities on Earth. As they developed, they sometimes – but not unfortunately always – managed to avoid some of the pitfalls that have been encountered in urban growth in Europe and North America.

7   So what might the future hold? Planners are increasingly aware of environmental concerns, particularly in relation to the costs and availability of energy sources. They are also disturbed by the regrettable division between rich and poor that has occurred in many of our cities, where you can see extreme wealth and great poverty existing side by side. Moreover, a beautiful natural location has often been destroyed, all in the name of progress. And this almost always goes hand in hand with desperate traffic congestion and a lack of green spaces. Taking all such issues into account may allow our cities to expand – as expand they must – in a more wholesome and rational way.

8   There are three essential ingredients for cities to be happy places for their inhabitants. There must be good standards of living, supported by stable economic growth. There must be a sense of equality for citizens. Cultural life must be able to thrive. For these conditions to be achieved, we need wise governments with the resources and foresight to ensure that urban planning is carried out responsibly and creatively.

Vocabulary

1 **Match these words to make collocations. You can check your answers in the article.**

1	rich	**a**	congestion
2	hustle	**b**	amenities
3	unique	**c**	concerns
4	modern	**d**	of living
5	traffic	**e**	recognition
6	beyond	**f**	character
7	environmental	**g**	and bustle
8	standards	**h**	in history

2 **Complete the sentences with a collocation from exercise 1.**

1 It's good to go to the countryside sometimes, to get away from the .... of the city.

2 It is hoped that the new bus service will ease ....

3 Kotor, in Montenegro, has a .... – a beautiful fjord in the heart of the Mediterranean.

4 .... have been rising in recent years – there is more employment, and health care has improved, too.

5 This town has changed .... – it used to be all green fields when I was a boy!

6 There are .... concerning plans for the new nuclear power plant.

7 This hotel has all the .... you need – wi-fi, 24-hour reception, and a regular shuttle bus to the city centre.

8 Singapore, with its Chinatown, Little India and Arab Quarter, is ....

3 **Choose three of the collocations. Write sentences about your own town or city.**

Listening

1 **You are going to listen to four people talking about living in large cities. What do you think they might say about how things have changed where they live and about what they enjoy about life there?**

2 **1 15 Listen and match each person with a photo.**

3 **Listen again and make notes in the table.**

Speaker	1	2	3	4
City				
Length of time there				
Change(s) mentioned				
Favourite aspect of city				

Kuala Lumpur

Dubai

Delhi

Bangkok

Future forms

1 **Identify the structures (a–j) used to express the future in sentences 1–10. There may be more than one answer.**

1 What are you doing this evening?
2 What will you be doing this time tomorrow?
3 What are you going to do for your next holiday?
4 What are you going to do when this course finishes?
5 What will you do if you pass the exam?
6 What would you do if you passed the exam?
7 What time does this English lesson finish?
8 Which country do you think is most likely to win the next football World Cup?
9 Is there anyone in the class who might eventually become internationally famous, in your opinion?
10 What will you have achieved by the age of 60?

a focus on one moment in future time
b looking back from a point in the future
c future probability
d future after time conjunction
e intention
f plan (with stated time)
g something fixed by a timetable
h a possible future using the first conditional
i a hypothetical future
j tentative prediction

2 **Choose the best form for each of these sentences.**

1 *I go* / *I'm going* / *I'll go* to the cinema on Saturday to see that new Brad Pitt film.
2 I'll call you when I *get* / *will get* / *will have got* home.
3 This time next week *we're going to lie* / *we'll lie* / *we'll be lying* on a tropical beach.
4 If he got the job, he*'ll leave* / *he'd leave* / he*'ll have left* for Paris next month.
5 Melissa is very likely *getting* / *to getting* / *to get* a good job as she is fluent in three languages.
6 My flight *is going to leave* / *leaves* / *is leaving* at 10.20 tomorrow morning.
7 When we *will be* / *are going to be* / *are* in London, *we are spending* / *we spend* / *we are going to spend* the first day on a tour.
8 If Barbara *gets* / *will get* / *is getting* a place at university, *she's studying* / *she's going to study* / *she studies* philosophy and politics.
9 By 2050 people *set foot* / *are going to set foot* / *will have set foot* on Mars.

3 **Work with a partner. Ask and answer the questions in exercise 1, using the correct verb forms.**

Speaking

1 **Work in groups. What are the pros and cons of life in a big city? Look at the topics below. How is each different in a city, compared to the countryside?**

TRANSPORT

shopping

leisure facilities

education

housing

HEALTH AND WELFARE

impact on the environment

social life

2 **What is the biggest advantage of life in a big city? What is the biggest disadvantage?**

3 **You are going to report your discussions back to the rest of the class.**

1 Think about how you will do this. Decide whether you will need any charts or other visuals as well as what to say and who should say it.
2 Now report your group's ideas to the class.
3 When you listen to other groups' presentations, make notes on what each group says.
4 In your groups, discuss the presentations you heard. Decide which ideas were best in relation to each of the topics in exercise 1.

Writing folder 4

Reports

In Part 2 of the Writing test, you may be asked to write a report.

1 Look at these statements about writing reports. Are they true (T) or false (F)?

1 Reports usually begin with *Dear*.
2 Reports are likely to open with a statement of the reason for writing.
3 If you are asked to write a report, you should also include a title.
4 The opening of a report should aim to catch the reader's interest.
5 Reports discuss what has happened, whereas proposals make suggestions about what the writer would like to happen.
6 Reports need to have a heading and sub-headings, whereas proposals do not.
7 Proposals make recommendations, while reports do not.
8 Reports and proposals are often written in informal English.
9 It is important to think about exactly who you are writing for.
10 Spending time planning what you're going to write is more important for a report than for an essay or a letter.

2 Remember that the Writing tasks also involve careful reading. You will lose marks if you do not do exactly as you are asked. Read this example of a task and underline the important elements.

> Your college has asked students to report on the sports facilities which students can use in their leisure time. Write a report for the college principal, commenting on the extent to which the facilities meet students' needs. You should also make recommendations about what you think the college should do to improve the facilities.

3 Answer these questions about the task.

1 Who do you have to write to?
2 Would you use a formal, neutral or informal register?
3 What information is needed?
4 What kind of text do you have to write?

4 Read two answers to the task (A and B on page 63) written by two students in the same class. Use the questions in the Exam advice box to analyse them. Which would score a better mark?

EXAM ADVICE

These are the kinds of questions the examiners consider when looking at a piece of writing.
- Does the writing do exactly what was asked for?
- Is the writing clearly organised?
- Is the writing accurate?
- Does the writer use a range of vocabulary and structures?
- Is the writing in an appropriate register (e.g. formal or informal)?
- Would the piece of writing have an appropriate impact on the target reader?

5 Now write an answer to this task.

> You have been asked to write a report for an international transport organisation on the public transport system in the area where you live. Your report should outline the public transport system available. It should comment on its strengths and should also make suggestions for improvements, explaining why these improvements are required.
> Write 220–260 words.

A

Dear Principal,

Thanks for your email. It was really good to hear from you. I've had a chat with a few of my mates and we agree that the leisure facilities here are really good. The sports facilities are great but they are very heavily used especially by people who want to play tennis or swim or use the gym to improve their fitness. It'd be better if the sports centre facilities were open longer hours and the booking system for the gym could be improved. The music block is also great. We all really like the practice rooms and the instruments you can use there. In fact, we think we are really lucky at this college that we have such good leisure facilities. Lots of students are not so lucky as we are. We are also very lucky that we have such a good library at this college too. I hope this gives you all the information you need. I look forward to hearing from you soon.

Yours

Ana

B

Leisure Facilities at Shamrock College

Level of satisfaction

In general most students have a high level of satisfaction with the leisure facilities here. We are all impressed by the sports centre, which is used by a large majority of students. The tennis courts, swimming pool and fitness gym are particularly popular. The music block is also appreciated by myself and all the many other students who make full use of the first-class practice rooms and are grateful for the range of high-quality instruments available for them to play there.

Recommendations

Because the facilities are well used, there is pressure on resources and that is the reason for these recommendations. The sports centre is currently open between 9am and 9pm. However, many students would like to use it outside these hours. Were it to open for longer, this would ease pressure on the facilities. A further way of achieving this aim would be to make the booking system for the gym more efficient. Double bookings frequently occur and this is frustrating for all concerned.

With regard to the music block, the sole improvement I would suggest is that the current concert hall should be extended. This would make it a much more flexible space, allowing it to be used for much larger events than is currently the case. This might enable the college to generate some useful income from ticket sales. Please let me know if you would like me to expand on these suggestions.

10 You live and learn

Speaking and Reading

1 **Work with a partner. Discuss these questions and give reasons and examples.**

  1 Look at the photos of students. What are they doing in each photo?

  2 Do you know anyone who has studied abroad? What have they told you about their experiences?

  3 Why might someone choose to study abroad?

  4 What impact might studying abroad have on a person?

2 **Read four extracts on page 65 in which four academics write about the topic of studying abroad.**

  Which researcher …

  1 focuses on students majoring in the same subject?

  2 focuses on students studying in one particular country?

  3 compares results from two different groups of students at the same institution?

  4 studied the same students at different points of time?

3 **Now read the extracts again and answer these questions.**

  Which researcher …

  1 shares reviewer D's opinion about the impact that international travel can have on future work opportunities?

  2 expresses a different view from the others in that he/she did not start from a concern about the impact of studying abroad?

  3 comes to a different conclusion from A about the parameters required for a beneficial period of study abroad?

  4 expresses a different view from the others in the way he/she hopes that studying abroad may prove useful in future?

⊙ Exam spot

In Part 6 of Paper 1 (the Reading and Use of English test), you need to answer four questions in which you have to compare four different texts in order to note what opinions they share and where they differ. Note that although you will need to understand all four texts in order to do the task, it is quite possible that one of the texts will not feature as the answer to any of the questions.

4 **Some vocabulary is found much more frequently in an academic context than in everyday English. Match the words from the box with the underlined words in the extracts.**

look for	main	choose	replies	views
develop	methods	before	given	

5 **Complete the sentences with the underlined words from the extracts.**

  1 The aim of the course is to help students .... the skills they will need in their future careers.

  2 The study skills guide recommends a number of useful .... to help with revision.

  3 The researchers .... the new drug to one set of patients and a placebo to a control group.

  4 The .... aim of the research was to obtain evidence that could usefully inform government policy.

  5 We only got 308 .... from the questionnaire.

  6 The study .... to establish the reasons why some students find it easier to adapt to a new culture than others do.

  7 The study compared samples taken .... the operation with those taken afterwards.

  8 The value of gaining your degree in another country can be considered from several different ....

  9 Most of the students decided to .... the intensive programme rather than the part-time one.

STUDYING ABROAD

Four researchers present their findings on the impact and effects of studying in another country.

A Studying abroad is an area that is becoming increasingly interesting for researchers, as more students are choosing to do a semester, a year or even a degree in another country. In my research, I set out to establish whether young people attending a course abroad <u>acquire</u> more global awareness than students enrolled on similar courses in their home country. Using a comparative study of 50 Canadian undergraduates, half of whom studied abroad for varying lengths of time, there were shown to be considerable gains in global awareness and these were not only self-perceived by the students but also noted by their tutors.

B My research project asked ten students embarking on a year of study abroad to keep a daily record of their experiences. Having begun the diary a month <u>prior to</u> leaving home, they continued it for a month after they returned. The <u>primary</u> reason for studying abroad in all cases was to polish their language skills. The students were allowed to write as freely as they wished but were asked to include comments on their language learning experience as well as on the <u>strategies</u> they used to cope with living in a new culture, with a view to helping others in the same situation in future. Analysing the diaries, we found remarkably similar patterns. All the participants demonstrated a gradual recognition and acceptance of difference in other cultures and a new objectivity about their own culture as a result of their experience.

C This paper reports on some research carried out last year into why students <u>opt for</u> a period of study abroad, their reasons for selecting a specific destination, their behaviour when abroad and the extent to which the experience matches their expectations. Having <u>administered</u> a questionnaire to 1,000 international students studying at a number of universities in Australia, we got 696 <u>responses</u>. An initial analysis of the responses has revealed some interesting data suggesting that the key factor affecting all the areas we were investigating was the individual's personality and study interests. Country of origin and gender proved less significant than anticipated.

D This research looked at the career paths of 35 young business people who had spent part of their university course at a foreign educational institution in order to ascertain whether those people had acquired greater cross-cultural <u>perspectives</u> through their experience of study abroad. Concerned about the lack of cultural awareness of their staff, a group of US business corporations prompted the research. The results are less conclusive than expected, but they do suggest that a period of study in a foreign country may help students to develop the cross-cultural awareness that US employers currently <u>seek</u>.

Vocabulary

1 **Many words in English come from a set of words formed from the same root. Complete the table. Sometimes there is more than one possible answer.**

Verb	Noun	Adjective
	acceptance	
	assumption	
attend		
	competition	
conclude		
	contribution	
determine		
establish		
opt		
signify	significance	significant

2 **Rewrite these sentences using the words in capitals. Do not change the form of the word.**

1 The results of the survey do not allow us to draw any clear conclusions. (CONCLUSIVE)
The results of the survey are not conclusive.

2 In my opinion, the research falsely assumed certain things. (ASSUMPTIONS)

3 The idea was initially controversial but it rapidly gained acceptance. (ACCEPTED)

4 A lot of people try to get a place at this university. (COMPETITION)

5 The government's inadequate response to the economic crisis contributed to their election defeat. (CONTRIBUTORY)

6 Very few students attended the last lecture of the course. (ATTENDANCE)

7 The party's aim was the establishment of a fairer distribution of wealth in society. (ESTABLISH)

8 I admire this student because she is so determined to succeed. (DETERMINATION)

Participle clauses

1 **Participle clauses are clauses beginning with either a present, a past or a perfect participle. Look at these underlined examples from the abstracts.**

1 <u>Analysing the diaries</u>, we found remarkably similar patterns.

2 <u>Concerned about the lack of cultural awareness of their staff</u>, a group of US business corporations prompted the research.

3 <u>Having administered a questionnaire</u>, we got 696 responses.

2 **Participle clauses can be expanded to make full clauses. Expand the underlined participles in the above examples to make full clauses.**

1 When *we analysed the diaries, we found remarkably similar patterns*.

2 Because they ...., a group of US business corporations prompted the research.

3 After ...., we got 696 responses.

3 **Expand the underlined participle clauses, using the words in brackets. Make any other necessary changes to the sentences.**

1 <u>Hoping to encourage people to respond</u>, the researcher offered the chance to win a prize to anyone who returned his questionnaire within two days. (because)

2 <u>It being a Sunday</u>, most of the shops were shut. (since)

3 <u>Generally considered a weak king</u>, Charles I was eventually beheaded. (who)

4 <u>Ignored by many scholars until recently</u>, Charlton's work is at last receiving the recognition it deserves. (although)

5 <u>Seen from a distance</u>, the university looks like something out of a fairy tale. (if)

6 <u>Having previously learned their language</u>, Picton was able to communicate with the tribe. (as)

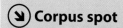 **Corpus spot**

Take care with perfect participle clauses. The *Cambridge English Corpus* shows exam candidates often make mistakes with these.

Having been in England for the last three years, I have a good knowledge of the language.

NOT ***Being*** ~~in England for the last three years, I have a good knowledge of the language.~~

4 Rewrite these sentences, starting with the words given.

1 While I was walking round the exhibition, I caught sight of an old school friend. (Walking)

....

2 Because Marti had made so many mistakes in her homework, she had to do it all over again. (Having)

....

3 She's a child – she doesn't know what's happening. (Being)

....

4 As Jack didn't have anyone to spend the evening with, he decided to have an early night. (Not)

....

5 If you look at it from a sociological point of view, the problem can be seen as one of tension between social classes. (Looked)

....

> **⊙ Exam spot**
>
> It will create a good impression in the Writing test if you occasionally make use of appropriate participle clauses.

5 Complete three or four of these prompts.

1 Having studied English for some years now, …
2 Having spent a lot of time trying to, …
3 It being a … day today, …
4 Not wanting to appear boastful, I …
5 Knowing what I know now about …

G → page 167

Speaking

1 Read the conversations and underline the words which Speaker B would be most likely to stress.

1 A: Did you go to the cinema last night?
  B: No, but I went to the theatre.
2 A: Did you go by bike to the theatre last night?
  B: No, Marco was using my bike last night.
3 A: Did you go to the theatre by bus last night?
  B: No, I went to the theatre by taxi last night.
4 A: Did you go home by taxi last night?
  B: No, I went home by taxi two nights ago.
5 A: Anna's wearing a lovely green dress.
  B: It's a green blouse and skirt, actually.
6 A: Did you have a good time at the party last night?
  B: Yes, we had a brilliant time.
7 A: Are you hungry yet?
  B: I'm not hungry, I'm starving.
8 A: Are you hungry yet?
  B: I'm not hungry but Tina is.

2 **1 16** Now listen and check.

3 Write three more conversations like those in exercise 1.

4 Work with a partner. Practise your conversations.

5 Look at the pictures. Work with a partner and take turns to suggest sentences about the differences you can see.

In B, the students are in a lab and in A, they are in a seminar.

> **⊙ Exam spot**
>
> In the Speaking test, you will have to compare pictures. Using the stress patterns practised here can help you sound more natural.

Units 6–10 Revision

Topic review

1 Work in pairs and discuss the questions.

1 What things – apart from making calls and texting – do you use your mobile for?
2 How do you feel when someone hangs up on you?
3 Which invention could you not live without?
4 What are some of the rewards and challenges of studying abroad?
5 What subject have you always wanted to study?
6 What do you hope you will have achieved by the year 2030?

Grammar

2 Think about last year and next year. Write at least one sentence in answer to each of these questions.

1 What changes are going to take place in your life next year?
2 What must you try to do next year?
3 What special things did you have to do last year?
4 What should you do next year if you have the possibility?
5 What should you have done last year but were unfortunately unable to?
6 What do you think will have happened by the end of next year?

3 Think about something that happened last year and the results it has had or is likely to have. Write a sentence to link what happened with its effects or likely effects.

Last year there was a change of government and this has resulted in less money being spent on the health service this year.

4 Now write a sentence using a participle clause about the events from last year that you thought about above.

Having won last year's election, the prime minister now has to try to implement his pre-election promises.

Reading

5 'Telecommuting' means working from home. With a partner, discuss what you think would be the advantages and disadvantages.

6 Read the text below and decide which option (A, B, C or D) fits each gap. What helps you to decide?

When the office is your best bet

I look back on my days spent working at home with (1) .... feelings. Sure, it was great not to have to fight through traffic to get to my desk. The (2) .... was, once I'd started working, I couldn't stop. When there was more work to do, I just kept doing it. Then I spoke to an expert, who explained the three laws of telecommuting.

'First of all, you should (3) .... that you have a self-contained office,' he said. 'Next, you should have a separate phone line, both from a business and a psychological point of view. And then you need to keep your work and your home life (4) ....'

My score: zero out of three. Dedicating a room to work is not (5) .... in a small flat. My computer was squeezed into a corner of the living room, which made drawing a (6) .... between home and work even harder: even when I was relaxing, all that equipment would be glowering at me from across the room. I'd pick up my email in the evening, and half of it would be work-related.

John, a friend who used to work from home, didn't have a separate room, so he couldn't get away from his work either. 'At one stage,' he says, 'I had to go through my "office" to get to the toilet.'

He likes to tell the story of the artist Magritte, whose studio was at home. Each morning, Magritte would (7) .... and put on his suit. He would then go out of his house, re-enter the house and go into his studio, where he would change into his artist's smock and spend the day painting. At the end of the day, he would change back into his suit, leave the house again and go once round the house in the opposite (8) .... and 'return' home for the evening.

It seems Magritte had the right idea. Unless you can stick to the three laws, stick to the office.

1	A combined	B distinct	C mixed	D opposite
2	A trouble	B matter	C doubt	D question
3	A assure	B insure	C reassure	D ensure
4	A aside	B aback	C apart	D away
5	A adequate	B feasible	C logical	D likely
6	A limit	B mark	C line	D border
7	A raise	B rise	C rouse	D arouse
8	A path	B indication	C way	D direction

Vocabulary

7 **Use the word given in capitals to form a word that fits the gap in each line.**

1 Sarah is very .... – she's always thinking up original ideas. INVENT

2 Tom's life changed beyond .... when he moved to the country. RECOGNISE.

3 You look like a top business .... in that smart suit. EXECUTE

4 What an utterly stupid .... idea! POINT

5 The teacher said one of the students had been .... rude to her. APPAL

6 Our business prides itself on receiving very few .... about our products. COMPLAIN

7 The students have all expressed a high level of .... with their course. SATISFY

8 There's no point in arguing over such a totally .... issue. SIGNIFY

9 You shouldn't make .... about someone just because of their appearance. ASSUME

10 The police were unable to charge the man because there was no .... evidence against him. CONCLUDE

🡖 Exam spot

In the word formation exercise in the Reading and Use of English test, it is important to understand what the missing word is likely to mean as this will help you to put the word in the right form.

8 **Complete the article with one word in each gap.**

Toys for the boys

There are lots of adult men who will happily **(0)** ...*spend*...... hours and huge sums of money on the latest gadget, standing in long queues overnight, hoping to grab the latest release before it sells **(1)** ....

Is this normal adult behaviour? Or are these men just refusing to **(2)** .... up and stop playing with their 'toys'?

According to Adam Shreck, editor of a leading electronics website, many men are devoted **(3)** .... gadgets. He believes they are an extension **(4)** .... a man's personality.

For Shreck, gadgets are also a **(5)** .... of personal wealth – instead of going to a toy shop, grown-up men can take out their wallets and go and buy something a lot more expensive.

Maybe it's not childish after **(6)** ...., but true macho behaviour.

Some men take a lot of pride **(7)** .... their gadgets. They like to know they have the best, the most expensive, the most up-to-date. It's like a male survival instinct – wanting to show they have something better **(8)** .... the next man.

Reading

1 Work with a partner. Discuss these questions.

1 Do you like to keep up with modern trends?

2 How often do you buy clothes and how do you decide what to buy?

3 Do you think people's tastes are influenced by what they read in magazines or see on screen?

4 Do you read articles on the internet? Which do you think is better: reading 'real' magazines or their electronic versions?

2 Read the article. Six paragraphs have been removed. Choose from paragraphs A–G the one that fits each gap. There is one extra paragraph.

3 How did you select the missing paragraphs? For example, did you find:

- the same or a similar word in the article and the missing paragraph?
- a noun in the article and its pronoun in the missing paragraph?
- a problem described in the article and then a solution in the missing paragraph?
- a logical development of the 'story'?

4 Complete these sentences. Use the useful words/ phrases in bold in the article to help you.

1 Before the technology was launched, the company .... several .... in the area.

2 The store's innovative approach gives them the edge .... their competitors.

3 This new scanning technology could mean .... customers not knowing whether clothes will fit properly or not.

4 These jeans are extremely .... money.

5 Some people are .... wool and can't wear this range of sweaters.

6 These clothes have been designed with the younger generation ....

7 A Japanese company has taken the technology .... and added several new applications.

8 Mark was talked .... buying the shirt by his brother.

Talking clothes get our measure

Can you imagine trousers that **talk you into buying** them? Customers in a top international clothing store may soon find their prospective purchases telling them whether they would be a good fit.

The system, which can be applied to jackets, skirts and almost any other garment, is seen as the most exciting innovation in retailing in years. It could cut out hours spent trying on clothes that will never fit and, once perfected, could **mean the end of** the changing room.

1 ....

A version of the technology is already being worked on by a leading clothes retailer, whose next big sizing survey, the first in more than 10 years, will make use of the latest three-dimensional scanning technology. The shop will use the information to determine the shapes of its future clothing and it will also **run a trial** in which selected shoppers can use the data collected from the scanner to order clothes.

2 ....

The technology has already been **taken further** in the United States. Smart cards holding an individual's scan details are being designed to plug into a portable device that shoppers carry round the store with them. This enables people to enjoy their usual browsing experience.

3 ....

For some customers, the prospect of successive pairs of trousers – in sizes that once might have fitted – loudly announcing that they are far too small could turn shopping into a humiliation. But the system is likely to be **designed with these people in mind**.

4 ....

Stephen Gray, an expert in computer clothing research, explains that it will be possible for shops to allow customers to use their smart cards to order made-to-measure clothing. 'Translating three-dimensional images into two-dimensional clothing patterns is a skill we have lost as traditional tailoring has disappeared,' said Gray.

5 ....

Both clothing retailers and manufacturers are keen to be involved with this new technology. They are always looking for ways to **give them the edge over their competitors** and increase their market share. Those businesses which are among the first to embrace this technology may well attract new customers, especially those drawn to innovative technology.

6 ....

If this technology takes off, it will be interesting to see if it is taken up by other sectors, such as the food industry. In the future, could food tell us its nutritional value and whether it is suitable for us and how much of it we should consume per portion? This could be extremely useful for people who are **allergic to** nuts or wheat, for instance. 'Talking technology' is also of course enormously helpful to people who are visually impaired.

As a result, several disabilities groups have also expressed interest in the technology and are looking into how it could make shopping easier for their members. Internet shopping, talking labels and spoken or videoed cooking instructions could revolutionise our lives.

These trousers will make your hips look big!!!

A As they pass racks of clothing in the store, tags on the clothes programmed with a selection of pre-recorded responses interact with the device and talk to the customer. They will be able to advise on the item of clothing's likely fit, or otherwise.

B By doing so, the device will also enable customers to shop by mail order more satisfactorily. This is something which customer groups have been pressing for.

C Any item of clothing, from a top-of-the-range suit to underwear, could be programmed to chat to its buyer, with warnings such as 'This is nice but not quite right for you,' or encouragements along the lines of 'I'm a perfect fit,' or 'It suits you, sir.'

D Interestingly, clothing manufacturers are extremely interested in the new possibilities this offers them. They are going to have to relearn the skills associated with making clothes by hand and then find a way to automate them. A challenge they are willing to take on in order to stay in business.

E Instead of loudspeakers, customers can opt for a small earpiece, so that their potential trousers, suit or even underwear would not need to talk. They could just whisper softly in the ear and avoid any potential embarrassment.

F Customers who agree to take part in this pilot scheme will be led to a special booth by a shop assistant, who will ask them to strip off and stand still while intense beams of white light are played over their bodies. A computerised scanner will turn the results into a 'virtual reflection' – an electronic recording of their exact shape.

G However, they must remember that the average customer is extremely sophisticated these days. They will not just buy clothes because of the novel technology involved; the goods will have to be stylish, high quality and **good value for money**.

Vocabulary

5 Match the phrases in the box to their definitions 1–10.

> to suit someone   designer labels   to fit someone
> a rack   out of fashion   a look   a changing room
> item of clothing   fabric   stylish

1 something you wear
2 a style or fashion
3 to be the right size
4 no longer considered stylish
5 a place in a shop to try on clothes
6 a frame or shelf used to hang clothes
7 look good on someone
8 clothes made by famous stylists
9 fashionable
10 material

Listening

1 **Work with a partner. Is there a dress code where you work/ study or in some of the places you go? If yes, are you happy with it?**

2 **You are going to listen to a manager. She is not happy with the way some employees dress. What do you think she will mention?**

3 ¹ 🔲17 **Listen and complete sentences 1–8.**

1 First, the manager singles out those who work at the .... for criticism.
2 Men have to wear a ....
3 Clients may come in to see .... at any time, so the way they dress is important.
4 The dress code is relaxed in this company on the day called ....
5 She is unhappy about the way employees dress when they take part in ....
6 She was appalled to hear that someone had worn .... to the Business College.
7 She recognises that employees may complain because this is a .... issue.
8 She suggests employees take complaints to the .... department.

4 **What do you think of the company's dress code and the way the manager addresses the staff?**

Reported speech

1 **Imagine that you were one of the people the manager was talking to. Change these sentences into reported speech. Start each sentence with the words given.**

> It's been brought to my attention that certain members of staff have been flouting the dress code.

She said that it had been brought to her attention that certain members of staff had been flouting the dress code.

1 'I want to make it crystal clear to everyone just exactly what's expected.'
  She clarified ....

2 'Those of you who work on reception must be businesslike at all times.'
  She insisted that ....

3 'Don't forget, in many people's eyes, sloppy clothes means sloppy work.'
  She reminded ....

4 'I'm not at all happy about the way some people dress for training days.'
  She pointed out that ....

5 'It seems as though some of you have got the idea into your head that when you're on a training day, you can dress like a student.'
  She said that ....

6 'I've even heard remarks about one person who turned up wearing a nose ring.'
  She criticised someone who ....

7 'What I want to emphasise is that it's a matter of professional pride, the way you dress.'
  She stressed that ....

8 'You have to toe the line.'
  She said ....

9 'If anyone feels particularly aggrieved by any of this, all I can say is that you should take it up with the Human Resources department.'
  She suggested that ....

10 'I hope I don't have to refer to this again.'
  She hoped ....

2 **Match verbs 1–14 with the structures from the box. More than one answer may be possible.**

> doing it   to do it   me (not) to do it
> that I (should) do it

1 He promised
2 She suggested
3 We agreed
4 They told
5 She asked
6 He offered
7 She advised
8 He recommended
9 He denied
10 She invited
11 They warned
12 I insisted on
13 He threatened
14 I regretted

3 **Work with a partner. Interview each other about fashion.**

1 Here are some questions to ask. Add another two of your own.
  • Where do you buy most of your clothes?
  • Do you prefer dark or light colours?
  • Have you ever bought something quite expensive which you later regretted buying?
  • Do you prefer going shopping for clothes alone or with a friend?
  • Have you got any brothers or sisters? Do you borrow each other's clothes?

2 Interview each other and make notes of the answers.

3 Write a summary of what your partner said, using reported speech.

G → page 168

↘ Corpus spot

The *Cambridge English Corpus* shows exam candidates often make mistakes with verbs like *recommend, tell, suggest*, etc. Correct these sentences written by exam candidates.

1 It is recommend to book in advance.
2 I would recommend to ask for further information.
3 It was told to us that the problems are going to be solved.
4 It has been suggested to have a film club once a month.
5 He suggested to ask Colin to make the opening speech.
6 He regrets having not enough time to play an instrument.
7 We promised it there would be 35 stalls at the charity day.

Speaking

⊌ Exam spot

In Paper 4 (the Speaking test) Part 2, you will be given the opportunity to speak for about one minute without interruption. You are asked to compare two photos from a set of three and also to comment on the photos. When you compare the photos, talk about their similarities and differences. After you have finished speaking, your partner will be asked a question about your photos and will have 30 seconds to respond.

1 **When comparing things, try to use appropriate connecting phrases. Work with a partner. Add as many words or expressions as you can to the lists.**

- Talking about similarities: *similarly, and, they both show …*
- Talking about differences: *whereas, but, in contrast …*

2 **1.18 Listen to Angela and Luciano commenting on two of the photos below.**

1 What connecting phrases does Angela use?
2 Does Angela think the suit the man is wearing in photo A is conventional, flamboyant or inappropriate?
3 Does Angela suggest that the man in photo B is a banker, a naturalist or a teacher?

3 **Work in groups of three: the Examiner, Student A and Student B. Examiners, follow these instructions.**

1 Ask Student A to choose two of the photos on this page, and to say which person follows fashion more and give reasons for saying this.
2 Then ask Student B whether he/she thinks young people follow fashion whereas older people don't.
3 Ask Student B to compare two of the photos on this page, and to say why the people might have chosen to wear these clothes.
4 Then ask Student A if he/she thinks the fashion industry is out of touch with reality.

Exam folder 5

Paper 1 Part 5

Multiple choice

1 **You are going to read an article about fashion. For questions 1–6, choose the answer (A, B, C or D) which you think fits best according to the text. Follow the procedure in the box below to help you.**

- Read and underline the key words in the questions or sentences to be completed by the option.
- Locate the part of the text which answers the question.
- Read the whole question carefully.
- Underline or highlight the part of the text which answers the question.
- Justify by close reading of the text why the other options are wrong.

1 According to the first paragraph, why does fashion change?
  A to satisfy business interests
  B to reflect developments in society
  C to increase the choices available to people
  D to make it hard for outsiders to reproduce it

2 The writer explains that people adopt a certain style as opposed to a fashion because
  A they wish to create a new image.
  B they enjoy the status associated with it.
  C they want to belong to an identifiable group.
  D they agree with the attitudes and values it represents.

3 Why does the writer give an example from nature?
  A to explain that fashion is not a new phenomenon
  B to imply that humans use fashion to hide their true identity
  C to emphasise the lengths some people go to to follow fashion
  D to question why men are generally less interested in fashion than women

4 In the fourth paragraph, the writer suggests that copies of famous brands
  A become desirable in their own right.
  B retain much of the quality of the originals.
  C fail to deceive true followers of fashion.
  D are looked down on by followers of fashion.

5 The word 'counter-signalling' in line 45 is used in this text to refer to
  A the way the difference between social groups is maintained.
  B the high group adopting the fashion of the low group.
  C the middle group imitating the low group.
  D the way fashion goes in cycles across groups.

6 What is said about fashion in the last paragraph?
  A There has been little development of new trends in the arts.
  B Differences in dress codes are becoming more exaggerated.
  C Many people find out about new fashions through music.
  D It takes a long time for society to adopt new ways of speaking.

2 **Work in pairs and discuss these questions.**

1 For question 1, you had to understand *the former* and *the latter*. Complete the gap.
  Both real fur and fake fur are used in fashion. However, the .... is disapproved of by animal lovers.

2 Sometimes you can work out the meaning of a word from the context and by thinking about word formation. Read the first paragraph of the article again. What does *mainstream* mean?

3 For question 2D, find synonyms for *attitudes and values* in paragraph B.

4 How can we use word formation to help understand the meaning of *underlying*?

5 What do you think *grooming* means in paragraph C?

6 The test focuses for questions can be: detail, opinion, attitude, tone, purpose, main idea, implication or text organisation features. What is the test focus of question 3?

Fashion

A New fashions and styles appear in all societies. First, we must understand the difference between fashion and style and how the changes in fashion and style happen for different reasons. The former are driven by insiders
5 to prevent others from copying the insiders' style. The latter are created by outsiders trying to invent alternative styles to the mainstream; the style of most people in a society. In order to succeed, a new style needs to completely reject one of the main indicators
10 of the mainstream style. This rejection means that most people will not accept or choose the new style, and it also means that it is rarely driven by big business.

B Let us identify the main factor that shapes a particular style before returning to the topic of fashion. Many
15 suggest that style is the main visible or outward component of group identity. However, research reveals that it goes deeper than that. Most studies conclude, and it is also my view, that style is the expression of certain underlying principles and
20 viewpoints. People decide to adopt a style only after careful thought. It is unlike buying a new coat to get a new look. Moreover, a new style does not necessarily involve showing wealth or class.

C Turning to nature, we all know that the male peacock bird displays his beautiful tail to attract a female. For a 25 male peacock, having a long, shiny tail shows strength and energy. Therefore, the strongest male peacocks have a better chance of attracting a mate than weaker males. In humans, in extreme cases, some people spend an unreasonable amount of time grooming themselves 30 and may even do without more essential items in order to be fashionable.

D Humans differ from animals in their ability to deceive. Almost as soon as a new garment by a top designer appears on the catwalk, fakes turn up on market stalls. 35 The original is out of financial reach of the majority. And so, copies are born. Some are so true to the original that they may be mistaken for the genuine article even by dedicated followers of fashion. Those who knowingly buy fakes rarely concern themselves 40 with the reaction of those who purchase the original article. The fake, in fact, carries with it so much of the image of the original that it becomes attractive in itself.

E Another interesting phenomenon is what is called 'counter-signalling'. We can divide society into three 45 groups: high, middle, and low. The middle group can easily imitate the fashion of the high group, so the middle group can be confused with the high group, to the detriment of the high group. Counter-signalling occurs when the high group imitates the fashion of the 50 low group. However, if the middle group imitates the low group, they take the risk of being confused with lower one. A typical example of counter-signalling is wearing jeans. Eventually, wearing jeans became popular with everyone. This partly explains why fashion goes 55 in cycles.

F The concept of changes in fashion relates to a much wider sphere than just clothes. It is evident in the evolution of language. What once was considered slang may become an accepted phrase. Interestingly, music 60 plays an important role in the development of fashion. It brings people together at festivals and people can see how others dress and speak. In other words, it provides a chance for people to be influenced by others. I do not argue that music alone creates a new 65 fashion. But music, dress and speech all work together to spread new ideas and trends.

EXAM ADVICE

- Read the title of the text. It might help you know in advance what type of text it is and what the subject is.
- Read the whole text quickly to get an impression of the content.
- Think about the question (perhaps without looking at the options) and find the answer in the text.
- Read the question again with the options and select the correct answer.
- To confirm, underline the part of the text which contains the answer.
- Think about why each of the other options is not correct so that you can justify your choice.

Making decisions

Speaking

1 **Work with a partner and discuss the questions.**

   1 Which of these photos would you choose to represent the way you feel about making decisions? Why?
   2 Approximately how many small decisions do you think you make in the first two hours after waking up? What are they?
   3 How do you make small decisions? Do you weigh up each possibility and then choose the most appropriate? Or do you use intuition?

2 **Work with a different partner. Discuss these questions.**

   1 What do you consider to be important decisions that people have to make in life?
   2 How do you make important decisions? Do you ask for advice?
   3 How hard do you think it is for most people to change their mind if they realise they've made the wrong decision?

Reading and Writing

1 **Read the magazine article about making decisions and discuss these questions.**

   1 Did the article change your mind about how you think decisions are made?
   2 What is the main idea of each paragraph?
   3 What conclusion does the writer infer from her personal experience in the last paragraph?

2 **Write a letter to the magazine.**

   1 You are going to write a letter to the magazine commenting on the views expressed in the article. What style do you think is appropriate?
   2 What do you think should be included in the first paragraph?
   3 You should write your letter in 220–260 words in an appropriate style. Make a plan of your letter.

3 **Write your letter.**

How do we make decisions?

In cafés, there's a wide range of coffees to choose from, from skinny latte to triple caramel frappuccino (that's coffee blended with caramel, milk and ice topped with a layer of dark caramel sauce, whipped cream, caramel drizzle and crunchy sugar topping, if you're wondering). How do you decide which coffee to have? Do you analyse or even know how much caffeine you'd like or need? Do you know or care how many calories are in the drink? Most people think the best option is the most expensive and if they can afford it, will choose it. There have been a number of studies where price tags have been switched and people's choices switch to the most expensive as a result. This would suggest that decision-making is not all rational.

Have you ever considered whether your decisions are influenced by the power of suggestion? If you were handed a warm drink on a cold winter's day and then asked your opinion of someone you'd recently met, the chances are you'd have a favourable opinion of the person. Conversely, if you were given a cold drink, your description of the person would be 'colder'. You would have literally been influenced by the warmth or cold of the drink and your judgement would have been clouded.

Our decisions are influenced in many different ways. We all know that the answers to questions in surveys depend largely on the wording of the question. A positively worded question will probably elicit a positive response. The human brain plays tricks on us too. In many cases, when we ask for advice, we don't really listen to and consider all of the advice, we just hear the parts that confirm what we wanted to hear. Our decision-making may also largely depend on our personality. An optimistic person may overestimate the positive outcomes of making a decision whereas a pessimistic person may decide against doing something for fear of a negative result.

Even when we believe we are making a rational decision based on previous experience, this may not be the case. If you went on holiday to a particular resort last year and had a great time, it does not necessarily follow that you will have a great time this year. The place may have changed, the weather might not be the same and your expectations will have been raised because of your previous positive experience. To help us make balanced and rational decisions, we are advised to make two columns and write down all the reasons for a decision in one column and all the reasons against in the other. But I don't know about you, but when I tried this, when I saw the 'against' column getting longer, I stopped trying to find negatives and found more positives. At least it made me realise that I really did want to do whatever it was but I still couldn't explain why. It was just a gut feeling and I was willing to manipulate the 'system' to get the outcome I wanted.

In my view, much of the discussion about how we make decisions is not very scientific at all. However, there do seem to be ways of explaining why we make certain decisions, if we look below the surface. For example, maybe we want to aspire to make more money, or maybe the power of suggestion plays a huge role, or maybe we always just go with our instincts. What do you think?

Vocabulary

1 Match these phrases to their definitions.

1	a gut feeling	**a**	to happen as a result
2	to raise expectations	**b**	to deceive or cheat
3	a favourable opinion	**c**	to feel that good things will happen
4	as a result		
5	a wide range	**d**	a good result
6	to follow	**e**	an instinct
7	play tricks on someone	**f**	a large selection
8	positive outcome	**g**	because of something
		h	a positive view

2 Complete these sentences with words/expressions from exercise 1.

1 I don't really know why I think Linda will be a good engineer; it's just a .... I have.

2 There is such a .... of courses on offer at the community college, it's hard to make my mind up which one to choose.

3 Although you enjoyed reading his last book, it doesn't necessarily .... that you'll like his latest one just as much.

4 If you meet someone when you're in very comfortable surroundings, there's a high chance that you'll have a .... of them.

5 Because of the positive testimonials by students at the college, my .... had been .... regarding the quality of the tuition.

6 My memory seems to be .... me – I'm sure I sent the email last night.

7 I find it hard to make decisions and ...., I prefer to ask for advice from trusted friends.

8 The meeting had a .... – everyone was satisfied with the decision.

Listening

1 You are going to listen to Jane Hurley, talking about how companies decide who to employ. How do you think employers choose the right job candidate?

2 🎧1.19 Listen and check your ideas.

⤵ Exam spot

In Part 2 of the Listening test, use the time before the recording starts to think about the type of information that is missing. The questions focus on concrete pieces of information that are usually not more than three words. Write down the actual words you hear on the recording that answer the question.

3 Listen again and complete these sentences.

1 Jane explains that employers read a candidate's .... before anything else.

2 Jane now finds jobs in .... for many students who graduate in arts subjects.

3 According to Jane, globalisation has resulted in a need for .... in employees.

4 Jane expresses concern about the level of .... required by some employers.

5 Jane recommends doing a .... because it may result in a job offer.

6 Jane quotes an engineering company where .... was an important part of being on their staff.

7 In Jane's experience, keeping to .... is crucial in all jobs.

4 Complete these phrases with *job* or *work*. What do the phrases mean?

1	...*job*... seeker	6	find the right ....
2	.... vacancy	7	the .... market
3	.... application	8	voluntary ....
4	.... placement	9	.... description
5	team	10	learn on the ....

-ing forms

1 Choose the correct options in these sentences from the recording.

1 Today I'd like *to share / sharing* some of my experience.
2 It means *be / being* prepared for searching questions at the interview.
3 It may *help / helping* you find the right job for you.
4 Get a friend to try *to read / reading* your letter of application to make sure it's got real impact.
5 It's worth *to get / getting* the job description for the job you're applying for.
6 An employee will need *to show / showing* they can meet deadlines, otherwise the company may lose its reputation.

2 There are several different uses of the *-ing* form. Match sentences 1–7 to uses a–g.

1 Learning keeps the mind active.
2 I avoid travelling on a Monday morning, if possible. The trains are too crowded.
3 I'm interested in seeing the job description.
4 If you keep on searching the internet, you're bound to find information about suitable courses.
5 It's worth making a detour to the west coast; it's spectacular.
6 I hope you don't mind my asking, but …
7 I can't imagine being paid that much money.

a We can use the *-ing* form after phrasal verbs.
b We can use *-ing* as part of a passive form.
c The *-ing* form can be the subject of the sentence.
d We can use the *-ing* form after some common expressions.
e We can use the *-ing* form after certain verbs.
f We use the *-ing* form after prepositions.
g In formal English, possessives are used with the *-ing* form.

Corpus spot

The *Cambridge English Corpus* shows exam candidates often make mistakes with *-ing* forms. Five of these sentences written by exam candidates contain a mistake. Find the mistakes and correct them.

1 Some people would probably burst out laugh.
2 Our generation has grown up in a society which is used to have greater access to information.
3 Have a break and doing something different is the best way to solve the problem.
4 I am looking forward to see you again.
5 I can't help thinking this is all a waste of time.
6 It was my fault not to tell you about our plans. You must have been very puzzled.
7 I miss not being able to have lunch with my family every Sunday.

G → page 168

Speaking

1 Look at this diagram, which shows the results of major decisions people sometimes make. Work with a partner and discuss these questions.

1 Which of the decisions do you think is the most important and why?
2 What might influence people most when they make these decisions?
3 When do you think it's important to stick to your original decision and when might it be better to change your mind?

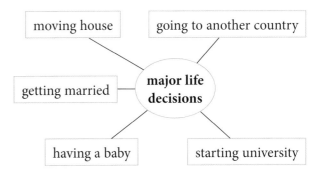

2 Work with a different partner. Discuss these questions.

1 Summarise what you discussed in exercise 1.
2 Discuss which situation in exercise 1 is the easiest to make decisions for, and why.
3 Which situation in exercise 1 do you think is the most difficult?

Writing folder 5

Letters / emails

1 Work with a partner and discuss these questions.

1 Approximately how many emails do you receive every day? How many do you send?
2 Are emails different from letters? In what ways? Is it appropriate to write emails in a formal style? Why? / Why not?
3 When was the last time you wrote a letter? Why?
4 Make a list of reasons why you might send a letter instead of an email.

2 In Part 2 of the Writing test, you may be asked to write a letter or email in 220–260 words. Look at tasks 1–3 and underline the key points. Think about these features.

- who the letter is for
- the purpose of the letter
- what you are required to include

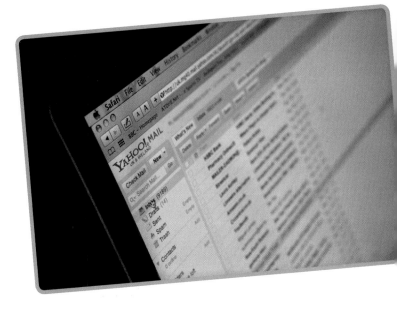

1

You see this announcement in your local newspaper.

Your city needs you!
As part of the city's summer festival we have invited singers and dancers from several countries to perform. We are now asking local families to host our guests during the one-week festival. We would like families not only to accommodate our guests but also to act as ambassadors for our culture. Write an email to the editor applying to be a host. You should explain which aspects of our culture you are interested in and what you think is the best way of showing it to our guests.

2

You have been offered a job in Australia during your college holidays. The job would help you improve your English and the work is relevant to your studies. However, the job will not finish until October 10 and you should be back at college on October 3.

Write a letter to the Principal of your college explaining the situation and asking for permission to delay your return to college in October.

3

You recently bought tickets for a trip to a concert from an events agency. The price included the coach to and from the venue, pre-concert dinner and the concert ticket. However, the dinner could better be described as a snack, the seats in the concert hall had a restricted view and the coach was late when it picked you up after the concert.

Write an email to the events agency outlining how the trip failed to meet your expectations and asking for a refund.

3 Read this letter. Which task does it answer? What are the main content points in the task? Underline the parts of the letter that cover the content points.

Dear Sir/Madam

I am writing regarding my trip to the Vivaldi concert in Chesterton on 14th March, which I booked through your events agency. Travel by coach from Linton to the venue in Chesterton and dinner before the concert were included in the cost of the ticket, £150. This was a significant amount of money especially as the concert ticket itself was only £42 but I was happy to pay this for a special occasion.

However, I would like to draw your attention to the aspects of the trip that did not live up to my expectations. Firstly, what was described as a dinner in your promotional material was no more than a light snack consisting of salad, bread and a drink. I had been looking forward to at least a two-course hot meal. Secondly, an even greater disappointment was my seat. There was a column between me and the stage which meant I was unable to see the orchestra and fully enjoy the event. Finally, after the concert had finished the coach driver had arranged to pick us up at 11pm but the coach did not arrive until 11.30. We were left waiting outside and no apology was offered by the driver.

The quality of these aspects of the trip did not reflect the price paid or indeed the information sent out prior to the trip. As a result, I expect a refund. I feel that your agency should offer this as a gesture of goodwill and to do something to redeem your reputation.

I look forward to your prompt reply.

Yours faithfully

Astrid Pett

4 Now read the task below. Work with a partner to underline the key points of the question. Then discuss what you would include in:

- the opening paragraph
- the body of the letter
- the closing paragraph.

A TV company is planning to make a series of programmes about how people make decisions. It has asked viewers to write letters to the company suggesting which sort of decisions should be focused on in the programmes.
They should also explain why this would be interesting for viewers and how it might help them make decisions more effectively.
Write your letter.

5 Write a first draft of your letter for this task in 220–260 words. Then give it to another student and ask for comments. Revise your first draft by checking through the Exam advice box.

> **EXAM ADVICE**
>
> - Make sure you have answered the question and covered all the points.
> - Use the conventions of letter writing (e.g. opening and closing salutations).
> - Check that your letter is clear.
> - Use a range of vocabulary, especially collocations, and grammatical structures.
> - Check for a range and appropriacy of vocabulary, and range and accuracy of grammar.

13 Colour

Speaking and Listening

1 Work in small groups and discuss these questions.

1 Which apple looks the most appealing to you and why?

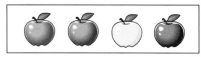

2 Look at the colours below. What do you associate them with? It could be things, people, feelings or situations.

2 You are going to listen to a talk.

1 Look at the left column of the outline below. How many sections will Jessica's talk have, and what are they?

2 Look at the right column and predict what Jessica is going to say.

3 Listen to Jessica's talk and complete gaps 1–10.

1 Which answers did you predict?

2 What do you think about Jessica's views on the use of colour in retail?

Introduction	
Instinctive reactions to colour: Colour has psychological and physiological influences.	e.g. (1) ....
Percentage of information we get through our eyes:	(2) .... %
Psychological influences	
People feel comfortable when colour suggests something familiar.	
Children prefer:	(3) .... colours
Cultural variations:	e.g. (4) ....
Variations according to climate:	e.g. (5) ....
Variations according to era:	e.g. (6) ....
Physiological influences	
Red results in:	(7) ....
White/grey results in:	(8) ....
Food retailing	
Reasons for fast-food outlets using red:	(9) ....
Sophisticated restaurants use:	(10) .... colours
Conclusion	

Vocabulary

⟳ Vocabulary spot

In English, words with the same meaning sometimes have different spellings depending on whether they are the verb or the noun. For example, in the recording you heard *Some of the top stores pay huge amounts of money for the advice of design consultants.* The word *advice* is a noun and is pronounced /ədvaɪs/. However, the verb form is *advice* and is pronounced /ədvaɪz/.

1 What is the verb form of these nouns?

bath belief licence relief proof loss life practice effect

2 Which words have the same pronunciation in their noun and verb forms?

3 Some words have the same pronunciation but there is a difference in spelling and in meaning. Try to work out the difference in meaning between the underlined words in these sentences.

1 a It's important that colours in a store or café <u>complement</u> other elements, such as product displays and lighting.

b My wife likes it when I <u>compliment</u> her on her new clothes.

2 a The city <u>council</u> is responsible for keeping the streets clean.

b In my job I <u>counsel</u> unemployed people about how to find work.

3 a Is it true that colour <u>affects</u> people's mood?

b I think I'm suffering from the <u>effects</u> of spending too much time in this bright red room.

4 a The organisation works on the <u>principle</u> that all members have the same rights.

b That was my <u>principal</u> reason for moving.

Reading

1 **You are going to read a blog written by Martin, who has colour vision deficiency (CVD), sometimes known as colour blindness. Discuss these questions with a partner.**

1 Make a list of situations when it is important to be able to tell different colours apart.

2 Look at the two photos of a stir-fry meal. The second shows the meal as seen by someone with CVD. What are the main differences?

3 How do you think having CVD might affect someone's life?

2 **Read Martin's blog to find out what he says about the topics in exercise 1.**

I've just had a brilliant weekend despite my CVD. Let me explain. Well, for a start, you'll have noticed that I prefer to call it *colour vision deficiency* rather than *colour blindness*. CVD is the inability or decreased ability to see colour, or perceive colour differences, under normal lighting conditions. There is no actual blindness, but there is a lack of normal colour vision. In northern Europe it affects about 8% of the male population and 0.5% of the female population. And it's usually a genetic thing. Now that I've got that basic stuff off my chest, I want to tell you about my weekend.

I've been going out with Emma for about four months now and I decided that this week I'd invite her round to my flat and cook her a meal. Now, you might just be thinking, that's nice … but I wonder if he can cook, but cooking a meal when you've got CVD is not exactly straightforward. I have problems with reds and greens. So, making sure that meat is thoroughly cooked and there are no unintended pink bits left is a bit tricky. So I decided to play it safe and cook a veggie stir fry and serve it with rice. I thought I'd be OK with rice because it's white – no problems there.

I'd got all the ingredients listed in the recipe from the market and I was assured they were really fresh. I had to trust the stall holder because quite honestly the red peppers, carrots, broccoli and other vegetables I'd bought all looked an unappealing shade of dull green. And I must admit at that point I was beginning to doubt the wisdom of my offer to cook dinner.

Anyway, Emma came round and looked happy. OK, she was puzzled when I said her blue jeans looked great and she had to reveal that they were purple. She knows I've got CVD and just accepts that she should never take my compliments about clothes seriously.

I started cooking and the recipe said I should make sure not to overcook the veg. I cooked them for just a couple of minutes and they still looked terrible to me. But when Emma saw the dish served up, she looked really impressed. And I know she wasn't just being polite because she asked for seconds.

So it was a wonderful success! Well it was until I went to turn on a lamp (to enhance the romantic atmosphere). I'd bought this really cool antique lamp and had had to put a new plug on it. And in the UK, you have to know which is the red wire and which is the green/yellow wire. Well, when I switched on the lamp it exploded and my flat was plunged into darkness! The next 30 minutes were spent trying to find a torch and fix everything. Anyway, Emma seemed happy. But she did seem a bit worried when I told her that I was going to start driving lessons next week, and mentioned something about red and green traffic lights …

Past tenses and the present perfect

1 In Martin's blog, a variety of past tenses was used. Look at this extract and underline the past tense verbs.

> I'd got all the ingredients listed in the recipe from the market and I was assured they were really fresh. I had to trust the stall holder because quite honestly, the red peppers, carrots, broccoli and other vegetables I'd bought all looked an unappealing shade of dull green. And I must admit at that point, I was beginning to doubt the wisdom of my offer to cook dinner.

2 When do we use the past simple and when do we use the past continuous?

3 Eight of these sentences contain a mistake. Find the mistakes and correct them.

1 I read several recipes before I had decided to cook a stir fry.
2 I decided that this week I've invited her round to my flat and cook her a meal.
3 Kate bought a new computer because she was been accepted on an Interior Design course.
4 The novel had been made into a TV drama last year.
5 My neighbour was owning an interesting collection of antiques.
6 Harry asked if he could borrow my laptop to do his essay, because his had crashed.
7 I've finished painting the kitchen just as Karen came in from work.
8 I worked as a marketing executive for two years.
9 The first paragraph of the blog was seeming very interesting, that's why I read all of it.
10 Are you sure Martin cooked the dinner? I thought it had been Emma.

4 Work with a partner. Look at the pictures and say what you think the person has done or has been doing.

A He's been studying all night. / He's been up all night.

5 Complete the sentences using the present perfect simple or continuous.

1 He .... (go out) with Emma for four months now.

2 I .... (go) to English lessons for about three years.

3 I .... (not use) my bicycle for a long time. I really should start again.

4 He .... (always be) careful with money – that's just his nature.

5 They .... (play) that music for three hours now. When are they going to stop?

G→page 169

Vocabulary

1 Put these adjectives in the most usual order.

1 a <u>vegetarian delicious</u> stir-fry

2 a <u>red beautiful silk</u> dress

3 a <u>black shabby</u> suit

4 an <u>extensive new exciting</u> menu

5 a <u>pale small</u> face

2 Describe the photos. Here are some phrases and adjectives to get you started.

sterile	elegant	clean lines	friendly
inviting	modern and efficient		
low-key	natural colours		

Speaking

1 Work with a partner. Choose two of the photos to discuss.

1 Look at the photos and describe the colours in each one.

2 Discuss how people might feel if they were in these places. Describe how the colours might affect a person's mood.

3 Say why the colours in each photo might have been chosen.

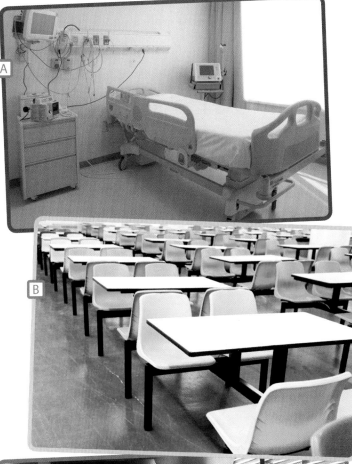

Exam folder 6

Paper 1 Part 6

Cross-text multiple matching

In Part 6 of the Reading and Use of English test, there are four short texts which are on a related theme. The prompts or questions require you to read across the four texts to understand the opinions and attitudes expressed in order to identify agreement or disagreement between the writers. Intertextual reading is an important advanced reading skill, in that people are often required to read several sources and compare, contrast and synthesise views in those different sources.

The questions may be of the following types:
- identify an opinion expressed in one text, and then identify which other text shares or contradicts this opinion.
- identify which text differs from the others in terms of an expressed opinion.

1 **You are going to read four reviews of van Gogh's sunflower paintings. Discuss these questions with a partner.**

   1 Have you seen copies or originals of any of van Gogh's paintings?
   2 Do you know anything about van Gogh?

2 **For questions 1–4, choose from the reviews A–D. The reviews may be chosen more than once.**

   Which reviewer:

   1 has a different opinion from the others about the influence of van Gogh's paintings on sunflowers on the art world?
   2 shares reviewer C's opinion of the impact of seeing the original works?
   3 expresses a different view from the others regarding the extent to which the paintings should be seen as a metaphor for life?
   4 takes a similar view to reviewer B on the quality of the colour in the paintings?

A

There are pieces of artwork around the world that have become synonymous with the artist's name and techniques. The paintings of sunflowers and Vincent van Gogh are a perfect example of this. Not only can one make a mental connection between the artist's name and paintings but also between the artist and his tremendous contribution to the development of art. His sunflower paintings have been duplicated many times by various artists (although never reaching the emotional intensity of van Gogh's) and are displayed everywhere; from households to art expos. The colours in these paintings express emotions typically associated with the natural cycle of sunflowers: bright yellows of the full bloom to arid browns of wilting and death. Perhaps this very technique is what draws one into the painting; the fulfilment of seeing all angles of the spectrum of the cycle and in turn reaching a deeper understanding of the transience of all living things.

B

On February 19, 1888, van Gogh leaves for Provence in the south of France. He rents a studio in Arles, and invites his artist friend Gauguin to join him. In anticipation of his arrival, van Gogh paints still lifes of sunflowers to decorate Gauguin's room. The flowers represent the sun, the dominant feature of the Provencal summer and doubtless the happiness he was feeling at that time. Inspired by the bright colours and strong light of Provence, he executes painting after painting and in so doing leaves a series of paintings which in later years are seen as a turning point by many an art expert. 'I am getting an eye for this kind of country,' he writes to his brother Theo. Whereas in Paris, his works covered a broad range of subjects and techniques, the Arles paintings are consistent in approach, fusing a master's technique with intensely saturated colour.

C

Although van Gogh's sunflower paintings are similar in many aspects, each stands out as unique and the series is considered a milestone in the history of art. The majority of his sunflowers were created in Arles, France during 1888–1889. Van Gogh did create some sunflower paintings prior to this time in Paris. This earlier series consists of sunflower clippings or sunflowers in vases. The sunflower paintings as a whole represent the lifecycle; a seed grows, blooms and finally dies. The overall layout of the paintings usually remains the same. However, differences can be noted. In one, the centre 'eye' of the main flower is filled with a greenish yellow, while in the second the centre is filled with black. Similar differences are also apparent in the leafy structure; being either yellow or more of a light brown. It is these subtleties that never come across in the numerous reproductions seen on kitchen walls.

D

This series of sunflower paintings by van Gogh was made possible by the innovations in manufactured pigments in the 19th century. Without the vibrancy of the new colours, such as chrome yellow, van Gogh may never have achieved the high reputation he enjoys today and many would not have been tricked into believing these paintings are truly significant with regard to the advancement of modern art. However, his paintings of sunflowers captivate many of his admirers and leave them astounded in their simplistic beauty. The flowing wilted stems and the burst of lovely yellow draws ones attention around the painting, without disrupting the balance of the piece. When the whole series of his sunflowers is viewed together, along with earlier paintings of dried sunflower heads the imagery becomes obvious; the flowers are a kind of shorthand for our time on earth. Each painting on its own reflects one particular moment in van Gogh's difficult life.

EXAM ADVICE

- Underline the key words in the questions (e.g. *similar*, *different*) and then key content words (e.g. *impact*, *art world*).
- Read all the texts quickly to get an impression of the content.
- Think about the question and find information relating to the question in the texts (the information may not be in each text).
- Read the first question again paying particular attention to your underlined words and select the correct answer.
- To confirm, underline the part of the text which contains the answer.
- Continue the process for each question.

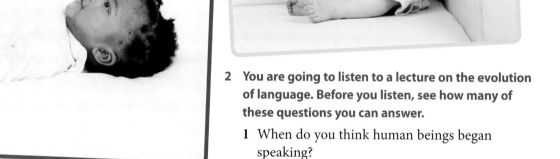

Speaking and Listening

1 **Work in pairs and discuss whether you think these statements are true.**

1 Babies can begin to learn language before they are born.
2 Babies can make sounds in different accents.
3 Learning two languages from birth causes delays in language learning.
4 Second-born children are late to start talking because their siblings do all the talking for them.

2 **You are going to listen to a lecture on the evolution of language. Before you listen, see how many of these questions you can answer.**

1 When do you think human beings began speaking?
   A 1.3 million years ago
   B 50,000 years ago
   C 6,000 years ago
2 When do you think humans developed language?
   A 500,000 years ago.
   B 300,000 years ago.
   C 50,000 years ago.
3 Why do you think humans developed language?
   A The population expanded.
   B They needed to communicate more effectively.
   C It is a natural ability.
4 How did humans originally communicate?
   A by using gestures
   B by speaking
   C by using tools

3 **2 02 Listen and check your answers.**

4 Listen again and complete the notes.

1 People began writing .... years ago.

2 It is estimated that people began speaking between .... and .... years ago.

3 Tools from .... BC show people recognised the concept of space.

4 Tools .... years old show people were capable of abstract thought.

5 People first used .... to communicate.

6 Pettito and Marentette concluded that manual language (sign language) is more ...., and .... than spoken language.

7 People may have stopped communicating with sign language because they started using .... and wanted to communicate ....

Reading

1 Now read an extract from an academic paper on the same topic. Answer these questions.

1 The importance of the shape of human teeth is that they
   A form a barrier to the throat.
   B allow certain sounds to be produced.
   C make chewing food easier.
   D allow the lip muscles to develop.

2 The structure of the human larynx means
   A the mouth cavity has space for the tongue.
   B it blocks air exiting from the mouth.
   C humans cannot breathe and swallow at the same time.
   D breathing requires effort in humans.

3 Why is it suggested that the human gestation period is so short?
   A to allow humans to learn more from the environment
   B to limit the size that humans grow to
   C to take full advantage of our genetic make-up
   D to ensure children learn speech

2 Work in small groups and discuss these questions.

1 Did you learn anything new? If so, what?

2 Do you think animals 'talk'? Give reasons or examples.

3 Why do you think it takes such a long time for babies to learn their first language and for adults to learn a foreign language?

Turning to the biological limitations affecting language development, if we assume that all humans are able to speak a language, a number of biological facts fall into place, suggesting that the human body is particularly adapted to the production of language.

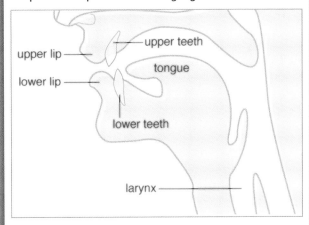

Human teeth are different to those of other animals – being even and forming an unbroken barrier, they are upright; they do not slant outwards and the top and bottom set of teeth meet. This is not necessary for eating. Yet evenly spaced equal sized teeth which touch are useful for producing the sounds /s/, /f/, /v/, /ʃ/ and /θ/ as well as several others.

Human lips have well-developed muscles which are linked in a more complicated way than those of other primates. The human mouth is small and can be opened and closed rapidly, allowing the sounds /p/ and /b/ to be made.

The human tongue is thick, muscular and mobile. This means that the size of the mouth cavity can be varied, allowing a range of vowel sounds to be made.

The human larynx, also known as the voice box, is simpler in structure than that of other primates; air can move freely past and then out of the mouth without being blocked by anything. The 'streamlining' of the larynx may be a sign of adaptation to speech – however, a disadvantage of this is that we cannot breathe while we eat, unlike monkeys. If food becomes trapped in our windpipe we could choke to death.

Our breathing is well adapted to speech; during speech, we are able to alter our breathing rhythm without noticing discomfort.

Humans have a long childhood compared to other animals. If factors like size, lifespan and gestation are taken into account, compared to other animals, humans appear to be born too early. For humans to follow the general trend, they would require a woman to be pregnant for 18 months. Thus, with other factors taken into account, the human gestation period is only half as long as those of other animals. This means that less information is inherited genetically. In effect, human babies are given more opportunity to learn from the environment. Perhaps humans are biologically disposed towards language, but they need the environment to make use of their brains.

The passive

1 Look at these extracts from the lecture you heard. Why is the passive used?

> Primitive tools **have been found** that date back to 1.5 million years BC.

> Tools **had been planned** in three dimensions.

> Hands **were needed** to manipulate tools.

2 Match examples 1–9 to statements a-i.

1 Research has been carried out into when babies start to learn language.
2 I attended some presentations given by several experts in our field.
3 You will arrive in Madrid, which is 450 kilometres from my hometown.
4 The lecture room should be air-conditioned.
5 The lecturer should have been given more time.
6 He enjoys being recognised in the street.
7 We were given a lot of important advice in the lecture.
8 In my culture, it is considered rude if you don't eat the food they give you at a wedding.
9 Several people are said to have been injured in the accident.

a Passive constructions can be made with *it* + passive + clause.
b Intransitive verbs cannot be made passive.
c When a verb has two objects, it is more usual to make the 'person object' the subject of the passive verb than the 'thing object'.
d This is an example of the passive *-ing* form.
e We use the passive when the action is more important than the person who carried it out or the person is unknown.
f We can use: subject + passive + *to* + infinitive.
g This is an example of the passive of a past modal.
h We use *by* + the person who carried out the action when this provides useful information.
i Modals can be followed by the infinitive passive.

3 Rewrite the underlined sentences in the passive.

Recent studies have revealed three important areas in the study of the evolutionary factors of language. 90% of humans are right-handed and have language in the left hemisphere of their brain. The second is that humans freed their hands in order to make and use tools, which meant having to find a method of communication other than sign language. Thirdly, syntax developed which increased the quality and quantity of the message.

People say that we can teach chimps to speak but there are several biological factors which make humans more predisposed to speech. You should note that the form of the human teeth, lips, tongue and larynx are all important when it comes to speech.

4 Make notes on the topics below.

Write two things …

1 which are considered rude to say or do in your country.
2 you should have said or done recently, but didn't.
3 you were told about the English language, or language learning, when you were at school.
4 which were written or sung by your favourite writer/singer.
5 you were given recently.

5 Work in pairs and compare your notes. Ask questions to find out more information about each other.

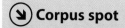 **Corpus spot**

Take care with active or passive forms of the present perfect. The *Cambridge English Corpus* shows exam candidates often make mistakes with these.

Many skyscrapers **have been constructed** *over the years.*
NOT *Many skyscrapers* ~~**have constructed**~~ *over the years.*

G → page 170

6 We can use phrases with *under* as an alternative to using the passive. Rewrite these sentences using the passive form.

1 This webpage is under construction.
2 The case is under investigation.
3 The situation is now under control.
4 I was under orders not to tell anyone the company's future plans.
5 The prime minister was under attack for the statements he made.

7 Work with a partner.

1 Explain the difference in the use of *had* and *got* in these two sentences.
   a *I **had** my handbag stolen while I was on holiday.*
   b *She **got** her fingers trapped in the door.*
2 Explain the use of *won't* in this sentence.
   *I **won't** have you staying out so late at night.*
3 Explain the meaning of the second sentence.
   Put your money somewhere safe.
   We don't want it stolen.

8 Complete the second sentence so that it has a similar meaning to the first. Use the word given and do not change it. Use between three and six words.

1 Has anyone ever recorded your voice?
   HAD
   .... your voice recorded?
2 We hired a professional photographer to take wedding photos.
   HAD
   We .... a professional photographer.
3 She asked the artist to produce a suitable illustration for her article.
   PRODUCED
   She wants .... for her article.

Vocabulary

(↘) Vocabulary spot

When you learn a word, you can increase your vocabulary even more by learning all the forms of the word (e.g. the noun, verb, adjective and adverb). This will help you in the Reading and Use of English test, where in Part 3 you need to fill each gap in a text with the correct form of a given word, as in the exercise below.

1 Use the word given in capitals at the end of some lines to form a word that fits in the gap in the same line.

Oral communication

Effective oral communication is an important – but often (0) ...*overlooked*... and	**LOOK**
(1) .... – skill in scientific and academic endeavours. This tutorial has been developed to serve as an	**PRACTISE**
(2) .... guide and as a general	**INTRODUCE**
(3) .... for use when formulating a talk.	**REFER**
The principles should be applied whenever you are faced with making a public presentation, whether it's an informal or a more formal talk, such as a conference presentation or interview. There are very few people who have a natural talent for delivering (4) .... presentations.	**STAND**
On the other hand, foresight, hard work and practice can carry most of the rest of us into the 'very good' level of presentation skills. The standards for public speaking in the (5) .... and academic realms are	**SCIENCE**
(6) .... low, so a good presentation will be	**RELATE**
(7) .... Few audience members expect	**MEMORY**
presenters to demonstrate real (8)	**EXPERT**

Speaking

1 Discuss these questions with a partner.

1 How much importance was given to speaking and writing your language correctly in your school?
2 Do you agree that being able to express yourself clearly is more important than having subject knowledge (e.g. knowing facts about history)?
3 Do you think that changes in a language, its grammar and vocabulary are a good or a bad thing? Why?
4 Do you agree that many people in modern societies speak less well because their parents spent less time talking to them when they were babies?

Writing folder 6

Essays (2)

In the Writing test, you will always have to write an essay in Part 1.

An essay is very often written for a teacher or tutor and may be a follow-up activity to a panel discussion or watching a documentary. In the exam you will be given a topic and some notes on the topic which will include three bullet points. You have to select two of the bullet points and base your essay on those two points. You will be asked to explain which of the points is more important in a given respect, and give reasons and opinions.

Your essay should be well organised, with an introduction, clear development and an appropriate conclusion. The main purpose of the essay in the exam is to outline relevant issues in a topic, and put forward an argument with supporting information and reasons.

Organisation

1 **Look at the table, which shows the organisation of a typical essay. Complete gaps 1–7 with the points below.**

	Content	Purpose
Introduction	General statement	(1)
	Definition(s) – optional	(2)
	Scope of essay	(3)
Body	Arguments	(4)
	Evidence	(5)
Conclusions	Summary	(6)
	Relate the argument to a more general world view	(7)

- to explain what is understood by some key words/concepts
- to introduce the reader to the topic
- to put the writer's point of view into a wider context
- to remind the reader of the key ideas
- to express important ideas
- to support ideas with reasons
- to tell the reader what you intend to cover in this essay

2 **Look at this sample essay. In the table above, tick the purposes which have been included.**

3 **In any piece of extended writing, we need to link our ideas so that we produce coherent and logical language.**

  1 Underline the connecting words/ phrases in the essay.
  2 Are most of the connecting words/ phrases formal or informal?

Developing good language skills

This essay will examine the role played by parents and teachers in the development of language skills. These two influences, in addition to others, were discussed during a recent panel discussion. Good language skills are seen by many as vital to a person's future prospects in education, and in employment and also as a means of enjoying the world of literature.

Research has demonstrated that babies start learning language even before they are born. They hear sounds and their brains can recognise the difference between familiar and unfamiliar sounds. As soon as a baby is born, it hears language and is encouraged to make sounds and eventually words and sentences. Therefore, I suggest that the family is the most crucial element in learning to speak and to write. Many children spend years at home before they ever go to school.

However, teachers then help children to make progress in their learning and it is their responsibility to make sure that a child reaches as high a level as possible in their language development. In fact, teachers can in some cases compensate for a lack of learning at home. For many and varied reasons, not all parents are able to give a child a good start in life.

In conclusion, parents are key in the development of a child's language skills. Secondly, formal education provides further support to ensure that young people are ready to face the world when they leave school.

4 **Make a plan for the following essay by making notes on points 1–3 and complete the table below.**

1 Which two points have you chosen?
2 Which point is more important?
3 Reasons/opinions?

In your English class, you have watched a documentary about why people study a second language. You have made the notes below:

What are some of the reasons for studying a second language?
- education
- employment
- travel

Some opinions expressed in the discussion:
Every country offers good courses delivered in that country's language.

More companies use English, so it is necessary for those seeking top-level jobs.

These days, it is not necessary to learn a second language for travel – people just need to learn a few phrases in the language of the destination country.

	Content	Purpose
Introduction		
Body		
Conclusions		

Vocabulary

When planning the main body of your essay, write down the two main points you want to include. Then, make a list of key words and phrases connected with the topic. For the essay in exercise 4, you could make notes like the following.

Education: access to research written in another language; increased choice for university selection; academic papers, research findings, intercultural awareness, well-educated/ qualified; scholarship

Employment: globalisation; multinationals; job prospects/offer; promotion, managerial position; recruit; apply for; vacancy; fill a vacancy/job; CV

5 **Look at the tips for essay writing. Add two more tips of your own.**

- Highlight the key words in the question.
- List the points you want to include.
- Plan carefully.
- Give examples or reasons for your views.
- Link ideas.
- Deal with each point equally.
- Use a range of formal/neutral vocabulary appropriately.
- Use a range of grammatical structures accurately.

6 **Write an essay for the question in exercise 4 in 220–260 words. When you finish, check your work using the criteria below.**

Content	Are there clear content points? Is the reader fully informed?
Communicative achievement	Is the reader's attention held? Is there a mix of straightforward ideas and complex ideas?
Organisation	Does it follow a typical essay format? Does it have paragraphs? Does the essay use appropriate connecting words/phrases?
Language	Is there a range of grammar forms? Is the grammar accurate? Is there a range of vocabulary? Is there appropriate use of vocabulary?

15 In my view ...

Speaking and Reading

1 Match the speech bubbles to the photos above.

1 At home, I had no say in what we had for dinner and I remember I used to complain about the food mum gave me, but now I really miss all that home cooking.

2 It's lovely having the children round for an afternoon, but it's also good when they go home to their mum and I can settle into my armchair and put my feet up.

3 They're always going on at me to tidy my room and do chores around the house when I just want to chill out.

4 I can't tell you how lucky I am having mum and dad living nearby. They've been a real help since the children were born. They can be a real handful sometimes.

2 Match phrases 1–7 with definitions a–g.

1	have round	a	not be involved in a decision
2	can't tell you	b	relax
3	a handful	c	a boring job you have to do
4	put my feet up	d	talk in an annoying way for a long time
5	go on	e	difficult to describe
6	have no say	f	a person who is difficult to control
7	chore	g	arrange for someone to visit you at your home

3 Discuss these questions.

1 What kind of things do you and your family tend to talk about?

2 Among your family and friends, who gets their opinion across most effectively? How?

4 You are going to read about a father's opinions on bringing up three children. Look at the title of the article. Do you agree?

5 Read the article and answer the questions.

1 Jon wants to be like his father in that he'd like
   A to have the same profession.
   B his children to be proud of him.
   C to show his children how to be successful.
   D his children to feel secure.

2 In the fourth paragraph, Jon explains that he is strict because he is
   A trying to set a standard in his community.
   B teaching his children where the limits of behaviour are.
   C making time to spend with his wife.
   D bringing up his children according to his beliefs.

3 Jon fears society may influence his children so they
   A cannot come to their own decisions.
   B will not cope with life's challenges.
   C will grow up far too quickly.
   D resent their parents' authority.

4 Jon finally bought a tablet because
   A his son felt he had been unfair.
   B Jacob had been behaving well.
   C Jacob had been patient and waited a year.
   D other pupils had been making fun of Jacob.

5 Jacob has been having some difficulties because
   A he is not good at playing football.
   B his top-of-the-form position is hard to keep.
   C his academic abilities set him apart from other children.
   D demands on him are becoming unbearable.

What kids need today is discipline

Jon Myerson explains why he has decided to be strict with his children.

I'm a very old-fashioned and strict parent, like my own father. He wanted me to become a lawyer, like him, but I used to say to him that he'd made me feel safe enough not to worry about having a proper job. He was very disappointed when I said I was going to be a writer, but I think that was out of anxiety – he didn't know how I would survive in the world.

As a child I was really proud of my father. I have an image of him, tall, broad-shouldered, wearing a smart suit and tie and behaving maturely – an image I feel I should live up to. My father had status in other people's eyes. I worry that I don't give my children that. They don't see me wearing a suit and going out to work or having status: they see me wandering around at home in shorts and no shoes.

I have inherited from my father a strong sense of the importance of doing the right thing. In the right context, my children are allowed to be rude to me – they might call me 'fat face' in a jokey way, when I would never have dared. But I'm also very authoritarian: I believe strongly in proper bedtimes, that chores have to be done and that certain times of the day – when Julie and I have an evening drink – are reserved for adults, which the children are not allowed to interrupt.

Some parents of our children's friends have told Julie that their children are scared of me because I am so strict with my own children. I know I have quite a severe image in a few families' eyes. But I want to make my children into the sort of children I want them to be.

I don't think that children should make up their own minds – and saying that is about as unfashionable as you can get. But if you don't influence them, they will only be influenced by others. I don't believe in reasoning with my children. They do what mummy and daddy say. If you say to a child, 'Would you like to go to bed now?' no child in his right mind will agree.

Julie and I don't let our children watch television after 6 pm, ever. It's important to think through why a programme is being made. If it's fun, that's fine, but I can't stand all those Saturday morning programmes, supposedly appropriate for children, that are really just to promote the latest toys. Our children watch it for an hour after school and then it's turned off. I think it's a parent's job to preserve childhood for as long as possible. We are proud of the fact that Jacob, at 10, still likes cuddly toys.

In our house we never buy toys which are fashionable crazes. We hold out against getting the latest gadget or toy, even if everyone else in Jacob's class has one. But I gave in when he said, 'I don't understand why, if I'm good and I do all my homework and I do everything right, I don't have a tablet and all the bad boys do.' I thought that was a very strong argument and admired his sense of justice. Jacob could not believe it when we got him a tablet for his birthday. But we still lay down rules about when he uses it, which he has never argued with, because that is the atmosphere in the house.

I am strict about homework. At the moment, the older two are doing well at school and sometimes I try to raise the amount of homework they are given. Jacob protests because I make him take it into school, which makes him look clever. He is already at the top of his class – and that in itself is very difficult for him.

I don't watch football, so nor does Jacob. That is also hard for him. Last year he had a tough time at school in terms of low-intensity bullying. Had he been interested in football, he would have had something in common with the others in his year. I was not prepared to change, however. I don't like the attitudes in football.

Vocabulary

1 Work with a partner. What do you think about the opinions in the article on page 95? Use some of the phrases below.

- I don't really feel that *Jon's ideas on raising children match my own.*
- In my view, …
- What I think is that …
- As I see it, …
- If you ask me, …
- The way I see it, …

2 Work in small groups. Discuss how important the things in the box are. As a child, were your priorities different? Support your opinions with reasons and examples.

> love   living up to family expectations   pride
> job status   strong moral sense   money
> friends   security   fun   discipline

 Exam spot

In Part 3 of Paper 4 (the Speaking test), you are given a spoken instruction and written prompts which you use in a discussion and decision-making task. During this task, you are expected to exchange ideas, express and justify opinions, agree/disagree, suggest, evaluate, negotiate, etc. It is a good idea to have a selection of phrases already prepared which help you do this.

3 Work with a partner. Discuss whether you agree or disagree with these statements using phrases from the table (below).

1 Having their mother at home all day with them makes children feel more secure.
2 Parents should set high educational goals for their children.
3 Children from large families seem to do better at school.
4 Children want to be the same as their friends and different from their parents.
5 Parents should let their children make their own decisions from the age of eight.

Agreeing	Disagreeing
I couldn't agree with you more.	I don't think so.
That's so true.	I'm afraid I disagree.
You're absolutely right.	I totally disagree.
Absolutely.	Oh? I'd say the exact opposite.
Exactly.	Well, not necessarily.
No doubt about it.	That's not always true.
You have a point there.	That's not always the case.
I was just going to say that.	I'm not so sure about that.

4 Work with a partner.

1 Look at the prompts in the diagram below, which reflect people's goals in life. Discuss with your partner how important these goals might be for having a happy life.
2 Look at these phrases. Decide which would be more appropriate when you start your discussion.

A You start.
B Would you like to start or shall I?

A I don't know what to say.
B OK, so we're going to talk about each of these goals and say how important they are for a happy life. Well, this …

A Shall we go through all the goals one by one and discuss them?
B OK, a quick read and then decide. Simple!

A I think it's obvious that this is the most important.
B What do you think about …?

3 Now decide which two goals are most important.

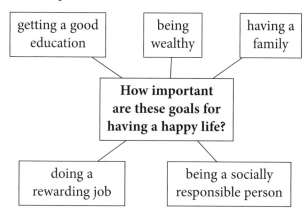

5 How did you start the discussion? Which phrases did you use to give your opinion? Did you support your opinions with reasons?

The infinitive

1 **Look at these sentences from the article on page 95. Which verbs in bold are followed by the infinitive with *to*? Which by the infinitive without *to*?**

1 I think children **want** to feel proud of their parents because it makes them feel secure.

2 I don't think that children **should** make up their own minds.

3 My children are **allowed** to be rude to me.

4 Jacob **could** not believe it when we got him a tablet for his birthday.

> **Corpus spot**
>
> Take care with infinitives and *-ing* forms. The *Cambridge English Corpus* shows exam candidates often make mistakes with these.
>
> *Please do not hesitate to phone me should you want **to know** further details.*
>
> NOT *Please do not hesitate to phone me should you want **know** further details.*

2 **Correct these sentences if necessary.**

1 I don't want you think I'm complaining, because I am not.

2 Students are not to use phones in class.

3 I must to go home before I miss the last bus.

4 In my opinion, parents should not let their daughters to wear make-up until they are 16.

5 The trip definitely seemed to be too short.

6 I was helped to get on in my career by one of my lecturers from university.

7 Please write it down not to forget.

8 It was fantastic see so many young children enter the competition.

9 The school made students do their homework on a computer.

G → page 171

Listening

1 **Work with a partner and discuss these questions.**

1 Do you watch more or less TV now compared to when you were a child?

2 Do you and your family/friends have the same taste in TV programmes?

2 **2 03 Listen to five people giving their opinions about TV. Which programmes are being talked about? Three programmes are not needed.**

A Naturally Yours

B Elizabeth I: the16th-Century Queen

C Food Master

D Star Voyagers

E Walking with Dinosaurs

F Crime City: New York

G We've Got Talent

H I Love the 80s

3 **Listen again. Which opinions are stated? Three opinions are not needed.**

A This isn't the kind of show I would normally watch.

B I'm not sure all the facts are correct.

C I don't know why the original pieces weren't used.

D I think the focus of the programme is all wrong.

E I don't think the title reflects the programme's content.

F I admit to feeling a bit nostalgic

G The jokey undertones and use of special effects made it work for me.

H The music was poor quality.

4 **Work in small groups. Discuss these questions.**

1 Why do you think so many people enjoy reality or talent shows, while others can't bear to watch them?

2 What makes a good comedy? Is it the characters, the acting, the plot or the dialogue?

3 Do you think it's easy to become a celebrity? Is it something to aspire to?

Topic review

1 Work in pairs and discuss these questions.

1 Do you think you can judge a person by the way they dress?

2 What was the last difficult decision you had to make?

3 Do you believe that colour affects our mood? Why? Why not?

4 How important do you think the use of colour is in paintings and photographs?

5 Which languages would you like to be able to speak? Why?

6 Have you ever had anything stolen? If so, what?

7 What are your views on children playing computer games?

8 What would you like your children to achieve in their lives?

Reading

2 Read this article. For questions 1–3, choose the answer (A, B or C) which you think fits best according to the text.

1 Why was the writer surprised at the results of the survey?

   A He had been influenced by previous surveys.

   B They do not reflect his personal experience.

   C He had thought people disliked change.

2 What does the writer say about technology?

   A It has enabled people to move away from their home town.

   B Family members have less personal contact than before because of it.

   C People use different forms of technology for different purposes.

3 What does *it* in bold in the last paragraph refer to?

   A the opinion poll

   B family life

   C the explanation

What is the future of the 'family'?

You might think that people's closest relationships are suffering as a result of the decline in traditional family structures. But you would be wrong. According to recent research, most people actually have a very optimistic view of their family's future. In a survey, the majority of those interviewed said they were still very close to members of their family. They also said they had great respect for their parents, and hoped their children would feel the same about them, one day. Indeed, the vast majority of those surveyed said they were very happy with their family.

However, it is also true that the structure of the family is undergoing a rapid change. The number of people choosing not to get married (and lead a 'traditional' family life) has risen rapidly. Why is this?

Technology plays a large part in this change. Today, physical distances between people have become psychologically much smaller, thanks to increased ownership of cars, access to public transport, or the internet.

However, due to modern communications, and the almost universal possession of a mobile phone, people do not actually make use of this technology to keep in touch more with their loved ones. According to the survey, only a very small number of people contact their family on a daily basis.

Yet, as research shows, we still value family life, and indeed, we are placing far more importance on **it** than ever before. Why is this? Perhaps because there is a greater need, in the modern world, to understand who exactly we are, and where we come from. As the world becomes smaller, and increasingly globalised, clear personal identities can easily become blurred.

Grammar

3 Read this article about Levi jeans. Complete the gaps with the correct form of the verbs in brackets.

The $25,000 pair of jeans

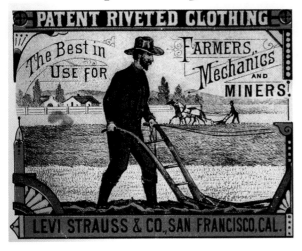

The men who wore them didn't come much tougher and neither did their jeans.

One battered pair of Levi's is reckoned **(0)** ......*to be*...... (be) the oldest in the world – a remarkable survivor of the Wild West. Such is the rarity of the jeans that, even in their washed-out and torn state, they are expected **(1)** .... (fetch) $25,000 when sold at auction. These Levi jeans were found **(2)** .... (lie) in a pile of mud some years ago in an old silver mining town in Nevada. The owner, who wants **(3)** .... (remain) anonymous, has refused **(4)** .... (say) exactly where they were found, or how he came by them. Tests have shown, however, that they were made around 1880, when they probably cost about one dollar, when the miners came flocking to the American frontier in search of their fortune. As they worked **(5)** .... (find) silver in the harsh conditions of the Nevada desert, the miners needed clothes **(6)** .... (stand up) to the job – and they found them in the durable, riveted trousers invented by Levi Strauss and partner Jacob Davis. Metal rivets were used **(7)** .... (secure) the pockets because miners kept **(8)** .... (complain) their pockets were ripping off as they worked.

Speaking

4 Work in small groups. Create a questionnaire for other students. Below are some headings for your questionnaire and one example for each heading. The aim is to revise past tenses, the present perfect, the passive, *-ing* forms and the infinitive, so you should devise questions using these forms.

Vocabulary	Did you start a vocabulary notebook or file at the beginning of this course?
Grammar	How much grammar had you studied before starting this course?
Listening	How much do you think your listening skills have improved?
Speaking	Have you taken full advantage of the speaking activities?
Reading	Do you think you have been given too much, too little or just enough reading to do?
Writing	Do you enjoy doing the writing tasks?
Exam preparation	Have you been given enough information about the content of the Cambridge English Advanced exam?

5 Take turns to ask and answer questions with someone from a different group.

Vocabulary

6 Read this article. Use the words given in capitals to form a word that fits the gaps.

New research has revealed some controversial and surprising results. Apparently, some teenagers have difficulty with their **(1)** ...., and their **(2)** .... to do activities for a long time. However, this is not because of **(3)** .... – it is in fact a natural biological process. The **(4)** .... of this research has found that teenagers' brains continue developing far longer into **(5)** .... than previously thought. Using MRI scans, the brain **(6)** .... of adolescents was monitored as they tried to solve a problem in their heads while ignoring **(7)** .... distractions. The scans suggested that the brain was working less **(8)** .... than that of an adult.

CONCENTRATE
ABLE

LAZY
COME

ADULT
ACTIVE

ENVIRONMENT

EFFECT

Speaking and Reading

1 Work with a partner and discuss these questions.

1 What topics did – or do – you study in biology lessons at school?

2 Look at the body parts in the diagram below. What does each organ do?

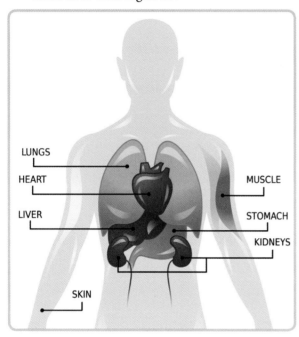

LUNGS
HEART
LIVER
MUSCLE
STOMACH
KIDNEYS
SKIN

3 How many cells do you think there are in the human body? How long do they last?

2 Scan the extract from a book about cells in the human body. What is the significance of the following numbers or times?

1 10,000,000,000,000,000

2 billions

3 approximately one month

4 several years

5 every few days

6 approximately 100,000,000,000

7 500

8 nine years

⤵ Exam spot

In the texts used in the Cambridge English Advanced exam, it is very likely that there will be some words you are not familiar with. Don't let this worry you. You should be able to use the context (as well as clues in the words themselves) to help you work out what the words mean.

Your cells are a country of 10,000 trillion citizens, each devoted in some intensively specific way to your overall well-being. There isn't a thing they don't do for you. They let you feel pleasure and form thoughts. They enable you to stand and stretch and caper. When you eat, they extract the nutrients, distribute the energy, and carry off the wastes – all those things you learned about in school biology – but they also remember to make you hungry in the first place and reward you with a feeling of well-being afterwards, so that you won't forget to eat again. They keep your hair growing, your ears waxed, your brain quietly purring. They manage every corner of your being. They will jump to your defence the instant you are threatened. They will unhesitatingly die for you – billions of them do so daily. And not once in all your years have you thanked even one of them. So let us take a moment now to regard them with the wonder and the appreciation they deserve.

Surprises at the cellular level turn up all the time. In nature, nitric oxide is a formidable toxin and a common component of air pollution. So scientists were surprised when, in the mid-1980s, they found it being produced in a curiously devoted manner in human cells. Its purpose was at first a mystery, but then scientists began to find it all over the place – controlling the flow

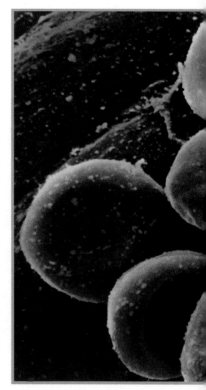

of blood and the energy level of cells, attacking cancers and other pathogens, regulating the sense of smell. It also explained why nitroglycerine, the well-known explosive, soothes the heart pain known as angina. (It is converted into nitric oxide in the bloodstream, relaxing the muscle linings of vessels, allowing blood to flow more freely.) In barely the space of a decade, this one gassy substance went from extraneous toxin to ubiquitous elixir.

Rarely does any living cell last more than a month or so, but there are some notable exceptions. Liver cells can survive for years, though the components within them may be renewed every few days. Brain cells last as long as you do. You are issued with a hundred billion or so at birth and that is all you are ever going to get. It is estimated that you lose five hundred of them an hour, so if you have any serious thinking to do, then on no account should you waste a single moment. The good news is that the individual components of your brain cells are constantly renewed so that, as with the liver cells, no part of them is actually likely to be more than about a month old. Indeed, it has been suggested that there isn't a single bit of any of us – not so much as a stray molecule – that was part of us nine years ago. It may not feel like it, but at the cellular level we are all youngsters.

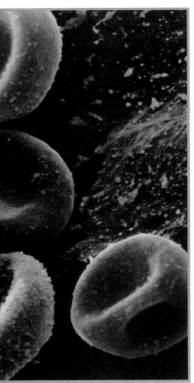

Listening

1 **Look at the inventions in the photos. What do you think they do? Use the words in the box to help you.**

> 17th century   microscopic
> magnify   275 times

2 **2 04 Listen and check your ideas.**

3 **2 04 Listen again and complete the sentences with a word or a short phrase.**

1 It was Robert Hooke who first described .... in his book *Micrographia* in 1665.

2 By using microscopes, he discovered that .... contained billions of tiny cells.

3 He estimated that a one-inch square of cork wood contained 1,259,712,000 cells – this was the first time that such a .... had appeared in science.

4 Hooke's microscopes could magnify things by up to ....times.

5 Later, an uneducated draper called van Leewenhoek managed to look even more closely at small things, just by using basic ....

6 We don't know how Leewenhoek achieved his results, because he was very ....

Vocabulary

Vocabulary spot

In the text you listened to, you heard the idiom *be a dab hand at*. This means 'to be good at'. There are many idioms based on parts of the body.

1 Complete the sentences (1–8) with a body part. Then match them with cartoons (A–H).

1 Working with such a bright team of people certainly keeps me on my ....
2 He's set his .... on becoming a dancer.
3 Don't carry all that on your own. Let me give you a ....
4 Tell me what happened last night. I'm all ....
5 She hasn't a clue what's going on. She's always got her .... in the clouds.
6 Put your .... up for an hour – we haven't got to rush.
7 Try and catch the waiter's ....
8 Giacomo is bound to know who we should ask – he's got .... in every pie.

2 Here are more idioms connected with parts of the body. Match idioms 1–8 to definitions a–h.

1 to bite your tongue
2 to be down in the mouth
3 to keep your fingers crossed
4 to get on your nerves
5 to keep an eye on
6 to put someone's mind at rest
7 to break someone's heart
8 to fall head over heels in love

a to make someone annoyed or irritated
b to make someone stop worrying
c to make someone who loves you very sad
d to hope things will happen the way you want them to
e to stop yourself from saying something you want to say
f to start to love someone passionately
g to feel miserable
h to look after something or someone

A

B

C

D

E

F

G

H

3 Complete this short story with idioms from exercises 1 and 2. Make any necessary changes to verb forms.

As soon as Luis met Fernanda, he (**1**) .... with her. They got to know each other when Luis noticed her loaded down with shopping and offered (**2**) .... Fernanda is a bit of a dreamer and her mother always says she (**3**) .... Nevertheless, she has a very good position as an office assistant and she (**4**) .... on getting promoted. She says that she finds working in a busy office really (**5**) .... Fernanda talks a lot about her job and at first Luis (**6**) .... But now he has to (**7**) .... to stop himself from telling her how bored he is with hearing about everything that's going on at work. Today when I bumped into him in town, Luis (**8**) .... because Fernanda had to go to a conference rather than on the holiday they had planned together. 'I love her but I don't know what to do,' Luis said, 'because I'm sure she likes her job more than she likes me.' I thought carefully but I couldn't think of anything that would (**9**) .... All I could do was promise (**10**) .... for him.

Inversion

1 Notice the use of inversion in these sentences to make them more emphatic. How might you write them without inversion?

1 Rarely does any living cell last more than a month or so.
2 On no account should you waste a single moment.

2 Use inversion to make these sentences more emphatic.

1 There was never any reason to doubt the results of the experiment.
2 Credit cards are not accepted under any circumstances.
3 The public did not appreciate the significance of this research until much later.
4 The scientist only realised what had happened when he arrived back at the lab.
5 The report included recommendations not only for this company but also for many other businesses.
6 The press only discovered her secret after she died.

3 Make six sentences about health and fitness using these phrases.

little	never	only after	not until
under no circumstances		not only	

4 Compare your sentences with a partner.

⬊ Corpus spot

Take care when using inversion. The *Cambridge English Corpus* shows exam candidates often make mistakes with this.

Not only does fashion reflect changes in how people live, it affects lifestyles, too.

NOT ***Not only fashion reflects*** ~~changes in how people live, it affects lifestyles, too.~~

Correct the mistakes that exam candidates have made with inversion in these sentences.

1 Never I could have imagined how many arrangements were necessary.
2 Not only the family was kind, but also helpful.

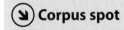 **G → page 171**

Paper 1 Part 7

Gapped text

In this part of the Reading and Use of English test, you read an article from which six paragraphs have been removed. The paragraphs are placed in a jumbled order after the main text. You need to decide where in the text the paragraphs have been taken from. This tests that you can recognise how a text is structured, and how a text creates meaning across paragraphs.

1   **You are going to read an extract from a magazine article. Six paragraphs have been removed from the extract. Choose from the paragraphs A–G the one which fits each gap 1–6. There is one extra paragraph which you do not need to use.**

2   **Work in pairs. Discuss the words/phrases which helped you to decide what fits where.**

Is your glass half full or half empty?

Are you happy? Did you open the curtains this morning, see that it's yet another day of sunshine and bounce out of bed? Or are you the kind of person who sees the sun and starts worrying about getting sunburnt and the problems it may cause for gardeners?

1 [ ]

But a television documentary, which is to be broadcast next week, suggests that in fact they play only a very small part and that you can, in fact, train yourself to have a more sunny attitude to life. It argues that it may indeed be simple to change negative people into positive ones.

2 [ ]

Next week's programme is timely, because the happiness of individuals is something that policymakers have started to take very seriously indeed. Indeed, yesterday, a new charity called MindFull suggested that mental health should be taught in schools. And later this month, the Office for National Statistics (ONS) will publish its National Well-being report. This will draw on a number of studies which suggest that our positivity has an impact on our health and our educational achievements.

3 [ ]

In other words, being happy could add years to your life. It doesn't just benefit your health, either. Educational attainment, too, seems to be linked to attitude. Nick Baylis, a consultant psychologist, works with the pupils at a school in London that, five years ago, had very poor academic results. Now, 87% of its pupils are leaving school with good qualifications. Baylis believes that teaching both the staff and pupils 'well-being' and coping strategies was key to this success.

4 [ ]

'Through monkeys, humans and lots of animals, the amount of activity in the front cortex does seem to be a good marker for positivity and negativity.' Positive people have a more active left frontal cortex; the presenter was found to have a substantially more active right frontal cortex – proving his assertion that he is one of life's pessimists. 'When I look into the future, I see all the things that are going to go wrong, rather than the things that will probably go right,' he says. He also suffers from insomnia. Professor Fox is among a growing number of psychologists, however, who believe that he and others like him can change this brain asymmetry and thus their personality through a series of exercises.

5 [ ]

It seems simple. But surely, trying to pick out a smiling expression isn't going to make me more optimistic. Professor Fox tells me: 'I was very sceptical when I got into this initially. But the task we used in the show has been used with kids with self-esteem issues. And it does seem to have very powerful effects. It's early days, but the signs are that it is definitely effective.'

6 [ ]

Of course, many psychologists argue that relentless happiness is neither normal nor healthy. Professor Fox says: 'There are situations when things go wrong, and having a healthy dose of pessimism can be good. But the evidence shows that, broadly, having a positive attitude really does boost your well-being.'

A The most striking example comes from Oxford, Ohio, which in the 1970s conducted a study of its inhabitants, then aged over 50. So who has survived in good health? Those who had a positive outlook on their life and impending old age have lived, on average, 7.6 years longer than those with negative views.

B It worked for the presenter, who over a couple of months of exercising was able to recalibrate his brain. He says that he is sleeping better 'though I wouldn't call myself a heavy sleeper yet', and that he is more optimistic. So should we all be doing the exercises? 'I think anyone could do them, but I suspect a fair number who start then let it slide,' he says.

C If the show touches a nerve in the same way as last autumn's documentary by the same director about fasting – which kick-started the phenomenally popular 5:2 diet – many of us could soon be undertaking mental workouts in our lunch hour.

D Professor Fox gives her views on the subject in next week's programme, pointing out that the research has very significant implications for schools and for health professionals. 'However, more work needs to be done before the results can be considered conclusive.'

E The most basic one is called Cognitive Bias Modification. To do it, you look at a screen for 10 minutes every day over several weeks. During those minutes, a series of 15 faces are flashed up. All (except one) are either angry, upset or unhappy. You have to spot, and click on, the one happy face.

F For years, many scientists believed that your personality was predetermined. They were of the opinion that it was your genes which were responsible for whether you were an optimist or a pessimist.

G Next week's documentary will try to provide a physiological explanation for their achievements. For the programme, the presenter had his brain scanned by Professor Elaine Fox, a neuroscientist at Oxford and author of *Rainy Brain, Sunny Brain*. She says brain asymmetry is very closely linked to our personalities.

EXAM ADVICE

- Read the whole of the text first.
- Read through paragraphs A–G and notice the differences between them.
- Pay careful attention to connecting words throughout the text and paragraphs, as well as at the beginnings and ends of paragraphs.
- Consider each paragraph for every gap. Don't assume you have been correct in your previous answers as you go along!
- Read the whole of the text again when you have completed the task.
- Don't rely on matching up names, dates or numbers in the text and paragraphs just because they are the same or similar.
- Don't rely on matching up individual words or phrases in the text and the paragraphs just because they are the same or similar.

Speaking

1 Work with a partner and answer the questions.

1 What kind of review is a *rave* review?
2 List as many things as possible that may be reviewed in the media.
3 What sorts of things do you read (or listen to) reviews of?
4 Has a rave review ever affected you?

Reading

1 Look at the headlines below, which are all from reviews.

1 What do you think the reviews might be about?
2 Can you tell from each headline whether the review would mainly praise or criticise?
3 Look quickly at the reviews (A–E) and check your answers.

[A]

Base for backpackers

[B]

Standing the test of time

[C]

Still fun, still challenging, still not changing much

[D]

An album of mystic love

[E]

Under one digital umbrella

2 Read the five reviews again. Are these statements true (T), false (F) or is the information not given (NG)?

Review A

1 The writer has no complaints about Base.
2 The writer found the architecture of Base unappealing.
3 The writer stayed in the 'Sanctuary' area of Base.

Review B

1 The writer has seen *Casablanca* more than once.
2 The issues at the heart of *Casablanca* seem rather outdated today.
3 The writer was moved to tears when he watched *Casablanca*.

Review C

1 *Mad Boys* is the fourth version of a computer game.
2 The writer thinks the new version shows little improvement.
3 The writer thought the original game did not need improving.

Review D

1 Pool Sounds' new album is based on a true love affair.
2 The writer thought the video accompanying the album was poorly filmed.
3 This new album presents a story in a very clear way.

Review E

1 The website gives information about different types of entertainment.
2 The website has just been created.
3 The writer finds this website difficult to use.

[A]

It's not brand new any more, but Base is still as distinctive as ever in its shiny red colour scheme (the colour, we're told, is called 'hot lips red'). Base has a futuristic feel, with an architecturally interesting environment and lots of unusual angles. Clear skyways connect different sections of the building and a sky-lit atrium on the ground floor has a pleasant indoor/outdoor feel. Shared facilities include a kitchen and TV lounge, plus an exciting bar. All rooms have air-conditioning and en-suite bathrooms, and there's a girls-only level called the 'Sanctuary'. The staff are young and hip and provide help tips for visitors to Melbourne.

B Little background is needed to appreciate this film. *Casablanca* does what only a great film can: it envelopes the viewer in the story, creating an unbreakable link with the characters, and only letting go with the end credits. The first time I saw *Casablanca*, I remember vividly how 'modern' it seemed. While many movies from the '30s and '40s appear horribly dated when viewed today, *Casablanca* stands up remarkably well. The themes of sacrifice and heroism still ring true. The dialogue has lost none of its cleverness. The atmosphere (enhanced by the sharp black-and-white cinematography) is as powerful as ever. The characters are still as three-dimensional as they were more than 60 years ago.

C When you've managed to find a formula through luck the way that J-Games did with *Mad Boys* it's hard to break too far from the original idea. Because of this, if you were to take a look at *Mad Boys 2* you might think nothing has changed. And in terms of basic game play, virtually everything is the same. But in terms of structure *Mad Boys 2* is a big improvement. The biggest change is that *Mad Boys 2* is much easier to play, if you give it some time. The original game was over-complicated at times, but with three difficulty settings, this second outing gives players much more freedom.

D Occasionally, an album arrives which is simple, but at the same time, is mysterious for the listener. Chords, dynamics, lyrics, harmonies and instrumentation all combine to send you back to an age when you experienced the deepest of emotions, but were unable to express them. Pool Sounds' second album was inspired by the end of the relationship between songwriter Jesse Lowe and singer Carly Sewell. Yet, what makes *Last Nights of Summer* a triumph is not what it communicates, but how it embraces the break-up. There's a film to go with the songs, but this album is already visual enough. It is a masterpiece. That, at least, is crystal clear.

E *Digital Skies* combines several popular entertainment sites under one roof. News and reviews have been seamlessly integrated into three main categories – Music, Cinema and TV – which makes it easy to browse the well-written content. The site also features a Cult section that covers *Doctor Who* and other popular shows and people, as well as links to lively forums. There's lots for music, TV and film buffs to enjoy, although you need to register to post comments.

Articles

1 **Discuss these questions about the use of articles in the reviews on pages 106–107.**

Review A

1 Could it be *a* colour instead of *the* colour in the first sentence?

2 Would it change the meaning if the review mentioned *one* kitchen instead of *a* kitchen? How?

3 Would it change the meaning if the writer had written *the* visitors instead of *visitors* in the last sentence? How?

Review B

1 Which would convey the same meaning as *a great film* in the first sentence: *one great film*; *this great film*; or *the great film*?

2 Which would convey the same idea as *the viewer*: *viewers* or *a viewer*?

3 Which would convey the same meaning as *the themes of sacrifice*: *themes of sacrifice* or *its themes of sacrifice*?

Review C

1 What could the writer have written instead of *through luck* in the first sentence: *through a stroke of luck*; *through a luck*; *through the luck*?

2 What could the writer have written instead of *some* time in the penultimate sentence: *a bit of* time or *a time for*?

Review D

1 What could replace *the* listener in the first sentence: *a* listener or *listeners*?

Review E

1 Could the writer have written *the* Music, *the* Cinema and *the* TV?

2 What could replace *to post comments*: *to post the comments* or *to post any comments*?

G→page 172

Listening

1 **Work with a partner and look at the photos.**

1 What kinds of film do you think they are from?

2 Which kind do you like best and least?

2 **205 Listen to two people discussing films they have recently seen.**

1 Which films are they discussing?

2 List all the facts that you learn about the films.

3 What words and expressions do the speakers use to make their feelings clear?

Vocabulary

> ⬊ **Exam spot**
>
> In the Speaking test, you need to give your opinions and perhaps suggest how things could be done differently or improved. The vocabulary you focus on in this unit is the kind of language that can be useful when reviewing something. The chunks here are particularly useful in this part of the exam.

1 **Choose the correct words to complete these sentences.**

1 Film *supporters / buffs* usually prefer less commercial films to Hollywood blockbusters.

2 This movie *made / gave* me an insight into life in the city of Mumbai.

3 You have to pay *attention / thought* if you don't want to miss some of the clues in this gripping detective drama.

4 Robinson has a talent for expressing complex ideas and making them *crystal / diamond* clear.

5 It's an old film, but it *stands / ages* up very well for modern audiences and hasn't dated at all.

6 The poet expresses feelings that we have all *experienced / done* but could never put into words so effectively.

7 The book's male characters are convincing but the female characters don't *make / ring* true.

8 I wouldn't say I enjoyed the film but it was certainly thought-*provoking / making*.

9 There have been other biographies of Charlie Chaplin but this one succeeds in showing him in a fresh *view / light*.

10 I couldn't *follow / catch* the plot at all – I had no idea what was happening.

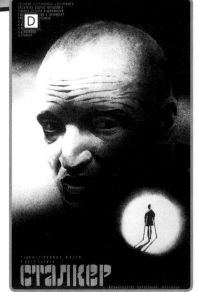

2 Choose two categories from the box. Choose one example from both categories that you would recommend to a partner and one that you would not. Explain your choices.

film   website   novel   theatre production
computer game   singer   restaurant   TV show

3 After reading or listening to a review, you might want to react to the opinions it gives. Complete the gaps in these expressions.

1 Why d.. we stay in this hotel? It has good reviews.

2 I might as w.. buy the album – I have all their other ones.

3 So am I r.. in saying that this software can be used with a Mac as well as a PC?

4 In other w.., we should have plenty of opportunity to publicise the concert.

5 Isn't it mainly a m.. of careful planning?

6 I'm not entirely c.. that we should ask the author to change the ending of the book.

7 I agree with you on the w..., but there are a few things I'd like to t.. issue with.

8 I'm in two m.. as to whether we should cut that scene or not.

4 Work in groups. You are going to discuss what reviews to include in the next issue of a class blog. Give your opinions and suggestions.

1 Discuss what you personally are going to review (e.g. restaurants, films, websites, etc.).

2 Discuss whether you are going to write a strongly positive review, a strongly negative one or a more balanced one. What language might you use to convey your opinions?

3 Present your plans to other students.

Writing folder 7

Reviews

In Part 2 of the Writing test, you may be asked to write a review. This could be for a book, a film, a play, a computer game, music, a restaurant, etc. Whatever kind of review you are writing, you need to be able to describe accurately and concisely and to convey your opinion in a clear and interesting fashion.

1   What is the purpose of a review?

  1 to interest and entertain the reader
  2 to describe the subject of the review to the reader
  3 to convey the writer's opinion about the subject of the review
  4 to promote the subject of the review
  5 something else

2   Read the film review. Then make notes on the topics below.

- facts about the film and its plot
- phrases that convey the writer's opinion of the film
- things included to interest and entertain the reader

GETTING ECO-FRIENDLY WITH ALIENS

When choosing the best film of the last decade, James Cameron's *Avatar* has to be up there among the most successful (at least in terms of how much money it made). With this movie, the director took a flying leap into another dimension – super-sleek 3D – leading those in the know to breathlessly declare a new level had been reached in the art of film-making. The film emerged as an eminently watchable and hugely entertaining sci-fi spectacular, but it did seem unable to decide if it wanted to wipe out every blue-skinned extra-terrestrial in sight or get all touchy-feely and eco-friendly with them.

The movie takes us one hundred years or so into the future, when planet Earth is trying to solve its energy issues by mining the rarest of all minerals – the charmingly named 'Unobtainium'. Naturally, this mineral is only to be found on one particular planet far, far away, deep in jungles swarming with quirky-scary CGI creatures, under a giant tree. This tree, unfortunately, just happens to be the spiritual home of the planet's native race – the Na'vi. These hugely tall, blue aliens have pointy ears and flat noses, ethnic beads and dreadlocks. A mining company from Earth has set up a quasi-military base there, and is preparing to drive the aboriginal inhabitants off their land, led by the psychotic Colonel Quaritch (played by Stephen Lang).

But the mining corporation also has a scientific unit led by Dr Grace Augustine (Sigourney Weaver), which seeks merely to study the inhabitants, get to know them, and (importantly) to make 'Avatars' in the shape of Na'vi. These 'Avatars', which the humans remote-control from their base into their jungle, can communicate peacefully with the blue giants in their own exotic, subtitled language and attempt to convince them to leave of their own free will.

Our hero – and 'Avatar pilot' – is Jake Sully (Sam Worthington) a retired soldier, now wheelchair-bound after dreadful injuries. He is blown away by the liberating virtual reality that his new-found Avatar alien body affords him. He revels in his jungle adventures, and although he at first schemes alongside the mining corporation to facilitate the upcoming military invasion, he soon falls in love with the beautiful female alien, Neytiri (Zoe Saldaña) and switches sides. Sully sees a glimmer of hope: a chance to be happy and in love. When the invasion comes, he sides with the Na'vi.

The digitally created world integrates seamlessly with real-life actors, and it's all undeniably impressive. The film's special effects are certainly spectacular, especially on the big screen. However, it's difficult to tell if cinema as a genre has really evolved or not. But take away the mind-blowing special effects, and the director's huge reputation, and you have a truly fascinating story about a money-obsessed company developing technology in order for humans to sneak into the lives of aliens and destroy their natural habitat. What an interesting idea it is – and this is what makes the film worthwhile.

3 **Is there anything else about the language of the review that you think in some way reflects the content of the film?**

4 **The sentences below use some collocations that are common in reviews. Choose the correct word to complete each sentence.**

1 As the plot *unwraps* / *unfolds*, you slowly realise what a complex *character* / *nature* the hero is.
2 The film was *shot* / *fired* in less than two weeks on *place* / *location* in New York.
3 The plot of the film *misses* / *lacks* originality but the *special* / *particular* effects are amazing.
4 George Clooney plays the *chief* / *lead* in a superb new *romantic* / *love* comedy.
5 The novel is *set* / *placed* in South Africa at a *turbulent* / *fierce* time in its history.
6 Helen Mirren *gave* / *made* a *stunning* / *hitting* performance as the Queen.
7 The play has taken the theatre-going world by *storm* / *lightning*, *lifting* / *winning* praise from all the critics.
8 The curtain *dropped* / *fell* to *thunderous* / *thundery* applause from the audience.

5 **Work with a partner. Look at the list below. Discuss which features are most important in a review and why.**

- an eye-catching title
- basic details about what you are reviewing
- further information about key details (e.g. people, location, etc.)
- a detailed summary of what you are reviewing (e.g. the plot)
- a mixture of past tenses (e.g. to give information about a film) and present tenses (e.g. to make a plot sound exciting)
- a style that is suitable for a specific audience
- evocative adjectives
- a balanced discussion of any positive and negative aspects
- a recommendation about what you are reviewing or a summary of who might enjoy it

6 **Now try this exam task. Read the instructions and write your answer in 220–260 words in an appropriate style.**

You see the following announcement on a website, Cool Reviews.

Reviews wanted

We are preparing a feature on TV programmes that viewers find particularly original or unusual.

Have you seen anything recently which caught your attention? Why was it unusual? What do you think the programme makers wanted to achieve? Were they successful?

Write your **review**.

18 Telling the truth

Speaking

1 Work with a partner and discuss these questions.

1 Look at the photos. Who are the people and what are they doing?

2 Would you expect these people to tell lies? If so, in what circumstances?

3 Below are the most frequent lies told by men and women. When do you think they might say each of these things? Have you ever said these things?

The top lies told by men

1 Nothing's wrong, I'm fine.
2 No, you look great in that dress.
3 Sorry, my battery died.
4 But, it wasn't that expensive.
5 I'm stuck in traffic.

The top lies told by women

1 Nothing's wrong, I'm fine.
2 Oh, this isn't new. I've had it for ages.
3 I'm on my way.
4 I don't know where it is – I haven't touched it.
5 Sorry, I missed your call.

Reading

1 Read the article and write one sentence summarising what it is about.

2 Complete each sentence about the content of the article with one word only.

1 The writer suggests that people tell lies surprisingly ....

2 He also expresses surprise at how .... people find it to identify whether someone is lying or not.

3 Scientists believe that certain beliefs about how people behave when they are lying may be

....

4 Current research is focusing more on how people .... questions.

3 Work in pairs and discuss these questions about the article.

1 What three reasons does the writer give as to why people lie? Which of these reasons do you think is 'more serious' than the others?

2 What three physical signs are often interpreted as indicating someone is lying?

3 In what four types of situation could it be useful to know whether someone was telling the truth or not? Give a specific example for each situation.

Truth or lie?

How do we know when someone is telling the truth?

So why are humans not better at detecting lies? And how can people get better at spotting fibs? One of the problems is that people don't know what to look for. Across societies, there are false beliefs that certain behavioural clues can indicate someone is lying. For instance, many people think liars shy away from making eye contact, blink a lot or fidget as they speak. Yet scientists now believe that, in reality, with those three things, it's exactly the opposite. It may indeed be the case that people who are experienced at lying learn that the easiest way to make it seem like they're telling a truth when they're not is to look you in the eye.

During the last decade, psychology researchers have been looking for ways to turn humans into more accurate lie detectors. If more accurate lie-detection methods can be developed, they could provide valuable applications in a variety of settings, ranging from criminal justice to intelligence gathering to financial or business situations.

Currently, the idea of human lie detection is being approached from a different angle. Rather than simply observing someone's behaviour, which has been shown to be unreliable, psychologists are looking at whether certain interview methods can prompt liars to respond in ways that reveal their deception in a more telling manner.

In other words, if we want to identify whether someone is telling the truth or not, we should move away from paying close attention to their behaviour to thinking more about the questions we ask and the way we ask them.

For example, maybe by asking the same question several times in several different ways to see if the answers given are always consistent, we can catch someone out.

Or perhaps we could pose very detailed, focused questions. Someone telling the truth would be able to answer quickly and directly, whereas someone lying might have to talk around the subject a bit while they thought up an answer.

It is believed that this major change of tactics represents a more promising approach, because it should make it easier to distinguish between the behaviours of liars and truth-tellers.

It has been claimed that people tell lies — whether small or large — in roughly 25% of their social interactions. People lie for all kinds of different reasons: to create a good impression, to obtain an advantage, to avoid punishment, and some of these reasons are obviously more serious than others.

Lying may be a common human behaviour, but despite its frequency, humans are surprisingly unskilled when it comes to separating fact from fiction.

In 2006, Charles Bond Bella DePaulo found that untrained observers are correct only 54% of the time when trying to distinguish between true and false statements. These results indicate that people are no better or worse at detecting lies than if they had left their judgments up to chance.

Vocabulary

1 The writer uses a number of words and expressions that are often used in more academic writing. Match the words in the box to these meanings.

> major   pose   interactions   identify
> claimed   currently   applications   indicate
> consistent   frequency

1 occasions when two or more people communicate with each other
2 at the moment
3 said that something is true although it cannot be proved
4 find out
5 show
6 the number of times that something happens
7 important
8 ask
9 practical uses
10 being the same

2 Form collocations used in the article.

1 to separate fact from   **a** angle
2 to leave something up to   **b** fiction
3 to make eye   **c** attention
4 to look someone in the   **d** contact
5 to approach something from a different   **e** chance
6 to pay close   **f** eye

3 Complete these sentences with language from exercises 1 and 2.

1 We wanted to .... whether people tell more lies when they communicate online.
2 On observing the children's behaviour I was surprised by the .... with which they changed activity.
3 I prefer to make careful plans for a holiday rather than ....
4 If you don't .... to what you're supposed to be observing, you may miss something important.
5 The professor is .... working on a very complex experiment.
6 I felt sure he wasn't telling the truth because of the way he refused to ....
7 The preliminary results of the survey .... that there have been some considerable changes in public opinion over the last decade.

Emphasis

1 What is the difference between these sentences?

1 I must not tell lies.
2 What I must not do is tell lies.
3 Telling lies is what I must not do.

2 Make these sentences emphatic in as many ways as you can, using the same technique as in exercise 1.

1 Paulo loves Maria.
2 Katya had an accident.
3 Rolf won a million dollars.

3 **2 06** Listen to nine sentences and decide what techniques are used to add emphasis.

1	auxiliary verb *do* added
2	
3	
4	
5	
6	
7	
8	
9	

4 Make these sentences more emphatic by using a stressed auxiliary verb.

1 Jake admires her work.
2 I love you.
3 Mary did her very best.
4 I used to be able to dive quite well.
5 They've agreed to help us.

5 Work in pairs. Write appropriate two-line dialogues using the emphatic sentences from exercise 4.

A: *They won't consider you for that post. You haven't got any qualifications.*
B: *I don't care. I am going to get that job.*

6 Respond in a natural and emphatic way to these sentences, using a stressed auxiliary verb.

1 You can't be sure you're right.
2 You didn't give me the right information.
3 Why don't you ever help me with housework?
4 I think your friend cheated in the exam.
5 I know you won't be able to kick the habit.
6 You've forgotten your purse, haven't you?

G → page 172

Listening

1 **2:07** You are going to listen to two students making 'small talk' with their tutor.

   1 Listen and write down the eight questions you hear.
   2 Think about how you could answer them.

2 **2:08** Listen to the full conversation. Who gives a more appropriate answer to each question? Give reasons.

3 **2:08** Listen again and make notes of the main points made by the person giving the better answer.

 Exam spot

In the Speaking test, you may be asked questions about yourself and you must try to answer the question asked, not some other possibly unrelated question.

You must, if at all possible, avoid giving just two- or three-word answers. The examiner can't give you a good mark if he or she doesn't hear much English from you.

4 Work with a partner. Take it in turns to ask and answer the questions you wrote down in exercise 1.

5 Think about when you meet someone for the first time. What kinds of thing do you often talk about?

6 **2:09** Now listen to a different conversation. Answer these questions.

   1 Who are the people?
      A friends
      B work colleagues
      C fellow students
   2 What do you think is the main purpose of their conversation?
      A to establish a friendly relationship
      B to find out about each other
      C to check that each person is telling the truth

7 Listen again and note what you learn about Jason and Sophie.

Speaking

1 Work with a partner. Ask and answer these questions. Answer some truthfully and at least three with a lie. Be prepared to expand on your answers.

   1 What did you do last night?
   2 What's the best present you've ever been given?
   3 What's your favourite kind of music?
   4 When did you fall in love for the first time?
   5 What did you want to be when you were a child and why?
   6 What's your ambition for the future?
   7 What's the most exciting thing that you have ever done?
   8 What would you do if you won a large amount of money?

2 Now write two extra questions to ask your partner. Don't show them to each other.

3 Take turns to ask each other the extra questions. Listen carefully to each other's answers and decide whether your partner is telling the truth or lying.

4 Tell each other whether you thought each answer was true or invented. Were you right?

Exam folder 8

Paper 1 Part 8
Multiple matching

> In Part 8 of the Reading and Use of English test, you have to match questions or prompts to bits of text. This is a multiple-matching task. Two reading skills are: scanning and skimming. Scanning means reading for specific information, while skimming means reading quickly through a text to get a general impression of the content. You will need to make use of both these skills in this part of the test.

1 **Read the Exam information. Discuss with a partner why each of the bullet points provides good advice.**

EXAM ADVICE

- Read the subtitle to get a general idea of what the text is about.
- Read the questions before you scan for the information/ opinions needed.
- Read each question very carefully.
- Skim the whole of the text before you scan for the information/opinions needed.
- Don't rely on matching up individual words or phrases in the question and the text just because they are the same or similar.
- Don't rely on finding all the information you need for a question in just one part of the text.
- Don't read the texts carefully before looking at the questions – as you then probably won't have enough time to answer the questions.
- If you are not sure of the answer, eliminate any options you are confident are wrong and choose one of the remaining ones.

2 **Now read the article on page 117 and answer the questions. Choose from the films (A, B, C or D). A film may be chosen more than once.**

Which of these films

1 does the writer see rather differently now than at first?
2 manages to avoid one of the common pitfalls of its genre?
3 made the writer wish to lead a life like that of its main character?
4 depicts relationships resembling those the writer has experienced?
5 made the writer feel it had helped them to become an adult?
6 has influenced the writer's own mannerisms?
7 appealed to the writer because of the way it reflected her own life?
8 made someone change her plans for the future?
9 does the writer say she admires despite its flaws?
10 has strong contrasts in mood?

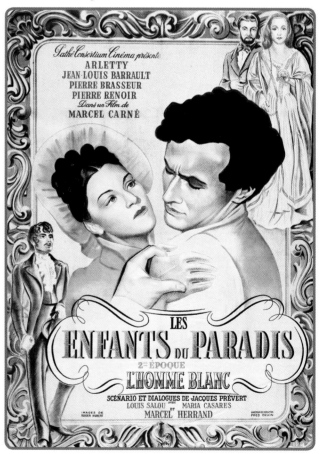

Which film changed your life?

We asked four well-known women to tell us about the films that have had a significant impact on their lives.

A Les Enfants du Paradis

Paula Rankin, the Oscar-winning actor, told us that her decision to try for a career on the stage was determined by watching this ever-popular French film when she was a teenager. 'I had always enjoyed taking part in school drama productions but had been planning to study law. Then my parents took me to see *Les Enfants du Paradis*, set in the theatrical world of 19th-century Paris. Its romance and passion captivated me but it also made me realise that people could devote their adult lives to the theatre. I suddenly knew that I wanted to be part of that world of art and emotion. I can't say my life has in any way resembled that of the heroine of the film, as I perhaps hoped it might, but I've certainly never regretted taking the path it turned me towards.'

B East of Eden

This was the film chosen by popular crime writer, Maria Cruikshank. 'It's certainly not the best film I've ever seen but it had a huge impact on me. It's such a powerful story, based on John Steinbeck's novel about the warring relationship between two brothers at the time of the American Civil War. I saw it when I was about 15 and I've always felt as if that was the day I grew up. I became aware of how tragic life can be and somehow I felt as if, on leaving the cinema, I had put childish things behind me forever. I must admit that when I see the film these days, it feels rather sentimental. But, even so, the simple camerawork combined with what strikes me now as the innocence of the acting still have the power to move me to tears.'

C The Women

This film was picked by comedian, Teresa Gordon. 'I've loved this film ever since I was 12. It's a 1939 film with an entirely female cast. Even the pictures on the walls are of women. It's about a group of friends, one of whom discovers her husband is having an affair. Some of the friends are sympathetic and supportive while others are simply gleeful at having something to talk about. It's hilarious but you can't laugh too much - you'd miss something because it goes at such a fast pace. It's also very moving at times. It's taught me a lot about female friendships, preparing me for the way in which our love for someone doesn't stop us gossiping about them. When I saw a video of my own show the other day I realised I'd borrowed some of my gestures and turns of phrase from my favourite characters in it.'

D Paper Moon

Film director, Amelia Forest, chose this 1970s classic. 'It's an adult film about a little girl in a grown-up world. As a child I didn't spend much time with other children. My mother used to take me to lots of movies and I saw *Paper Moon* first when I was about ten. I felt as if it was speaking directly to me. I loved the tough tenderness in the relationship between the girl and her con-man father. The story is set in the 1930s and many period films tend to idealise the past. This one is clever enough not to do that. It shows how fear and hunger drove people to desperate actions. Of course, I'd no idea when I first saw it that I'd have a career making films myself, but I'd love to feel that one of my films might move and impress a ten-year-old as much as that one did me'.

Reading

1 Read the adverts and decide what type of people would be most likely to apply to each one.

2 Work with a partner. Discuss which advert you would be most likely to respond to. What would you want the money for?

3 Imagine that you and your friends are considering applying to the college in advert A. What would you need to do before writing your personal statements to give yourselves a better chance of success?

> **personal statement** a kind of proposal; a piece of formal, persuasive writing in which someone proposes him or herself as a suitable candidate for a course of study

4 Now look at the article on page 119 about things to avoid in personal statements. Match mistakes 1–9 with the problems in paragraphs A–I.

1 The statement made the point that the writer hoped that qualifying as an engineer would help him to buy his own flat within a few years.

2 The writer wrote *it's* instead of *its* throughout.

3 The writer concluded her statement by saying 'Getting a place on this course is the stuff that dreams are made of'.

4 The writer said he was excellent at science but his application form showed poor chemistry exam results.

5 The statement said the wrong college.

6 The statement was presented as a set of photos with captions.

7 The writer submitted five pages, although she was asked for just a paragraph.

8 The writer gave details about what subjects he studied at school.

9 The writer began her statement by saying that her marks throughout school had been badly affected by the fact that she came from a poor family and had nowhere quiet to study at home.

(↘) Exam spot

You may be asked to write a proposal in the Writing test and you may also have a negotiating or discussion task in the Speaking test. This unit helps you with the language needed for such tasks.

 A

 **Newmore College**

A prestigious college with world-class facilities and staff.

We teach a full range of subjects.

Funding is available for:

★ travel and living expenses

★ computers, books and other relevant study equipment

★ fees.

If you are interested, write us a personal statement in 500 words, telling us what you want to study, why you wish to study it and why we should offer you a place.

B

Have you got a good business idea but no funds to put it into practice?

We can offer set-up grants to people with original and viable ideas.

All proposals must be submitted by the end of this month.

C

TIME FOR A CHANGE?
WHY NOT RETRAIN?

Grants available for deserving applicants who would like to do one of a wide range of retraining courses at a number of local further education colleges. Send us a one-page proposal explaining what you would like to do and why.

How *not* to write a personal statement

To prepare an effective personal statement, you need to know what to do, as well as be aware of what not to do. These tips are based on real personal statements that have been rejected by universities.

A My first tip for you might seem obvious, but it is one that a surprising number of candidates ignore. Make sure that your statement is long enough to get your point across, but not so short that it makes you look careless (or worse, dismissive). Admissions officers read hundreds, if not thousands, of applications, so be sure that you write a statement that keeps to the word limits or space restrictions that have been set.

B Don't forget to proofread your statement very carefully. Most people don't apply to just one college, but to several at the same time, and so they inevitably copy and paste from one application to the next. That's understandable. What is surprising is how many people forget to change key bits of information (for example, the title of the course they are applying for).

C It gives a poor impression if your statement contains spelling or grammar mistakes, so don't be too lazy to check your work carefully. Ask someone to look through it for you, if possible – it's always easier to pick up on someone else's mistakes. Don't rely on your computer's spell-check, as it will not identify all the errors and may suggest corrections that are inappropriate.

D The above tips are all technical matters. The ones that follow relate more to the content of your personal statement and these are at least as important. First of all, you should not, for example, just include facts about yourself that we will already have read in your application forms. We know what school you went to, for example. What we don't know is what motivates and enthuses you or what your reasons are for choosing our college and our course.

E However, what you say should not be at odds with what is contained elsewhere in the application. Don't claim in your statement that you are passionate about learning languages if there is no evidence of your having taken any language courses or passed any language exams on your application form. It's always worth checking back to make sure that everything is consistent.

F Don't try to make the admissions tutor feel sorry for you. Resist the temptation to use the statement as an opportunity to complain about how hard life has been for you, how unfair your school has been to you, how your parents do not understand you, how no one has ever given you a lucky break … It may sometimes be appropriate to briefly refer to some specific problem, but the focus should be on how you overcame any obstacles you have met. In that way, you may impress by demonstrating your resilience.

G It's best not to focus on potential earning power as being your main motivation for doing the course. Even if part of your reason for wanting to do a degree in dentistry or law is the salary you should eventually earn, admissions tutors are much more impressed by those students who appear to be motivated by a love of learning and an enthusiasm for the academic discipline they are applying to study.

H Don't try to attract the reader's attention by being gimmicky. I've seen several applications written in verse. One applicant submitted her statement in the form of a short story. Another based his on an abstract painting he had done, explaining how it represented his life so far and his ambitions for the future.

I Finally, don't fall into the trap of thinking that a good writing style is only important if you are applying to do an English degree. So avoid clichés 'first things first' or 'at this moment in time'. We don't expect personal statements to be works of literature, but there is no doubt that we are impressed when they are written in a polished and succinct way.

---

5 Look again at college advert A on page 118. Write a personal statement for yourself.

1 When you have finished, exchange your statement with a partner. Write three things that you like about your partner's statement and one suggestion for improving it.

2 Take back your statement and improve it in the light of your partner's comments.

Vocabulary

1 **Match the words to form verb + noun collocations from the article. Sometimes there is more than one possible answer.**

1	to get	a	an obstacle
2	to give	b	a degree
3	to resist	c	attention
4	to overcome	d	a salary
5	to fall	e	your point across
6	to do	f	the temptation
7	to earn	g	an impression
8	to attract	h	into a trap

2 **Choose one of the collocations from exercise 1 to complete each sentence. You will need to change the form of the verb. There may be more than one possible answer.**

1 After he left school my brother .... in Zoology.

2 Sally .... me .... that she didn't approve of my decision.

3 Chloe's unconventional style of dress always .... a lot of ....

4 Having some good slides would help you .... at the meeting.

5 These days most doctors .... good ....

6 I couldn't .... to have another cream cake.

7 Mark .... of thinking he could manage without help from anyone else.

8 Alex .... many .... before he was able to fulfil his lifelong ambition.

⬂ Vocabulary spot

The meaning of a word might differ from one collocation to another. We can write a proposal where *proposal* means a formal, written suggestion, but if we talk of a woman accepting or refusing someone's *proposal*, we may be referring to a *proposal of marriage*. In *get your point across*, *point* means *opinion* or *important fact* whereas *the point of a pencil* means *its sharp end*, and *the point of doing something* means *the purpose or reason for doing it*.

Language of persuasion

⬂ Exam spot

Knowing what language can be used to persuade someone is vital for a proposal. It is also important when you are asked to discuss a topic or negotiate something during the Speaking test.

1 **Work with a partner and discuss these questions.**

1 List some situations when you had to persuade someone to do something.

2 How did you persuade them? How easy was it?

3 What technique can be used to persuade people to do things they are reluctant to do?

2 **2.10 Listen to eight people and complete the table.**

	What the speaker wants others to do	How the speaker tries to persuade them
1	a mother wants baby to eat vegetables	encourages, plays games, praises
2		
3		
4		
5		
6		
7		
8		

3 **Match the sentence halves. Pay attention to the phrases in bold.**

1 Surely, **the most sensible thing to do would be**

2 **There is a very good reason why**

3 **It's always worth**

4 **Make sure you**

5 **Don't forget to** explain

6 **I would urge you to** reconsider

7 **Don't make the mistake of** thinking that you

8 **You need to** think a lot before deciding

9 **It's probably better to** do it yourself

a it might be advisable to try to save money.

b to stay at home this evening?

c to your parents exactly how you feel.

d your decision.

e can succeed without making any effort.

f planning an essay before you start writing it.

g than to rely on other people for support.

h take everything you need with you.

i what it would be best to do.

4 Look at these different ways of persuading someone. Which is the best alternative in each situation?

1 A teenage girl wants her father to change his mind and let her go to an all-night party.
   a Are you quite sure you won't reconsider?
   b Just this once. Please!

2 The manager of a sales department is trying to persuade his staff to work longer hours.
   a Couldn't you be persuaded to give it a try?
   b Come on, just do it for me.

3 A father is trying to persuade his young son to swim the length of a pool.
   a Oh come on, have a try. It's not as hard as it looks.
   b It's in your own best interests to do what I suggest.

4 A woman is trying to put an end to a small quarrel with a friend.
   a Surely the most sensible thing would be to take some independent advice?
   b Don't be like that. Please!

5 A businessman is trying to persuade fellow workers at a meeting.
   a You're a load of idiots if you can't understand what I'm driving at!
   b The best course of action would be to survey our markets for their reactions.

5 Look at statements a–e below.

1 First, decide which statements are more formal.

2 Now, work with a partner. Discuss ways in which you can make the formal statements informal, and the informal ones formal, using a range of expressions and grammatical forms.
   a Could you possibly find time to check through this report for me, please?
   b Come on! Don't be so stubborn!
   c I'd be really grateful if you could lend me some money until Monday.
   d Go on. Don't be scared. It'll be OK.
   e I was wondering if you would mind coming with me this afternoon?

G → page 173

Speaking

1 Work in A/B pairs. Role-play this situation.

Student A You are a company manager. There is a conference next week in an industrial city 300 km away. It will last for five days. It is extremely important that someone from the office goes. Unfortunately, you are busy because there is a deadline. Student B (a junior employee) is the only other person knowledgeable about the conference.

Student B You are a junior company employee. Ask Student A (your boss) if you can have some time off next week. It is your wedding anniversary and you would like to take your partner away for a romantic break. You have been working so hard recently that you haven't had much time together.

2 Work with a new partner. Role-play this situation.

Student A You are a parent.
There is going to be a party to celebrate your mother's 80th birthday next Friday. You would like everything in the house to be as nice as possible, but you are busy. Ask Student B (your teenage son/daughter) to clean everything and also to cut his/her hair to look smart. You have bought new clothes for him/her.

Student B You are a teenager.
Ask Student A (your mother/father) if you can borrow some money. There is an important party next Friday and everyone will be there. You would also like to colour your hair because you are bored with the style you have.

Writing folder 8

Proposals

Proposals are similar to reports in many ways. Both set out information in a formal and clear way, often so that someone else can make a decision based on the information.

The main differences between a report and a proposal are:
- a proposal looks forward while a report looks back
- a proposal always presents the writer's viewpoint, whereas a report focuses more on facts (although a report may have a persuasive element to it, this is not always the case).

1   Work with a partner. Discuss these questions.

   1   Name five possible kinds of proposals (e.g. a proposal to a university department from a student who would like to do a piece of academic research).

   2   Have you had any experience of writing a proposal?

   3   What do you think are the characteristics, format and language of a proposal?

2   Work with a partner and choose a task below that interests you. Discuss what you would include in your proposal.

   1   Write a **proposal** for your college principal in which you ask for support to travel to another country in order to gain some useful experience there. Explain what you would like from the college and why it would be of benefit.

   2   Write a **proposal** to your college principal suggesting that your college set up (or make improvements to) its own website. Explain why it would be a good idea and what it should contain.

   3   Write a **proposal** for your college principal suggesting a college event that you would like to organise. Describe what you would like to do and give reasons why it would be of benefit to the college.

3   Discuss these questions about the task you chose.

   1   Why do you think what you are proposing would be a good idea?

   2   Remember that the college principal is likely to be more concerned than you are about costs, potential organisational problems and college prestige. How will you address these issues in your proposal?

4   Discuss the presentation of your proposal.

   1   It is important to open with a clear statement of what the proposal contains. How will you do this?

   2   It is also important to close effectively. How will you do this?

   3   What headings would be appropriate in your proposal?

5   **Look at these sentences used in other proposals. Which might you be able to adapt for your own proposal? How would you adapt them?**

1   The aim of this proposal is to put forward a piece of academic research that I would like to undertake.

2   This proposal outlines the scope of the new course being recommended, explaining why it would be of benefit to students. It then concludes with some suggestions as to how the course could be implemented most effectively.

3   There are a number of reasons why I wish to put this proposal forward.

4   There are a number of overwhelming arguments in favour of extending the computer centre at the college, rather than the sports facilities.

5   Firstly, the proposed new college magazine would help to create a stronger feeling of community within the student body.

6   Secondly, the proposed extension to the college library would serve the additional useful purpose of attracting more students to apply for courses here.

7   Despite the fact that the suggested programme might be expensive, the additional cost could be justified in terms of the benefits that participants would receive.

8   There are a number of recommendations that I would like to make.

9   Taking all the evidence into account, I recommend that the English Club should make some radical changes to its current programme.

10   I would urge you to give these recommendations serious consideration.

11   Please do not hesitate to contact me if you would like me to expand on anything in this proposal.

12   Having outlined the proposal in general terms, I would now like to discuss three key issues in more detail.

6   **Now work alone to write the proposal in 220–260 words in an appropriate style.**

1   Write the first draft of the proposal.
2   Exchange proposals with a partner for comments and suggestions.
3   Make any improvements suggested by your partner.

20 We are what we eat

Speaking

1 Work with a partner. Look at the photos and discuss questions 1–4 below.

1 What do you know about Chinese beliefs about yin and yang?

2 In what ways can what we eat or drink sometimes have a negative impact on health?

3 What situations can you think of when food has had a dramatic impact on history?

Reading

1 Read the four texts quickly. Each relates to a question in Speaking exercise 1. Match texts A–D with questions 1–4.

2 Now read the texts again. Match them with opinions 1–4 below.

1 Greater wealth has brought some new problems related to food consumption. A

2 Medical problems can be treated by choosing the right type of food for the given ailment. B

3 Most of us have lost the direct connection with, and understanding of, agriculture that people used to have in the past. C

4 Political and social issues relating to the provision of food for all must be taken very seriously. D

4 How many ways can you think of in which science has affected food production?

A For humans, food is both a basic necessity for life and a source of pleasure and problems. In the rich world, the basic needs have long been satisfied. Meals play a key role in social life and there is great interest in food and cooking. At the same time, there are problems of affluence such as obesity and diet-related cardiovascular diseases. Food serves as the agent of dispersal for many diseases, and food safety is therefore very important. The food we eat must be safe and we must exercise control over the entire chain from cultivation and animal breeding to processing and intake. Residues of preservatives and other toxic elements may occur in both what animals and what humans eat, and also in surface and ground water, our most essential basic necessity.

B The Chinese way of eating is characterised by the ideas and beliefs about food, which actively affect the ways in which food is prepared and taken. The overriding idea about food in China – in all likelihood an idea with solid, but as yet unrevealed, scientific backing – is that the kind and the amount of food one takes is intimately relevant to one's health. Food not only affects health as a matter of general principle, the selection of the right food at any particular time must also be dependent upon one's health condition at that time. Food, therefore, is also medicine. The bodily functions, in the Chinese view, follow the basic yin-yang principles. Many foods are also classifiable into those that possess the yin quality and those of the yang quality. When yin and yang forces in the body are not balanced, problems result.

C Many may ask why food science is important? Food science has a hand in every product that is consumed. I'd like to hit a few highlights that may unveil why we need food science within the industry. The world has progressed through hunter-gatherer, agricultural, and industrial stages to being a provider of goods and services. Along the way our reliance on a stable food supply has increased dramatically. This started with the domestication of plants and animals in order to feed our ever-growing population. The majority of the population of the US are no longer connected to the production of their food nor are they familiar with general agriculture practices that make food so readily available. The commitment of food science and technology professionals is to advance the science of food, all the while ensuring a safe and abundant food supply and contributing to a healthier people everywhere.

D The national and international security risks of failing to tackle the global food supply crisis are highlighted in a new report issued this week by a leading independent think-tank. This ground-breaking report highlights the very serious risks of failing to tackle the global challenge of food security – from human suffering and civil unrest to trade disruption and mass migration. Food supplies must increase by at least 70% to keep pace with the demands of a world population set to exceed 9 billion by 2050, and the report highlights the urgent need to increase agricultural productivity, reduce food waste and improve distribution networks. Innovations in plant science, from agricultural biotechnology to advanced crop protection products, offer major opportunities for Europe's farmers to deliver sustainable gains in agricultural productivity. With the security of UK food supply a central theme, the report examines a global supply chain under pressure, underlining the relationships between productivity, commodity prices, political stability and conflict.

3 **Answer these questions about the extracts.**

Which writer …

1 shares an opinion with A regarding the importance of maintaining the quality of food?

2 expresses a different opinion from C about the role of science in food preparation?

3 expresses a less optimistic point of view than C about the tasks facing food scientists in the future?

4 expresses opinions with a broader geographical focus than the other three texts?

4 **Which text do you find most interesting? Give reasons.**

⤵ Exam spot

Part 6 of Paper 1 (the Reading and Use of English test) requires you to compare opinions given in four texts on the same subject. It will never be possible to answer a question by looking at only one of the texts.

Vocabulary

1 Look at this summary of text A on page 125. Use the words given in capitals to form a word that fits in the gaps.

Food is a basic **(1)** .... of life. In rich countries there are some food-related problems because of **(2)** .... Eating too much, for example can lead to **(3)** .... and heart disease. Contaminated food is responsible for the **(4)** .... of many illnesses and it is important that we exercise control over the food chain from animal **(5)** .... and plant cultivation through to processing and on to the eventual **(6)** ....

NECESSARY

AFFLUENT
OBESE

TRANSMIT

BREED

CONSUME

2 Fill each gap with an appropriate word formed from the word in capitals at the end of each sentence.

1 Fruit and vegetables have been *scientifically* proven to provide some protection against cancer. (SCIENCE)
2 The student impressed her tutor by the *broadth of* her knowledge of the topic. (BROAD)
3 Although the investigation was time-consuming and costly, the results were *conclusive* and we still cannot be sure whether our basic hypothesis is correct. (CONCLUDE)
4 Nothing is more pleasant than spending a *leisurely* evening at a good restaurant with close friends. (LEISURE)
5 The research wanted to *clarify* the relationship between social background and eating habits. (CLEAR)
6 It is very important that food should not be prepared in *unhygienic* conditions. (HYGIENE)
7 We all need to eat enough, of course, but *overeating* can lead to obesity and all sorts of health problems. (EAT)
8 The sauce is rather *tasteless* – try adding some herbs to it. (TASTE)
9 Bananas are a very *nutritious* food. (NUTRITION)
10 Goose and duck are very *fattening* meats – much more so than chicken. (FAT) *fattening*

Hypothesising

 Exam spot

The essay that you have to write in Part 1 of the Writing test often involves an element of hypothesising. This language is, of course, also useful for other pieces of writing you may have to do as well as for Part 3 of the Speaking test.

1 Look at the phrases in boxes A and B. What grammatical structures can you identify? Match the boxes to headings 1 and 2.

1 Formal writing and formal speech
2 Neutral speech and informal writing

A

I wonder if …   Suppose …   What if … Just imagine …   If only …

B

Let us imagine …
Let us consider …
Let us suppose …
Let us assume …
If we were to …
Were we to …
If we had …
Had we …
If I may speculate for a moment, …
Speculating for a moment, …
Let us take a hypothetical case: …
On the assumption that …
Provided (that) …
Allowing for the fact that …
Given (that) …

Corpus spot

The *Cambridge English Corpus* shows exam candidates often make mistakes when hypothesising. Correct these sentences written by exam candidates.

1 I was wondering you could make it in July?
2 Imagine you would have to live with no central heating. My grandmother used to. It was a pretty tough life.
3 Suppose she takes the job in Moscow, how we would manage without her?
4 The best way to prepare for the driving test is to assume yourself as a driver.

G → page 173

2 Rewrite these sentences as more formal English. Use the prompts given to make different sentences.

1 If there had been enough food for workers in Russian factories in 1917, there might not have been a revolution that year.
  a Were there to …
  b Had there …

2 Had the government done more about food shortages, it would have been more popular.
  a If the government had …
  b If the government were to …

3 I'd like you to think about the different ways in which food science might help with feeding the growing population of the world.
  a Let us imagine …
  b Let us consider …

4 Most people would probably be prepared to do anything to provide food for their own children.
  a Let us suppose …
  b Let us assume …

Reading H.W

1 Look at the photo. Imagine that all restaurants and cafés had to provide information about calories and ingredients along with every food item they sold. How would you react to this?

  1 This would be very helpful.
  2 This would be a bit strange, but you would get used to it.
  3 This would be very bad. You wouldn't be able to enjoy your food.

2 Read a proposal from a politician, arguing for the introduction of a new law. What is he arguing for and what points does he make? Would you vote in favour of his law?

3 Which hypothesising phrases does the politician use? Are they mostly formal or informal?

4 Prepare to introduce a new law of your choice related to food or diet.

  1 Think about a new law you would like to introduce.
  2 Think of hypothesising phrases you can use.

5 Work in small groups. Take turns to introduce your laws and ask questions to find out more information.

PUMPKIN LOAF
380 Calories
$1.85

I propose that restaurants should provide menus which include the calorie content and the ingredients for each food item sold.

If I may speculate for a moment, I believe that this will be welcomed by the growing numbers of people who are concerned about what they're eating. We are all increasingly anxious to know precisely how much salt, how much fat and how much sugar we are consuming every day.

Speculating further, this type of menu should be welcomed by anyone who has a food allergy of some kind. Allergies appear to be on the increase, and my proposal will make it much more straightforward for customers to avoid those ingredients which cause their problem.

On the assumption that what we eat has a major impact on our health, I have every reason to suppose that the implementation of this proposal might well have far-reaching benefits for the future health of people in our society.

Provided that we are able to develop a clear and easily understandable way of presenting the required information on a menu, I think that there is no reason why this idea should not be implemented throughout the country within the next five years. Allowing for the fact that it would take some time for restaurants to design and print new menus, I think that it is possible to expect the proposals to be implemented within 12 months.

Topic review

1 Work in pairs and discuss these questions.

1 What is the best film you have ever seen?
2 Do you prefer to read reviews in a newspaper or a magazine or to trust your friends' opinions?
3 What do you find remarkable about human cells?
4 What does a personal statement aim to do?
5 Do you ever pretend to understand English when you really haven't?
6 Someone who says they always tell the truth is a liar. Do you agree?
7 What do you prefer: home cooking or eating in restaurants?

Writing

2 Your teacher has asked you to write a proposal for something the class can do in the last week of your course.

1 Write full details of what you are proposing and explain why you think it is a good idea.
2 Work in groups. Take turns to read out your proposals.
3 Vote on the best proposal in your group.
4 Take turns to present your group's best proposal.
5 Vote for the best proposal you heard from the class (you may not vote for your group's ideas).

Vocabulary

3 These sentences all contain idioms which refer to parts of the body. Fill the gaps.

1 I've been trying to catch Adam's .... for ages but he hasn't noticed me yet.
2 Judit has set her .... on getting married in Paris.
3 It's been a long day – sit down and put your .... up while I make a cup of tea.
4 Don't carry all that – let me give you a ....
5 I've been racking my .... for ages, trying to decide what to get Aki for his birthday.
6 Alejandro has fallen .... over .... in love with her.
7 Sarah wouldn't have got so upset if Joe's criticism hadn't touched a raw ....
8 Good luck with your driving test – I'll keep my .... crossed for you.

Grammar

4 Fill in the gaps with one word.

These days, (0) ....**with**........ contemporary art universally presented as the new rock'n'roll, a huge international survey has shown that people may not know much about art, but they know (1) .... they like: old pictures.

The director of the National Gallery saw no contradiction. 'Old master paintings speak powerfully (2) .... a contemporary audience,' he said yesterday.

From Melbourne to Tokyo, from Madrid to Rio de Janeiro, the pattern was (3) .... same: the exhibitions people queued (4) .... the block to see were of old masters or of long-dead craftsmen. The nearest to a contemporary artist in the international top 10 is Picasso.

One exhibition featuring the works of old masters is Seeing Salvation at the National Gallery. With more than 5,000 visitors a day, it has become the fourth (5) .... popular in the world. Within a day of it opening, staff knew they had a phenomenon. People were queuing for hours to get in, moving (6) .... a snail's pace because visitors were spending so (7) .... studying the works.

The director said 'Seeing Salvation investigated (8) .... theme that has shaped Western art through the centuries. This historical approach to familiar material clearly captured the public's imagination.'

Reading

5   Choose which paragraphs (A–G) complete the gaps (1–6) in this
    article. There is one extra paragraph you do not need.

Is honesty the best policy?

Lying is bad for your health, according to an American psychotherapist. But telling the truth is tricky.

'Does my bum look big in this?' asked my friend. It had to happen. The question I had been dreading for the past few hours needed an answer.

1 [ ]

Radical honesty therapy, as it is known in the US, is the latest thing to be held up as the key to happiness and success. It involves telling the truth all the time, with no exceptions for hurt feelings.

2 [ ]

'We all lie. It wears us out. It is the major source of all human stress,' says Brad Blanton, psychotherapist and founder of the Centre for Radical Honesty. The best-selling author of *Practising Radical Honesty: How to Complete the Past, Live in the Present and Build the Future with a Little Help from Your Friend*s has become a household name in the States, where he spreads his message via day-time television talk shows.

3 [ ]

Well, fibbing may be murderous, but honesty started becoming inconvenient for me just after breakfast, when I needed change for a parking meter. The cashier in the local shop looked at my $10 note wearily. Did I really want the newspaper, or was I after change for the parking, he wondered. If so, the shop always had a policy of refusal.

On a normal day, I would have lied. Traffic wardens in these parts show no mercy. Instead, I admitted everything and was shown the door, change-less.

4 [ ]

The alternative, he believes, is the stress of living 'in the prison of the mind', which results in depression and ill health. 'Your body stays tied up in knots and is susceptible to illness,' he says. Allergies, high blood pressure and insomnia are all exacerbated by lying. Good relationship skills, parenting skills and management skills are also dependent on telling the truth. So, honesty, according to Dr Blanton, brings many rewards, not least in business – and perhaps he is right. Gifi Fields, chief executive of Coppernob Communications, who has made tens of millions of pounds in a long career, insists that his own integrity has helped him succeed. 'I have always believed that honesty is the best policy. Obviously, there are moral and ethical values in business. If you want to make deals, you have to have trust.'

5 [ ]

Richard Wiseman, a psychologist at the University of Hertfordshire, agrees with her. He says that lies can protect people as well as harm them. He is also certain that people will continue to tell them because human beings follow the law of survival of the fittest.

6 [ ]

By the end of my day of telling nothing but the truth, I definitely regretted my honest approach. Forget personal gain. My big-bottomed ex-friend decided to tell some home truths of her own. I still haven't quite recovered.

A He certainly has his work cut out for him. In a recent survey of Americans, 93 per cent admitted to lying 'regularly and habitually' in the workplace. Dr Blanton is typically blunt about the consequences of being deceitful. 'Lying kills people,' he says.

B As she looked at me inquiringly, turning this way and that in a pink micro-mini at least one size too small for her, I mentally steeled myself before replying in a whisper. 'Yes, I'm afraid it does.' Hopes for a jolly afternoon's shopping fell, along with her face. So much for telling the truth.

C People who tell lies get so confused about what they have said to whom, they can sometimes get to the point where they no longer know what the truth is. This is very bad for their physical as well as their mental health and is one reason for the stomach complaints and headaches frequently reported by frequent liars.

D On the other hand, Anne McKevitt, an interior designer and television presenter, is happy to admit to frequent fibbing. She points out that the truth can sometimes be too painful. 'I think white lies are good,' she says. 'I tell them all the time.'

E Dr Blanton, who lives in Virginia with his wife and two children, is adamant that minor inconveniences are nothing compared with the huge benefits of truth-telling. 'Telling the truth, after hiding it for a long time, reopens old wounds that didn't heal properly. It hurts a lot. It takes guts. It isn't easy. But it is better than the alternative.'

F But, as I found out, this is not as easy as it might sound. Little white lies, rather than the conniving, self-aggrandising variety, are an essential part of polite society.

G 'I suspect Dr Blanton has devised an unstable strategy. If we all told the truth all the time, it would be fine, but the advantage would then go to the few who were prepared to lie.'

Listening

1   Work with a partner. How could the phrases in the box describe the scenes in the photos on this page?

> internationally recognised   spectacular
> the ultimate adventure   diverse marine life
> perfect for guided tours   luxury
> once-in-a-lifetime experience

2   Imagine the seven 'natural wonders' of the world. Suggest what you think might be on the list and why they deserve to be there.

3   **2.11** Listen to a talk about one of the seven natural wonders. How do the photos relate to what you heard?

4   Listen again. Are these statements true or false? Correct the false ones.

1   Cairns has the fifth busiest airport in the southern hemisphere.
2   Great Adventures is the name of a travel company.
3   Green Island is 100 years old.
4   It takes 45 minutes to fly to Green Island from Cairns.
5   A pontoon is a kind of underwater capsule.
6   You are only allowed to go to the pontoon once.

5   Work with a partner and list all the things that the destination described offers. Which three things appeal to you most?

Reading

1   You are going to read an extract from a book called *Running a Hotel on the Roof of the World*. What kind of place do you think it will be about?

2   Read the first part about two men, Dorje and Tashi, then make notes on these points.

• means of travel
• driver's aim
• how Tashi felt about the journey
• difficult aspects of the journey
• good aspects of the journey
• scenery
• what could be seen on the river

1

Dorje had an interesting driving technique which involved keeping the car off the ground for as much time as possible. 'Terrible!' Tashi called out whenever we were airborne, grinning from ear to ear and bracing himself for the inevitable impact whenever the Landcruiser would hit the tarmac again. It was hardly surprising that our car had practically no suspension. Dorje had an advantage which would have made his taxi comrades in the city I had just flown from green with envy: visibility. In the pure air of Tibet, the view is not hindered by smog or pollution. Mountains which are tens of miles away appear crisp against the horizon. Apart from a few army trucks, the roads are free of traffic and the only limiting factor on Dorje's driving was how hard he could keep his foot pressed down on the accelerator pedal weighed up against the likelihood that at any moment one of the rattles could lead to the total disintegration of the vehicle.

Just visible through the vibrating windows were rectangular coracles setting out across the river. Tashi saw me trying to look at them. 'Yak-skin boats,' he shouted over the roar of the Landcruiser engine. It seems that every part of the yak has a use. To make watertight boats, the skins are stretched over a wooden frame, sewn together with wool made from yak hair and the joins are then sealed with yak butter.

3 Now read the second part.

1 Imagine you wanted to paint a picture of the villages being described. Underline the things the writer mentions which would help you.

2 Then look at the photos connected with the story. Which of the things you underlined are shown?

4 Now read the final part and discuss these questions.

1 What problem is being discussed?
2 Who does not seem to help solve the problem?
3 Why is the dung mixed with water and straw?
4 Why is the dung put on walls?

2

Every now and then we would speed through a village lined with waving Tibetan children. Their villages looked wonderful and so inviting but Dorje was not showing any signs of slowing down. Small clusters of single and double-storey buildings with walled-in courtyards jostled together in the foothills to gain maximum exposure to the sun. The houses looked solid, built for the harsh environment. Walls were made of stone up to waist height and finished off with mud bricks to the roof. Tin cans lined the window ledges, with the bright orange of marigolds in full bloom livening up the black and white of the houses. Branches of trees adorned with colourful prayer flags stood high into the wind from the top of the flat roofs. The auspicious blue, white, red, green and yellow colours of the fabrics stood out against the rich blue of the Tibetan sky. Each prayer flag carries a picture of lungta, the jewelled dragon-horse, who carries the owners' prayers up to the divinities every time the flag flaps in the wind.

The larger villages had healthy trees, usually willows or poplars which looked quite out of place in the generally treeless landscape. Wood is a precious commodity in the highland areas of Tibet and is never wasted. The few shrubs which grow wild on the hillsides are harvested for use as brushwood and each courtyard wall is piled high with sticks to get a fire started gathered from the mountains.

3

The lack of solid fuel in the shape of wood is not a problem to the Tibetans, who have an ingenious wood substitute: yak dung. The dung is collected during the day by young children who are out on the hills tending to flocks of sheep or yaks. What better way to spend the time when out on the hills than by collecting every piece of dung which can be found? It certainly sounds more attractive than being locked up in a school room. When the children return in the evenings with their panniers of dung, it is usually the mother of the household, or an older sister, who has the task of mixing the raw material with a little water and, if available, some barley straw. This is then made into attractive chocolate chip cookie shapes and slapped against the whitewashed walls to bake in the sun. Once dry, the cookies are stacked in rows on top of the walls to be used as fuel throughout the year.

Vocabulary

1 Match idioms 1–10, which can be used to describe places, with explanations a–j.

  1 a black spot
  2 a tourist trap
  3 home from home
  4 no room to swing a cat
  5 picture postcard
  6 a stone's throw from
  7 as the crow flies
  8 hit the road
  9 off the beaten track
 10 put a place on the map

  a attractive in a slightly artificial way
  b crowded place selling souvenirs, entertainment, etc. at high prices
  c make a place important or famous
  d place where you feel very comfortable
  e very small
  f a bit of road that has seen a lot of accidents
  g distance if you go in a straight line
  h leave a place, begin a journey
  i very close to
  j where not many people go

2 Complete the sentences with idioms from exercise 1.

  1 I prefer to spend my holidays ...., far away from any other tourists.
  2 It's getting late and we've got a long drive home. It's really time we ....
  3 We stayed in a lovely .... village nestling in the valley.
  4 Take care on the drive across the mountains. There's a notorious .... just as you leave the main road to start the climb up to the pass.
  5 There was .... in our hotel room but the view we had was superb, so we didn't mind too much.

3 Which idioms from exercise 1 would you be most likely and unlikely to find in a tourist brochure? Why?

Range of grammatical structures

 Exam spot

In the exam, you are expected to produce a range of structures when writing and speaking. This not only means a range of tenses but also the use of the passive form, modal verbs and complex sentences with more than one clause.

1 Look again at part 1 of *Running a Hotel on the Roof of the World* on page 130 and underline the different tenses and grammatical structures. Compare with a partner. How many did you find?

2 Work with a partner. Complete this blog about a student's gap year with an appropriate form of the verbs in brackets. Sometimes, more than one answer is possible.

G → page 174

Looking back on it now, it seems like a dream – my year off after university travelling the world. The best bit (0) ....*was*........ (be) definitely Indonesia. Intuition (1) .... (tell) me, even before I left, that Indonesia was where something special was about to happen. A friend of mine (2) .... (cycle) through China with paintbrushes and a sketch pad and we (3) .... (arrange) to meet in Bali. We (4) .... (stay) on the beach for a day and then decided that what we really needed was more of a cross-Indonesia adventure. So we (5) .... (set) off for the island of Lombok. And it was there that I saw him. He (6) .... (sit) with his back to me under the shade of a palm tree, (7) .... (look) out to sea. He turned and smiled, which at once left me incapable of even (8) .... (think) of moving on to another island. And that is how I stayed for six months in the same place!

Writing

1 **Read the description of a hotel in Lombok below. Three sentences are from an informal letter and three are from a holiday brochure. Underline the informal sentences.**

The hotel has a magnificent location on the island and most of the bedrooms enjoy sea views. It's a great hotel with loads of character. The bedrooms get a bit chilly at night and the uncarpeted corridors can be noisy but it's worth putting up with a few minor inconveniences as it has so much atmosphere in other ways. Each room has its own luxurious en-suite bathroom and is individually decorated with many original finishing touches. The superb restaurant offers a wide range of delicious dishes to suit all tastes. The food is fantastic and you can stuff yourself at breakfast so you don't need to eat again till the evening.

 Exam spot

In the Writing test, you are expected to write in an appropriate register for your target reader and it is usually neutral or formal.

2 **Read these extracts from holiday brochures. Which place would you prefer to stay at?**

The exuberance of the islands appears in all its splendour at the Grand Ocean Hotel. Here, in an atmosphere of quiet elegance, every creature comfort is catered for with 24-hour room service. The lavishly appointed rooms and magnificent top-floor suites combine private luxury with spectacular views and, for those in search of the ultimate in luxury, there is nothing better than the Presidential Suite with its antiques, original paintings and a private terrace.

Dalhousie Farm offers its guests a charming home-from-home of cosy corners, comfortable sofas, polished antiques and warm, welcoming fires. Its eight guest rooms and two garden suites all enjoy an old-fashioned feeling with local hand-made fabrics and views over the magnificent gardens. Gourmet dinners, with an emphasis on freshly caught seafood, are served each evening in the restaurant, whilst snack lunches are available in the bar. The hotel boasts its own horse-riding centre with guided treks and other daytime pursuits, including tennis, shore walks, sea fishing and golf.

3 **Imagine that you spent a week in a hotel on this page. Some of the claims made in the advertisement were false.**

1 Write a letter of complaint, explaining why you are unhappy.
2 Describe how your holiday was affected and what you did. Remember to use a range of grammatical structures to explain what happened.
3 Explain what action you would like the hotel to take now.
4 Write your letter in 220–260 words.

Exam folder 9

Paper 3: the Listening test

1 Work with a partner. Answer the questions on page 160.

Parts 1 and 3: Multiple-choice questions

Both Parts 1 and 3 of the Listening test have multiple-choice questions. In Part 3, you listen to one long text and there are six multiple-choice questions, each with four options.

2 **2.12 Listen to an interview with a businesswoman. Choose the answer (A, B, C or D) which best fits according to what you hear.**

1 When Julia began her own company, she
  A listened carefully to male colleagues' advice.
  B made sure she came across as being professional.
  C avoided bringing family problems to work.
  D worked in cooperation with all the employees.

2 What did Julia learn from the work of Jennifer Alderton?
  A to make sure she was respected by all the staff
  B a concept of power that she found acceptable
  C the importance of persuading staff to do the right thing
  D that belief in what you are doing is essential

3 According to Julia, companies that have command-control management
  A waste productive time in dealing with conflicts.
  B work well in certain manufacturing industries.
  C do not offer their staff adequate facilities.
  D do not treat staff fairly when there are disputes.

4 Julia believes that encouraging criticism in a company
  A reduces the number of disagreements.
  B enables managers to get more varied experience.
  C allows managers to delegate more effectively.
  D creates opportunities for development.

5 Julia explains that the debate surrounding the work–life balance has been helped by
  A international barriers being broken down.
  B workers becoming more assertive in the way they communicate.
  C well-known people openly favouring time spent away from work.
  D an increasing number of women taking on top positions.

6 What is Julia going to be working on in the near future?
  A financially supporting small businesses
  B running communication skills courses
  C helping people come up with creative ideas
  D doing market research for small businesses

3 **2.12 Work with a partner and compare your answers. Then listen again.**

EXAM ADVICE

- Use the preparation time to read the questions and think about possible answers.
- Listen attentively to the first playing of the recording and lightly mark the answers you think are correct.
- Don't worry about missing a question – leave it and keep listening attentively.

Part 2: Sentence completion

4 **2.13** You will hear a fashion historian called **Gina Lombard giving a talk about jeans and culture. Complete the sentences.**

1 According to Gina, young people in the 1950s started wearing jeans as a symbol of ....

2 Because the older generation thought of jeans as .... they believed they were unsuitable for social occasions.

3 Jeans became internationally popular because they are what Gina describes as ....; they improve with age.

4 Jeans don't just look good – they also contain the idea of ....

5 Gina explains that the .... of jeans and music are in the United States.

6 Nowadays members of the establishment, for example ...., are seen wearing jeans.

7 There are .... of jeans which can be worn by anyone, not just one group.

8 Gina says you can show rebellion by wearing jeans to work with

....

5 **Read the Exam information below. Then listen again to check.**

EXAM ADVICE

- Read the title to find out what the context is.
- Read the questions carefully before you listen.
- Try to predict what sort of word(s) is/are needed in the gap. For example, is it a noun?
- Try to predict the answer using your knowledge of the context and your logic.
- Write down the word(s) you hear.
- Remember that the answers are short – one to three words – and very often concrete nouns.
- Check your spelling and that you have made a grammatically correct sentence.
- When you listen the second time, check carefully.
- Always try to write something, even if you're not 100% sure it's the correct answer.

Part 4: Multiple matching

Part 4 of the Listening test is a multiple-matching task. You hear five short extracts twice and there are two multiple-matching questions. You may be asked to identify the speakers, topics or opinions, to interpret what was said or to say what each speaker is doing when he or she speaks (e.g. apologising). There are eight options, so three options will not fit what you hear.

6 **2.14** You will hear five short extracts in which people are talking about friendship. For questions 1–5, choose from the list (A–H) who each speaker regards as a true friend. For questions 6–10, choose from the list (A–H) what each speaker appreciates most in a friend.

A a teacher
B a colleague
C a family member
D someone with the same hobby
E a former employee
F a neighbour
G an old school friend
H a member of the gym

Speaker 1 [1]
Speaker 2 [2]
Speaker 3 [3]
Speaker 4 [4]
Speaker 5 [5]

A being adventurous
B being sociable
C being efficient
D being sympathetic
E being eager to help
F being honest
G being modest
H being ambitious

[6]
Speaker 1 [7]
Speaker 2 [8]
Speaker 3 [9]
Speaker 4 [10]
Speaker 5

EXAM ADVICE

- Make sure you read the question and the options carefully in the time before listening.
- As you listen to each speaker, try to answer the questions in both tasks.
- Remember that the answer to each task may come at the beginning, middle or end of what each speaker says, so listen attentively all the way through.
- Listen out for paraphrases of what is in the question or listen and decide if there is a sort of summary of what the speaker says in the question.
- There are five speakers and eight options, so know why the ones that don't fit are wrong.
- Transfer your answers to the answer sheet carefully in the time given at the end.
- Don't forget that in the exam, you will be expected to do both tasks as you listen to the recording twice.

Under the weather

Speaking and Reading

1 Work with a partner and discuss these questions.

1 What area of the world do you live in? What are the features of its climate?

2 Do you think climate affects people's personalities or mood?

3 What would be your idea of a perfect weather climate?

4 Have you ever experienced conditions similar to the ones in the photos?

5 Look at the diagram. What does it tell us?

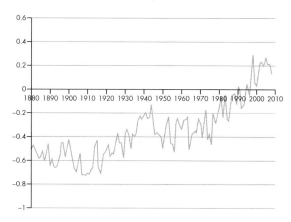

Comparison of temperature estimates

2 Read the article quickly. Would you say this article is mainly reporting fact, opinion or a mixture of both?

3 Read the article again. Underline phrases used to express how sure each person or group is that something is happening or will happen. Discuss whether the phrases are 'very sure' or 'not so sure'.

will bring ... very sure

It's not *if*, it's *when*

The world's scientists have given their starkest warning yet that a failure to cut greenhouse-gas emissions will bring devastating climate change within a few decades. As droughts affect more areas for more prolonged periods, it is estimated that global food production will fall by 10%. Conversely, we are experiencing more powerful hurricanes, which results in both human tragedy and costly damage to infrastructure. There are dire predictions of 80 million more people being exposed to malaria and 2.5 billion to dengue fever.

The latest report from the Intergovernmental Panel on Climate Change (IPCC) concludes that average temperatures could increase by as much as 2°C within the next 20 to 30 years if emissions continue to rise at the present rate. The Panel warns that 'substantial and sustained' reductions in greenhouse-gas emissions are essential if such a potentially disastrous rise is to be avoided.

Ban-Ki-Moon, UN Secretary General, is urging world leaders to heed the 'world's authority on climate change' and agree a new global deal on cutting emissions. John Kerry, the US secretary of state, said in a statement: 'This is yet another wakeup call: those who deny the science or choose excuses over action are playing with fire.'

Climatologist Dr Bateman warns that to hold warming to 2°C, total emissions cannot exceed 1,000 gigatons of carbon. Yet by 2011, more than half of that total 'allowance' – 531 gigatons – had already been emitted. Dr Bateman adds that the only way to avoid serious consequences will be to make sure that some valuable fossil fuels are left unexploited. But this is something that it will be hard to get everyone to agree to.

Jasper Purdy of Environment Watch goes to great lengths to point out that a disastrous outcome is not inevitable. If there were a significant switch to clean and resource-efficient technologies, we could cut expected temperature rises by half. He stresses that what is needed is international political commitment to take action – something which has been absent so far.

Vocabulary

1 Write a paragraph summarising the article using these key words and expressions.

melting

atmosphere

carbon dioxide

global warming

greenhouse gas

flooding

political commitment

emissions

drought

cumulative effect   absorb

climate change

2 Here are some more phrases related to the weather and climate. Match a word from the list (1–9) with a word which collocates (a–i).

1 torrential *(really heavy)*   a defences
2 high   b freezing
3 ice   c forecast
4 sea   d cap
5 below   e rain
6 long-range   f tide
7 ozone   g wave
8 heat   h footprint
9 carbon   i layer

(N) torrent.
(heavy shower)

3 Complete this blog with collocations from exercise 2.

It may be the start of spring here, but no one seems to have told the weather! We've just had a severe storm which even ripped roofs from houses. What's more, there has been (1) _torrential rain_ which has caused flood alerts to be issued for some areas. This makes you really believe what they say about the (2) _ice caps_ melting – floods seem to have been in the news a lot more over the last year or so. Coastal areas have been prone to flooding too – this spring, (3) _high tides_ have been at record levels in the Severn estuary. This means (4) _sea defences_ *mouth of the river* have been breached and waves have rolled into some village *=broken* centres. As if all this wasn't enough, night temperatures have been (5) _below freezing_ all week, leaving gardeners stuck as to what they should do with their spring plants.

A snapshot of today's weather around the world					
Country	Argentina	Brazil	Greece	Japan	Sweden
City	Buenos Aires	Rio de Janeiro	Athens	Tokyo	Stockholm
Temperature	18°C	26°C	18°C	17°C	8°C
Humidity	84%	26%	53%	58%	38%
Wind speed	9 (NE)	4 (NE)	4 (NW)	4 (SW)	6 (SW)
Visibility	good	moderate	very good	n/a	n/a

Interpreting and comparing

1 Look at the weather forecast above. Complete the summary by choosing the best alternative.

A This chart shows the (1) *main weather features* / *changing weather patterns* of a number of cities on a particular day.

B It can be seen that the warmest city was (2) *Buenos Aires / Rio de Janeiro / Athens*, whereas the coldest was (3) *Tokyo / Stockholm*.

C According to the information, (4) *humidity / visibility / wind speed* was very good in Athens; this is important as there is often concern about the levels of (5) *traffic / pollution / congestion* in large cities but, as we can see, this was not a problem in Athens.

D In conclusion, depending on your preferences, Rio de Janeiro or Athens might have been very pleasant places to spend that day as they both had reasonably warm (6) *atmospheres / temperatures / climates* and the (7) *wind speed / humidity* was not as high as in (8) *Buenos Aires / Rio de Janeiro / Stockholm / Athens* or Tokyo.

2 We can use different methods to interpret information from charts, graphics or statistics. Match the sentences in exercise 1 (A–D) with these methods (1–4).

1 discussing the important features (e.g. by providing examples or giving reasons)
2 making a general statement about the information
3 drawing a conclusion
4 commenting on significant features (e.g. by comparing and contrasting information)

↘ Exam spot

Language for interpreting and comparing is useful for the Speaking test where you have to describe and contrast pictures.

3 Complete this extract with words from the box. Think about the position in the paragraph as well as what follows each gap.

> because   contrary to   however
> on the other hand   whereas   indeed

On the one hand, some people say they feel cosy and secure when they are inside on grey days, reading in front of the fire. (1) *On the other hand*, others say they feel dull and gloomy when the weather is grey. *(Indeed)* (2) *However*, it is true to say that higher levels of light do raise the spirits. You know yourself that when you wake up and it's sunny, you feel brighter, (3) *Whereas* when you wake up and it's dull, you feel sluggish. Interestingly, recent research has shown that, (4) *Contrary to* popular belief, people are more creative in colder climates. For example, more inventions have been made by people living in colder climates than in hotter ones. *(However)* (5) *Indeed*, it could be that they stay at work longer (6) *because* the weather is so awful outside!

4 You are going to compare some photos showing the same place at different times of the year. Student A, look on page 160. Student B, look on page 161.

    1 Describe your pair of pictures to your partner.

    2 Discuss how the climate of the place in the two pairs of pictures differs.

    3 Discuss how the different climates in these two places might affect people's lives.

    4 Decide which kind of climate you prefer and why.

 → page 174

Listening

1 2·15 Listen to two people giving their views on climate change. Tick the topics they mention.

	Peter	Anna
• El Niño		
• global warming		
• endangered animals		
• greenhouse-gas emissions		
• pollution		
• sea levels		
• storms		

2 Listen again and make notes on each speaker's views.

3 Work with a partner and compare and contrast Peter and Anna's views. Say whether or not you agree.

Vocabulary

1 Complete the nouns (1–7) in the table. They all describe changes in quantity.

There was / has been a …
slight   gradual   small   significant   steep   sharp   rapid   sudden
(1) i _ _ _ _ _ e
(2) r _ _ e
(3) d _ _ _ _ _ e
(4) d _ _ _ _ e
(5) r _ _ _ _ _ _ n
(6) f _ _ l
(7) d _ _ p
in
temperature   humidity   rainfall   hours of sunshine   wind speed   the number of storms   the amount of damage   night-time temperatures

2 Which nouns talk about an upwards change? Which nouns talk about a downwards change?

3 Does the word *fluctuation* describe an upwards change, a downwards change or both?

4 Which adjectives mean the same as these words?

    1 minimal

    2 steady

    3 marked

    4 quick

Writing folder 9

Persuasive writing

In many Part 1 and Part 2 Writing tasks, there will be an element of persuasive writing.

1 **Work with a partner. Look at these situations and discuss:**
- who you are trying to persuade.
- what you are trying to persuade them to do.
- why you want to persuade them.
- appropriate arguments to use.

1 an essay for your tutor arguing for the need to take the issue of climate change seriously

2 a review for a website of a music album that you feel strongly about

3 a reference letter to a tour company on behalf of a friend who has applied for a job as a tourist guide

4 a report for your teacher about a book you have read in English, explaining whether you think it is an interesting and enjoyable book for other language students to read

5 a letter to a company complaining about a gadget you bought recently which no longer works

6 a proposal for your college principal about how to spend some funding the college has been provided with

2 **When writing persuasively, it is important to use language that is appropriate. Look at these sentences from students' answers on the topics in exercise 1. Decide which sentence in each pair is more appropriate and why.**

1 a On the other hand, to ignore climate change is to bury your head in the sand.
  b On the other hand, it's a bit silly to ignore the issue of climate change.

2 a However, the first track on the album is really rubbish.
  b The first track on the album is undoubtedly a catchy tune. However, it has little originality.

3 a Anna is a nice person; she has been my neighbour for six months and I really feel you should give her this job.
  b Anna and I have been fellow students and friends for over four years now. Because she is a charming person with excellent people skills, I have no hesitation in recommending her.

4 a I feel that there are other books which future students might find more appealing.
  b It was a boring book and I don't think other students should waste their time with it.

5 a As this item is defective, I hope that you will be able to offer me a refund.
  b If you do not give me my money back then I shall have to consult a lawyer.

6 a In conclusion, I would recommend spending the funding on an improved swimming pool as this would be of considerable benefit to both staff and students.
  b In conclusion, you would be well advised to spend the money as I have suggested on an improved swimming pool.

3 **Here are some steps to go through when planning your answer to a writing task. Put them in order.**

1 reorganise your brainstorming notes into a logical order
2 think about the reader
3 read the question
4 brainstorm the topic
5 think about the layout, including the number of paragraphs

4 You are going to prepare an essay in answer to one of the topics in exercise 1. First, underline the key words in this task.

You have attended a radio discussion on what needs to be done about climate change. You have made the notes below.

> **What needs to be done about climate change:**
> - Scientific research
> - Legislation
> - Education

> **Some opinions expressed in the discussion:**
> 'We need more scientific evidence to know exactly how significant climate change really is.'
> 'Governments have to take action for there to be any real improvements.'
> 'People must be made more aware of the problem.'

Write an **essay** for your tutor discussing two **of the things that need to be done about climate change** in your notes. You should explain **which you think is more important**, providing reasons to support your opinion.

5 Work with a partner and discuss these questions.

1 What do you know about the issue of climate change?
2 Who is the intended reader of your essay?
3 What style of writing would be most appropriate: formal and factual, lively and entertaining, chatty?

6 Now think about these points.

1 Which two of the three points will you discuss in your essay?
2 Discuss what to include in each paragraph.
- Introduction …
- Second paragraph …
- Third paragraph …
- Conclusion …
3 Think about grammatical structures. Mark these structures according to this key.

> ✓ I'm sure I will use
> ? I'm not sure I will use
> ✗ I won't use

- past simple
- past continuous
- past perfect
- present perfect
- present simple
- present continuous
- conditional forms
- passive forms
- *-ing* forms
- infinitives
- relative clauses

7 Write your first draft.

8 Exchange your first draft with another student and edit their first draft using this code.

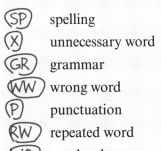

SP spelling
X unnecessary word
GR grammar
WW wrong word
P punctuation
RW repeated word
WO word order
S inappropriate style

9 Write your final version of the task and check it again.

23 I really must insist

Speaking

1 Work in pairs. Discuss these situations. When you have finished, look at the key on page 161. Do you agree?

1 You are in a restaurant. The waiter is taking ages to serve you and you've been waiting 45 minutes. The restaurant is busy. Do you
A walk out of the restaurant?
B go up to the waiter and demand to see the manager?
C try to smile at the waiter?

2 You paid a lot of money for a designer T-shirt. The first time you washed it, you followed the instructions, but the colour ran and ruined some other clothes. When it dried it had shrunk. You think the material is poor quality. Do you
A throw it in the bin and forget about it?
B phone the shop and complain angrily?
C go back to the shop with the T-shirt and ask politely for your money back?

3 You go to a concert with a coach company. The trip was advertised as using comfortable buses with friendly drivers. You arrive four hours late. The coach was dirty and the driver was rude. Do you
A get a taxi back home and pay for it?
B get a taxi back home and insist that the coach company pays for it?
C mention to the driver that you've missed the concert and write to the coach company when you get home?

2 Work with a partner and discuss these questions.
1 What sort of complainer are you? Do you just moan to your friends or do you complain to the shop or company?
2 Do you get angry when you have to complain?

3 What do you think is the best way to complain: face-to-face, by phone, by letter or email, or start a campaign on a social-networking site? Why?

Reading

1 You are going to read an article called *How to complain*. With a partner, make a list of the advice you expect to read.

2 Read the article below and match headings A–H to paragraphs 1–6. Two headings are not needed.
A Who will I complain to?
B How can I get my money back?
C How do I feel?
D Ask yourself: what are the facts?
E What do I do if I don't get satisfaction?
F What are my rights?
G How will I complain most effectively?
H What do I want?

3 Choose three pieces of advice in the article which are the most important.

How to complain

Most people love to complain, but while moaning to friends is a national pastime in Britain, when it comes to protesting to a retailer, for example, we often prefer to suffer in silence about faulty goods or services.

When we do decide to make our point, we can become aggressive, gearing up for battle and turning what should be a rational negotiation into a conflict.
To complain effectively, you need to be clear in your communication, specific about your problem and how you want it solved, and objective in the words you choose to make your point. Good negotiators tend to be calm and logical.

1 ☐
Was the product faulty or are you complaining about rude service or a delay? Sift out feelings from hard fact. This will help you to be concise and to the point.

2 ☐
What will it take to put the problem right? Most complaints become negotiation and it's important to know what you'll accept. Do you want your money back, or the product replaced? Or will an apology be sufficient?

Phrasal verbs (2)

1 Find these phrasal verbs in the article.

> gearing up   finding out
> go ahead   carry out

1 What do they mean?
2 Which verbs have an object?
3 Which verbs may be separated?

Corpus spot

Take care to use the correct prepositions with phrasal verbs. The *Cambridge English Corpus* shows exam candidates often make mistakes with this.

*Get off **at** the sixth bus stop, just after the bridge.*

NOT *Get off **on** the sixth bus stop, just after the bridge.*

3 ⬜

If the complaint is a serious one, you need to go armed with your legal rights.

4 ⬜

Have you ever begun to complain with the words: 'I know this isn't your fault, but …'? Spouting hot air to the wrong person is a waste of time and energy. Start off by finding out exactly who you should be speaking to, and who has the authority to handle your problem. Take the name of the person who deals with your complaint.

5 ⬜

In person, by letter, or over the phone? If face-to-face isn't possible or you feel you lack confidence, a phone call may be easier. Start by explaining the situation and stating your requirement clearly, without threat. If you are not satisfied with the response, remind the other person about the agreement that's been broken.

6 ⬜

Most complaints prompt an emotional response, but being reasonable is more likely to get the positive result you want. If you feel angry or upset about what has happened, go ahead and tell the company, but do it calmly. Demonstrate that you understand the situation from the other person's point of view. 'I appreciate that it might be difficult to arrange a special delivery, but I really need the order by tomorrow.' Do state clearly the consequences of your request being ignored. ('I'm going to place the order elsewhere and cancel my account with you'), but never make a threat that you can't carry out.

2 There are mistakes in three of these sentences. Find the mistakes and correct them.

1 Before you go to the shop to complain, jot down the points you want to make.
2 I looked the guarantee through but I couldn't find out how long it was valid for.
3 The engineer's explanations as to why it doesn't work just don't add up.
4 I didn't expect a problem to crop up so soon after buying a new computer.
5 We don't hold much hope out, but we are still trying to get compensation.
6 Trying to get a satisfactory answer to my queries took out the whole morning.
7 If you had taken out an extended guarantee, the cost of the repairs would have been covered.
8 I didn't really want to spend so much on a TV so I bought a cheap one.

3 Read the email to get a general understanding of what it says. Then fill the gaps (1–8) using the correct form of the phrasal verbs from the box.

> ~~put up with~~   bring up   build up   call on   settle in
> come up against   draw up   fit in with   give up

Dear Sir/Madam
I am writing to you with regard to a problem I am having with my new neighbours. I live in a block of flats and I am finding it increasingly difficult to **(0)** *put up with* the noise from the family who live in the flat above me. In particular, they play loud music all day and I find I often have to **(1)** .... trying to study as concentration is impossible. I have not **(2)** .... the issue with my neighbours as I do not want to interfere. Moreover, as they have made no attempt to **(3)** .... the local community, it makes it difficult for me to approach them.

The family have lived in the flat for about a month and at first I thought once their teenage children had **(4)** ...., the situation would improve but in fact it seems to be getting worse. I can relate to teenagers wanting to play music but when it impacts on my life in such a negative way I feel that I need to **(5)** .... your services. I have never **(6)** .... a problem like this before and would appreciate your advice.
I understand from the information on your website that you can provide noise measuring equipment so that I can **(7)** .... a body of evidence to support my complaints and that I should **(8)** .... a list of dates and times when the noise becomes intolerable.
Would it be possible for you to visit me so that I can explain the situation in more detail? I look forward to your reply.

Yours faithfully
Terry Foster

G➔ page 175

Listening

1 Work with a partner and discuss these questions.

1 What sort of person would your ideal boss be and why?

2 What do you think is the strongest reason for asking for a pay rise?

3 If your boss was rather 'difficult', how would you go about asking for a pay rise? Which of these suggestions might be useful?

- Make a formal appointment to discuss the matter.
- Wear more formal clothes for some time before asking for a pay rise.
- Go into your boss's office frequently and drop hints about how much work you are doing and how good it is.
- Make a list of all the reasons why you should have a pay rise.
- Tell your boss how much better you are than other employees.

⬇ Exam spot

In the Listening test, you will be asked to complete a multiple-choice task like the one on this page. Read all the questions before you start listening so that you are prepared to choose the right answer. You hear the recording twice.

2 ◄2 16 Listen to some advice on asking for a pay rise and choose the best answer according to what you hear.

1 The key factor when asking for a pay rise is
   A voicing your demands in a convincing way.
   B making it clear you feel undervalued.
   C proving you are an asset in the business.
   D comparing yourself to the rest of the staff.

2 If you have any failings, you should
   A check that no one knows about them.
   B put them right gradually so that it is not too obvious.
   C accentuate your strengths, to compensate.
   D make sure your boss likes you as a person.

3 When preparing what to say in your salary negotiation
   A put yourself in your superior's shoes.
   B do not forget that you really need extra money.
   C make a list of all the points in your favour.
   D focus on what you can do for the company in the future.

4 What should you do if your boss is likely to raise objections to your pay rise?
   A Prepare a counter-argument.
   B Make sure you can quote company rules to him or her.
   C Appreciate that your boss is only doing his or her job.
   D Accept any offer as it is better than nothing.

5 To maximise the chances of a positive outcome, it is important to
   A mention that the company is very successful.
   B ensure your boss is aware of how serious you are.
   C arrange to see your boss early in the day when he or she is fresh.
   D try not to put your boss in an awkward position.

6 What should you do if you do not get a pay rise or as much as you wanted?
   A Be prepared for a long drawn-out conflict.
   B Know that you might have to resign as a matter of principle.
   C Either have an alternative or ask for constructive criticism.
   D Either get a colleague to back you up or talk to your boss again soon.

Writing

 Exam spot

In the Writing test, you may be asked to write a letter in which you need to get your point of view across or an article complaining about something. Read the situation carefully and make the purpose of your writing clear.

1 **Read this situation and then work with a partner to discuss the questions.**

You recently bought a piece of electronic equipment from a shop but it didn't work properly. The shop promised to repair it but having taken it back twice, it still does not work. You decide the only solution is either for the shop to replace the item or to get a refund. You decide to write to the manager of the shop.

1 Which pieces of advice in the article on pages 142–143 might be appropriate in this situation?
2 Think about what you can write to the shop. Consider these points.
- the number of paragraphs you need
- the main content of each paragraph
- some formal phrases
- some grammatical structures
- the overall organisation

2 **Write to the manager explaining your situation and what you would like to happen next.**

Speaking

1 **Getting your views across is part of being a good communicator. Discuss which suggestions are important.**

- state your opinion clearly and concisely
- never say 'I'm not sure.'
- paraphrase and reformulate what you want to say so that the listener can understand easily
- use body language
- use phrases to try to persuade your partner to agree with you (e.g. *Isn't it true that …?*)
- don't let your partner interrupt before you have made your point
- be open to your partner's point of view
- periodically summarise what you have said
- use a wide range of vocabulary
- use grammar accurately so that the listener is not distracted or confused

 Exam spot

In the Speaking test, one of the things the examiner is listening for is your interactive communication. You are given an activity which you discuss with your partner. Then the examiner will ask you some more general questions which relate to the topic of the activity. You will need to show that you can get your views across.

2 **Work with a partner and role-play this situation.**

Student A, you recently bought an expensive music system but it has suddenly stopped working. You go back to the shop where you bought it and ask for a new one. Unfortunately, you lost the receipt. Fortunately, this is the only shop nearby where this kind of music system can be bought, so it should be clear to the shop assistant that you bought it there recently.

Student B, you are a shop assistant. You can't do anything without a receipt, but you can try to persuade the customer to buy a more expensive music system to replace the one that doesn't work.

Exam folder 10

Paper 4: the Speaking test

The Speaking test is quite short (only about 15 minutes for two candidates) and so it is important not to waste time with unnecessary silences. Don't worry too much about making mistakes – the important thing is to show that you can communicate in English both with the examiner and with your partner.

1 **Work with a partner and discuss the questions.**

1 What advice would you give a candidate who feels very nervous about the Speaking test?

2 What do you think the examiners are looking for in the Speaking test?

2 **Read the Exam information box and tick any points you mentioned in Exercise 1.**

EXAM ADVICE

- Smile at the examiners as you greet them – it will relax you and create a pleasant first impression.
- Try to relax – imagine you are talking to a new friend.
- Listen carefully to the instructions and do what you are asked.
- If you did not understand or do not remember all the instructions, it is fine to ask the examiner to clarify or repeat something.
- Answer the examiner's questions fully, not just with one-word answers.
- Speak clearly and loudly enough for both examiners to hear you.
- Give your partner a chance to speak too.
- Talk to your partner – you get marks for interacting, so ask each other questions, and react to what your partner says (as in a normal conversation) but try to do so without interrupting.
- When you ask questions, try not to use an intonation which rises too much as this can sound aggressive.
- Try not to repeat what you or your partner has already said – add something new.

Part 1

In Part 1, give reasonably full answers to the examiner's questions.

3 **Work in groups of three (one examiner and two candidates). The 'examiner' should ask each candidate one or two questions.**

1 How important is it for you to learn English?
2 How do you prefer to spend your leisure time?
3 What are your hopes and ambitions for the future?

4 **Now swap roles.**

Part 2

In Part 2, you need to talk about two photos and give your opinion on a topic represented by the photos.

5 **Work in the same group of three, but change roles. Focus on photos A–C.**

1 The 'examiner' should say to Candidate A:
Look at the photos of people doing activities for the first time. Compare two of the photos and say why the people might have chosen to do these things and how they might be feeling.

2 Then the examiner stops Candidate A after one minute, and asks Candidate B:
Which activity do you think is the most difficult to do for the first time?

6 **Now change roles and focus on photos D–F.**

1 The 'examiner' should say to Candidate A:
Look at the photos of people spending time alone. Compare two of the photos and say why the people are in this situation and how they might be feeling.

2 Then the examiner stops Candidate A after one minute, and asks Candidate B:
Why do people sometimes choose to spend time alone?

Part 3

In Part 3, you will have more to say if you do not simply agree with your partner but react either by taking their ideas a step further or by disagreeing.

7 **Look at the diagram below. Work in the same group of three, but change roles.**

1 The 'examiner' should say:
Here are some of the types of websites that students can access to learn English and other languages. Talk to each other about how useful these types of websites might be for people learning languages.

2 Candidates A and B speak for about two minutes. Then the examiner says:
Now you have a minute to decide which two types of websites would be most useful for students of all levels.

| online club with members around the world | online lessons with private teacher | online dictionaries |

How useful might these types of websites be for students learning languages?

| news in different languages | computer games in different languages |

Part 4

In Part 4, as with all the other parts, it is important to listen carefully to what the examiner asks you to do.

8 **Work in the same group of three, but change roles. The examiner asks both candidates these questions.**

1 Apart from the websites you have already discussed, what other types of websites do you think could be useful?

2 Do you think it is effective to learn a subject online?

3 How important is it to find a form of study that suits you?

4 Do you think it's a good idea to learn a language in the country where it is spoken? Why?

5 How important is it to keep learning new things throughout your life?

6 Do you think there is too much pressure on young people to achieve good results in exams?

Speaking

1 Work with a partner and discuss these questions.

1 How do you usually find out about the news?
2 What impact do you think the internet and 24-hour TV news have had on newspapers?
3 How do you think TV viewing will change in the future?

Reading

1 News stories are often about a new scientific breakthrough or discovery. You are going to read an article about the 'sweet-tooth gene'. Before reading, work in pairs and discuss these questions.

1 Have you come across any news stories recently about new scientific breakthroughs?
2 Have you got a sweet tooth? Does this trait run in your family?
3 If scientists could discover a sweet-tooth gene, what could they do with this information?

2 Read the article and choose the correct answer to each question.

1 What has the research described in the article discovered?
   A More people than expected have a gene which makes them want to eat sweet things.
   B A drug can modify genes so a person loses their desire for sweets.
   C The reasons why people like the foods they do are genetically determined.
   D Some mice have a gene which affects how they experience a sweet taste.
2 What are the implications of the research?
   A Some people are unlikely to be able to stop eating sweet things.
   B It may in future be easier to change people's eating habits.
   C Children should be discouraged from eating sweets.
   D Gene therapy may have some harmful effects.
3 In reaction to the research, Aubrey Sheiham
   A admires its originality.
   B is concerned about its accuracy.
   C is unconvinced of its value.
   D is interested in its potential.

3 Work with a partner and discuss these questions.

1 What do you think about newspaper articles which herald new 'wonder discoveries'?
2 What new scientific developments do you think we will see in the near future?

If bingeing on chocolate makes your trousers too tight, blame the genes

*Chocoholics no longer need to feel guilty about their desire for chocolate. They are simply the victim of their genes, scientists have **found**.*

The so-called 'sweet-tooth gene' has been **identified** by separate teams of researchers and helps explain why some find it harder to resist chocolate bars and cream cakes.

It also raises the possibility of designing a drug which could 'switch off' the gene and help people resist sugary foods. Children, in particular, risk their health by eating too many sweets and chocolates.

To identify the gene, the research teams – based at Harvard Medical School in Boston and Mount Sinai School of Medicine in New York – conducted almost identical experiments using mice which have differences in their ability to taste sweet foods. They **compared** the DNA of the two types of mice and noticed differences in a gene called T1R3.

Dr Gopi Shanker, of the Mount Sinai team, said: 'It contains information which produces a protein called the sweet taste receptor.

'This **recognises** the sweet content of food and **initiates** a cascade of events which signal to the brain that a sweet food has been eaten.' Dr Shanker added, 'Exactly the same gene **exists** in humans, so it means that if your parents have a sweet tooth then you probably will as well.'

Research by the Harvard team has come to the same conclusion.

But Aubrey Sheiham, professor of dental public health at University College, London, said the results did not provide chocoholics with an excuse to give up dieting.

He said: 'We have always known that some people have a sweeter tooth than others. But it has also been **proved** that if you gradually **expose** people to less sugar, then the body becomes accustomed to less. They will be satisfied with a lower level of sweetness.'

Mr Sheiham warned against any form of gene therapy which sought to deactivate the sweet-tooth gene.

'We have produced this gene through evolution because sweet foods in nature are not poisonous and also give us energy. We all need to have some sugar in our diet.'

The US researchers are using their discovery to **develop** artificial sweeteners without an aftertaste.

Vocabulary

1 The article uses a number of verbs that are useful for writing about academic experiments. Match the verbs in bold in the article with the definitions of their basic forms.

1 show to exist
2 be present
3 show to be true
4 discover
5 look for the resemblances and differences between two or more things
6 bring into being
7 make (someone) experience
8 start
9 know what something is

2 What is the noun form of verbs 1–9 in exercise 1? Add them to the phrases below.

1 to be working on the .... of some unusual insects
2 to discover the .... of a new type of beetle
3 the .... of a theory
4 some unexpected ....
5 a .... of two types of plastic
6 the .... of a new product
7 .... to light
8 the .... of a process.
9 .... of someone's abilities

3 Complete this article with the verbs that collocate correctly.

Pietro Tonioli is in the process of (1) *conducting / making* an experiment into the health benefits of honey. Other researchers have already (2) *come / come to* the conclusion that honey boosts our immune system. Tonioli's work, however, goes much further than this; he suggests that people may actually be (3) *risking / gambling* their health if they do not eat honey on a regular basis. Some politicians have expressed considerable interest in his work and have (4) *raised / brought* the possibility that honey should be supplied free to all schoolchildren. This, they say, would be of great benefit to families which (5) *have / find* it difficult to afford honey for their children.

Listening

1 **2 17 Listen to a presenter talking about next week's edition of a current affairs programme. Complete these sentences.**

   1 *News Weekly* will be shown next week on
     .... at 8.30.

   2 The title of next week's programme is
     '.............................' .

   3 The theme of the programme is the
     .... of modern teenagers.

   4 Most of the programme was recorded in
     .... areas.

   5 It focuses in particular on the attitudes of
     teenagers towards ....

   6 At the end of the programme there will be an
     ....

   7 There will also be a .... on the
     programme's website.

   8 Later programmes will deal with issues relating
     to .... and crime.

2 **Look at photo A, which comes from a news item. What do you think it is about?**

3 **2 18 Now listen to the news item and make notes on people, places, and the general topic.**

4 **Listen again and answer these more detailed questions.**

   1 What event happened last night?
   2 What happened during the event?
   3 Which three groups of people were present at
     the event?
   4 Which records does the news item say have been
     broken over the last few weeks?

5 **Look at photo B. You will hear a broadcast called *Those who break the labour laws*. What do you think this story will be about?**

6 **2 19 Now listen and answer these questions.**

   1 Is the problem of illegal employment confined
     to one country?
   2 What are the two types of illegal employment
     the journalist mentions?
   3 Give one reason why the employees do not
     complain.
   4 What happened when she said she might leave
     the job?
   5 Does the reporter think it is likely that she will
     go back to school?

7 **Do you think that investigative journalism can actually improve conditions by exposing exploitation? Why? / Why not?**

Connecting words

1 Complete the article below with the words from the box. Think about which phrase would be grammatically correct in each gap as well as its position in the sentence. There are two which do not fit.

> ~~no sooner~~   and what's more   as   but
> because   by then   in all   even   despite
> provided   resulted in   so   then

2 Have you ever taken part in a marathon or similar event? If not, would you ever consider it?

G → page 175

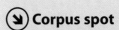

Corpus spot

Be careful with *and, or* and *but*. Although they are 'easy' words, the *Cambridge English Corpus* shows that exam candidates make mistakes with them.

*I was impressed by the good food in the café **and** also by the new exhibition.*

NOT ~~I was impressed by the good food in the café **but** also by the new exhibition.~~

I can stay at home without seeing anybody or speaking to a 'real' person for ages.

NOT ~~I can stay at home without seeing anybody **and** speaking to a 'real' person for ages.~~

30,000 runners take London in their stride

(H.W)

(0) ...*No sooner*.... had the gun sounded than we were all off, including me and my running flatmate, Fran, jostling for position (1) .... we crossed the starting line, which was awash with plastic bags, unwanted clothing, bottles and banana skins.

The real running began as Greenwich came into view and the crowds, which were already big, increased even further. People shouted at friends. Anyone with their name on their vest became public property (2) .... everyone wanted to be part of this event. Screams of encouragement mixed with brass bands and Beatles tribute bands.

The 12-mile point. I must have lived this part at least a dozen times from my armchair. I could hear a commentator murmuring about how plucky we all were.

(3) ...., the halfway mark was within reach and it was getting tiring. Tower Bridge loomed, magnificent, with thousands of people screeching encouragement.

I knew what was coming. At 13 miles out I saw a small flag fluttering and annoying someone's ear and then heard the words: 'There he is.' My parents had spotted me. I stopped for a chat, and went on my way.

(4) .... someone was watching after all.

(5) .... regularly ingesting isotonic fluid and strawberry and banana flavoured gels (350 calories a sachet), we were getting only fleeting benefits. Children were pressed to the barriers offering support and sometimes sweets. Through a haze of discomfort Canary Wharf appeared. It went on forever. Things were flagging. Knees were sore, ankles pinching, (6) .... my arms were tingling. Twenty miles gone and it was agony. I guessed this was my wall coming. Tall and slippery with broken glass on the top.

How I got past that point without hiring a cab I have yet to unravel.

Things worsened. The closer to home, the harder it became. My feet were sticking to the floor. Fran was looking worried. We did not stop and walk (7) .... just ran at a walking pace.

The last mile felt like the first 13. Nothing was much fun. I was gone. (8) ...., I was hungry.

(9) ...., turning past Big Ben I saw a man holding an advert for McDonald's bacon double cheese burger. Unbelievable cruelty.

(10) .... I would have eaten my hand if it was encased in a bun and covered in mayo with a couple of those gherkin-type things for relish. And I am a vegetarian.

The finish was in sight. Past Buckingham Palace and a couple of screeching friends and to the end. The full-stop finish, no more, never again. Around me people staggered, their faces covered in dry salt deposits from sweat, lips trembling, a few crying.

Strangers offered congratulations, touched our backs, smiled the brightest smiles, spoke the most beautiful words. I loved the world and it loved me.

NEWS AND VIEWS   **151**

Writing folder 10

The Writing Paper: general guidance

In other Writing folders you have worked on, you practised writing the different individual tasks tested in the Writing test. But this folder focuses on some general and very important aspects of the test.

1 **Discuss the following general pieces of advice about the Writing Paper. Which verb do you think is needed to complete each tip?**

   1 Before you start to write it is very important to .... the question carefully.
   2 It may be useful to .... the key words in the task instructions.
   3 It is important to allow time to .... your answer – think about how you are going to .... your ideas into paragraphs.
   4 In Part 2, make sure you .... the best question for you to answer.
   5 When you have completed your answer, don't forget to .... what you have written very carefully – if you find a mistake, ... it as neatly as you can.

Reading the question

2 **Look at this Part 1 task. Which aspects of the task would you underline or highlight?**

> Your class has watched a panel discussion on the benefits of young people doing voluntary work. You have made the notes below.
>
> **Benefits of young people doing voluntary work:**
> • contribute to society
> • learn about others
> • gain skills
>
> **Some opinions expressed in the discussion:**
> 'It's good for them to help others.'
> 'It can open their eyes to the problems some people face.'
> 'They learn how to do useful things.'
>
> Write an **essay** discussing **two of the benefits** in your notes. You should identify **which benefit is more important**, giving reasons for your choice.

3 **This is what some exam candidates do when they answer the question. Have they done anything wrong? If so, what?**

   1 Suzi compares the benefits of contributing to society, learning about others' lives and learning useful skills and explains how learning about others' lives is the most important from her point of view.
   2 Marco writes an entertaining article about his own experience of doing voluntary work, explaining what skills he learned from doing so.
   3 Lisa talks about the first two benefits, copying the words in the quotations so that she does not make any language errors.

Planning

4 **Work with a partner. Discuss how you would write an answer to the task in exercise 2.**

   1 Brainstorm some ideas.
   2 Note down some good expressions that you might be able to use.
   3 Decide how many paragraphs you are going to write and note down the topic of each paragraph.
   4 Compare what you and your partner decided with the work of other pairs.

Choosing the best task

> Part 2 of the Writing Paper is the only part of the exam where you have a choice of question. It is important to choose the best task for you.

5 **Discuss these questions with a partner.**

   1 Is it better to choose the most interesting question or the one that you know the vocabulary for?
   2 Is it better to choose to write a letter, a report, a proposal or a review?
   3 Is it a good idea to choose a task that is rather similar to one you already did for your teacher?

6 Look at these tasks. Discuss with a partner which task you think would be the best one for you to answer and why.

1 This is part of a letter which you receive from an Australian friend.

> We're doing a project at college about using websites rather than books for study purposes. How much do students use websites in your country? What's your favourite study site and what do you use it for? Do you think students will eventually stop using traditional libraries?

Write a **letter** to your friend replying to their questions.

2 You work for a travel company. Read this email from company management.

> We are planning to make our offices look much more stylish and inviting for customers and would like staff to submit proposals suggesting how you feel we should do this. Your proposal should outline your ideas, describing how they could be put into practice and explaining why this kind of office would be of benefit to the company.

Write your **proposal**.

3 The manager of a sports centre where you have been going for some time has asked you to write a report on what you see as the strengths and weaknesses of the centre and describing one or two improvements that could be made in order to attract new customers.

Write your **report**.

Checking your work

7 Here are some of the mistakes which the *Cambridge Learner Corpus* shows to be very frequently made by students taking the Cambridge English Advanced exam. Which of these mistakes do you tend to make?

- tense errors especially with present perfect
- articles
- dependent prepositions
- collocations with *do* and *make*
- misspellings

8 Look back through some pieces of writing you have recently done. Notice the mistakes you made. Make a list of errors that you need to try to avoid making in future.

9 Write an answer to one of the tasks in this Folder (the Part 1 task or one of the Part 2 tasks). When you finish, check it very carefully.

EXAM ADVICE

Remember that in both parts of the Writing test, it is important to think about the content, language and register of your answers. You will lose marks if you do not write in a way that is appropriate to the genre or the target reader.

Speaking

1 **Work in pairs and discuss these questions.**

   1 In what way are all the photos linked to the theme of intelligence?

   2 Do you think people are born intelligent, or can most of us study and become intelligent?

   3 Which animals do you think are the most intelligent? Why?

Reading

1 **You are going to read an article about using observation as a research method. Read this sentence from the extract and discuss what you think the text might be about.**

Hans answered questions by tapping with his forefoot or by pointing with his nose at different alternatives shown to him.

2 **Now read the first part of the extract and check your ideas.**

3 **Read the next part. How do you think Hans was able to answer the questions?**

Research methods in psychology

We can learn a great deal about behaviour by simply observing the actions of others. However, everyday observations are not always made carefully or systematically. Most people do not attempt to control or eliminate factors that might influence the events they are observing. As a consequence, erroneous conclusions are often drawn.

Consider, for example, the classic case of Clever Hans. Hans was a horse that was said by his owner, a German mathematics teacher, to have amazing talents. Hans could count, do simple addition and subtraction (even involving fractions), read German, answer simple questions ('What is the lady holding in her hands?'), give the date, and tell the time. Hans answered questions by tapping with his forefoot or by pointing with his nose at different alternatives shown to him. His owner considered Hans to be truly intelligent and denied using any tricks to guide his horse's behaviour. And, in fact, Clever Hans was clever even when the questioner was someone other than his owner.

Newspapers carried accounts of Hans's performance, and hundreds of people came to view this amazing horse. In 1904, a scientific commission was established with the goal of discovering the basis for Hans's abilities. The scientists found that Hans was no longer clever if either of two circumstances existed. First, Hans did not know the answers to questions if the questioner also did not know the answers. Second, Hans was not very clever if he could not see his questioner. A slight bending forward by the questioner would start Hans tapping, and any movement upward or backward would cause Hans to stop tapping. The commission demonstrated that questioners were unintentionally cueing Hans in this way.

This famous account of Clever Hans illustrates the fact that scientific observation (unlike casual observation) is systematic and controlled. Indeed, it has been suggested that control is the essential ingredient of science, distinguishing it from non-scientific procedures. In the case of Clever Hans, investigators exercised control by manipulating, one at a time, conditions such as whether the questioner knew the answer to the question asked and whether Hans could see the questioner. By exercising control, taking care to investigate the effect of various factors one by one, a scientist seeks to gain a clearer picture of the factors that actually produce a phenomenon.

4 Work with a partner. Discuss these questions.

1 To what extent do you think animals can communicate with humans?

2 Do you think that people these days are less likely to believe stories like the one about Hans? Why / Why not?

Vocabulary

1 The article contains many words and phrases connected to research and reporting on results. Find these words in the article and then match them to their definitions.

> observe systematic influence involve consider establish illustrate distinguish procedure investigate

1 using a fixed and organised plan *procedure* / *systematic*
2 examine a problem carefully *observe* *investigate*
3 watch carefully *observe*
4 include something in a process *involve*
5 effect of people or things *influence*
6 discover or get proof of something *establish*
7 a set of actions, the standard way of doing things *procedure*
8 spend time thinking about a possibility *consider*
9 show something more clearly *illustrate*
10 notice the difference between two things *distinguish*

2 How are the examples of informal language 1–8 written in a more formal way in the article? Match the informal words to formal versions a–h. Look back at the article to help you.

1 just		**a**	a great deal
2 lots		**b**	simply
3 wrong		**c**	observe
4 so		**d**	attempt
5 try		**e**	eliminate
6 get rid of		**f**	as a consequence
7 show		**g**	erroneous
8 look at		**h**	demonstrate / illustrate

3 Using as many words as possible from exercises 1 and 2, summarise the article about Clever Hans.

4 Quickly skim this article about 'Psychic Paul', an octopus who predicted football results. Decide which word (A, B, C or D) best fits each gap. Think about how each word collocates with other words in the article.

H.W

Fluke!

The octopus who predicted a World Cup final

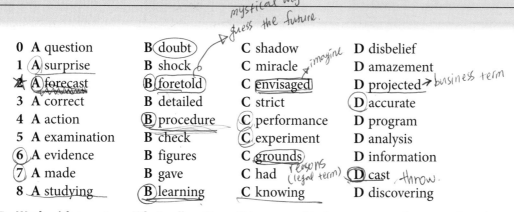

Our interest in animals' intelligence and possible psychic powers spans the centuries. For some people, Paul the Octopus proved conclusively, beyond all (0) *doubt* , that animals have intelligence. Spain's victory over Germany in the 2010 World Cup came as no (1) .... to many football fans, because the result had already been (2) .... by Paul. This was a creature that had achieved celebrity status with its incredibly (3) .... predictions.

Known as the 'psychic octopus', Paul seemed to demonstrate above-average intelligence. It seemed he could predict all of Germany's World Cup results every time he was asked. Such was the popularity of his selections that, just before the final, a German news channel broadcast Paul's prediction live on TV.

Paul's handlers, at an aquarium in the city of Oberhausen, turned him into an international superstar. A simple (4) .... was followed each time. Mussels were placed into two glass boxes. One box carried Germany's flag while the other had the flag of the opposing team. Paul then made his 'prediction' by swimming towards one of the boxes and eating the tasty mussel inside.

Aquarium staff never claimed that this was a carefully controlled scientific (5) .... There did indeed seem to be a lack of concrete (6) .... that Paul was making intelligent choices.

The day before the World Cup final, Paul at first swam towards the Spanish flag, before moving and hovering over the German box. After a few moments, the octopus

eventually returned to his first choice. Occurrences like this (7) .... some doubt over whether Paul really did have 'psychic' powers.

Not everyone appreciated Paul. When Argentina lost to Germany in the quarter-final, Argentine fans threatened to put him in a paella. The newspaper *El Dia* even printed a recipe for anyone who captured Paul: 'All you need are some potatoes, olive oil and a little salt.'

The octopus sometimes erred in his predictions, although not often. His most famous mistake was when he wrongly picked Germany over Spain in the 2008 European Championship. Spain won 1–0. Proof, perhaps, that he was capable of (8) .... from his mistakes. Paul lived a happy and celebrated life and died naturally in 2010. The world awaits the next animal oracle.

mystical way
→ guess the future.

0	A question	B doubt	C shadow	D disbelief
1	A surprise	B shock	C miracle *imagine*	D amazement
2	A forecast	B foretold	C envisaged	D projected *→ business term*
3	A correct	B detailed	C strict	D accurate
4	A action	B procedure	C performance	D program
5	A examination	B check	C experiment	D analysis
6	A evidence	B figures	C grounds	D information
7	A made	B gave	C had *reasons (legal term)*	D cast *throw.*
8	A studying	B learning	C knowing	D discovering

5 Work with a partner. What collocations did you need to know to complete exercise 4?

Complex sentences and adverbial clauses

Complex sentences have at least two clauses: a main clause and at least one subordinate clause. Adverbial clauses are subordinate clauses which give more information about the main clause (such as time, place, manner, reason, condition, etc.).

1 **Look at these adverbial clauses in bold. What extra information do they give about the rest of the clause?**

 1 Paul the octopus could predict Germany's World Cup results **every time he was asked**.

 2 Hundreds of people came to see Hans **wherever he appeared**.

 3 Paul made his 'prediction' **by swimming towards one of the boxes**.

 4 The horse became famous **because he could answer any question asked of him**.

 5 The scientists found that Hans was no longer clever **if either of two circumstances existed**.

↘ Exam spot

Using complex sentences in both your writing and in your speaking is a sign that you are working at an advanced level.

2 **Complete these sentences appropriately.**

 1 Some people thought Paul the octopus was truly intelligent because …

 2 Hans the horse could answer questions even if …

 3 Hans could not answer questions when …

 4 A scientific commission unravelled the mystery by …

 5 Although Hans was never denounced as a fraud, …

 6 People asking questions had to stand in front of Hans where …

3 **Work with a partner. Compare your sentences.**

G → page 176

Listening

1 **Work with a partner. Discuss these questions.**

 1 What do you think 'emotional intelligence' is?

 2 How far do you think it's possible to judge someone's intelligence by giving them a standard intelligence test?

 3 During this course what have you noticed about your style of learning? What time of day can you study best? Do you prefer reading, listening, speaking or writing? Do you like working alone or with other people?

2 **2 20 Listen to five speakers talking about intelligence and feelings. Match them to the statements (a–e).**

 a This person has discovered different styles of learning. ....

 b This person can remember things better when they are emotionally involved. ....

 c This person has an instinct for knowing how people are feeling. ....

 d This person feels uncomfortable when people openly display affection. ....

 e This person believes it's hard to say who is intelligent and who is not. ....

3 **2 20 Choose one of the topics the speakers talked about.**

 1 Listen to the recording again and note down any additional information about your chosen topic.

 2 Work with a partner. Take turns to give a two-minute talk on the topic.

4 **Work in small groups. Discuss these questions.**

 1 What are you going to do before the exam to make sure you are ready and well prepared?

 2 How do you feel about your exam preparation, the exam itself and getting your results?

 3 What can you do to support other students who are taking the exam?

 4 How can other people help you?

Topic review

1 Work with a partner and discuss these questions.

1 If you could go anywhere in the world, where would you go?
2 Would you like to be a travel journalist? Why/Why not?
3 Has the climate in your country changed since you were a child?
4 Do you agree that people are to blame for the world's climate change?
5 Have you ever taken anything back to a shop? If so, what happened?
6 What characteristics do you find difficult to put up with in your neighbours?
7 How much chocolate do you eat every week?
8 Who should decide what children should watch on TV and when?
9 How far can humans train animals to do different things?
10 Have you ever taken part in a survey? If so, what for and what did the results show?

Vocabulary

2 Complete each sentence with one word.

1 The hotel was ideally situated, only a stone's .... from the beach.
2 Unfortunately, the castle area has become a real tourist .... with many shops selling cheap souvenirs.
3 Travellers differ from tourists in that they prefer to find somewhere off the .... track.
4 Be careful when you drive through the mountains; that road has become an accident .... spot in recent years.
5 Building an internationally famous art gallery in Bilboa has certainly put the city on the

....
6 With the thatched cottages with roses growing round the doors, it's a picture-............................... village.

Grammar

3 Connecting words can be divided into different categories. Look at the book extract. Which category does each word/phrase in bold belong to?

Individual development

Effective teamwork seeks to pool the skills of individuals and to produce better results. **While** the effectiveness of the team can be greater than the sum of the parts, it **also** follows that effective teams need to pay attention to the development of individual skills. **Just as** different societies have different views of the developed group, different societies and cultures have had different views as to what constitutes the developed and effective individual. **That's why** the effectiveness of any team must in part be a function of individual ability, as teams are always a collection of individuals. So, **to summarise**, in aiming to develop any team, we must first aim to build individual strengths.

- Listing: *first and foremost*
- Concession and contrast: *despite* / *in spite of*
- Cause and reason: *because*, *due to + N*
- Result: *therefore*
- Summing up: *in conclusion*

4 Work with a partner. Add more examples to the categories above.

Reading

5 Read this extract quickly about the different roles people take on in group activities. What type of team member do you think you are?

6 Match the statements (1–9) with the types of team member. There may be more than one possible answer.

1 This member realises the importance of support from further afield.
2 If a team does not have this member, it may be satisfied with present results and not try harder.
3 This team member can see a creative way through difficulties.
4 Some team members find this person a destabilising influence.
5 This person smoothes the process towards the result.
6 This person makes sure the team is not swayed by someone's flights of fancy.
7 Although this team member makes an invaluable contribution, their influence is limited.
8 The whole team has to consider this member's advice in relation to the bigger picture.
9 The overriding concern of this team member is to guide the team in a favourable direction.

7 Work with a partner and discuss these questions.

1 What type of team member do you think you are? Have you changed your opinion since reading the descriptions? Does your partner agree?
2 Which types of team members are indispensable and which are dispensable?
3 What do you think causes the most conflict in teamwork?

The challenger

Often seen as the 'maverick' of the team, the challenger often adopts an unconventional approach. This is an individual who will look afresh at what the team is doing and why, and who will challenge the accepted order. Because of this, such an individual is often unpopular with those who prefer to conform and can be accused of 'rocking the boat'. The challenger provides the unexpected and while many ideas may prove to be worthless, some may become 'the idea of the year'. Without a challenger the team can become complacent, for it lacks the stimulus to review radically what it is doing and how it is doing it.

The expert

We live in an age of ever-increasing specialisation and the team may require several specialists whose primary role is to provide expertise which is not otherwise available to the team. Outside their area of specialisation, these people make little contribution; in meetings they assume the role of 'expert witness' giving a professional viewpoint which the rest of the team may need to evaluate in the light of other constraints and opportunities. The expert may be an accountant, engineer, marketing advisor, trainer, personnel specialist, corporate planner or any other specialist, whose primary role is to provide the team with the expertise required.

The judge

Like the judge in the courtroom, this team member listens, questions and ponders before making a decision. This character tends to keep out of the arguments and does not see himself or herself as an advocate for any particular view or cause, but is concerned to see that ideas are properly evaluated and that the right decisions are made. A judge will not be rushed, preferring to pay the price of slow progress to make sure that the team follows the right path. Down-to-earth and logical, regarded by some as slow and ponderous, this person provides a balance and check on those who may be carried away by their own enthusiasm; like the courtroom judge seeking out the truth and seeing justice done.

The innovator

Here is one who uses imagination to the full: an ideas person who is always proposing new ways of doing things. The innovator ensures that new ideas are evaluated, nurtured and developed and builds on the original ideas of others, visualising opportunities and transforming ideas into practical strategies. A fearless capacity to grapple with complex problems which demand new approaches provides the team with a rich source of vision, ingenuity, imagination and logic and can usually help the team to understand the unconventional and the new.

The diplomat

The diplomat is the team member who knows the diplomatic solution. This character generally has high influence within the team and is a good negotiator, and because of these skills plays a large part in the orientating of the team towards successful outcomes. Building alliances within and outside the team and trying to ensure that solutions are acceptable to all, the diplomat can sometimes be seen as 'papering over the cracks' in an effort to compromise, but is often dealing with the 'art of the impossible' rather than the ideal solution. Ways are found through difficult problems and in difficult times this is often the person who leads the team through dangerous ground.

Activities

Unit 5 Speaking page 34

These are the top ten jobs, according to the survey.

1 pilot
2 doctor
3 writer
4 photographer
5 musician/singer
6 sports trainer
7 Formula 1 driver
8 actor
9 journalist
10 artist

Exam folder 9 page 134

How much do you know about the Listening test?

1 How many parts are there in this test?
2 How many times do you hear each part?
3 What sorts of tasks do you have to do in each part of the Listening test?
4 Where do you have to write your answers?
5 How many marks can you get for each question?
6 Do spellings and grammar have to be correct?
7 How long is the whole Listening test, approximately?
8 What percentage of the whole exam is this test?

Unit 22 Interpreting and comparing page 139

Student A

Unit 22 Interpreting and comparing page 139

Student B

Unit 23 Speaking page 142

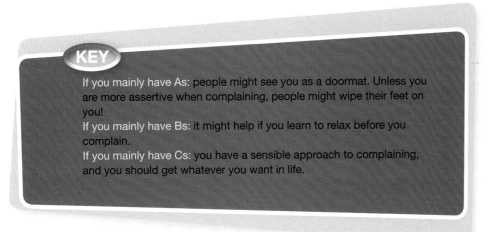

KEY

If you mainly have As: people might see you as a doormat. Unless you are more assertive when complaining, people might wipe their feet on you!

If you mainly have Bs: it might help if you learn to relax before you complain.

If you mainly have Cs: you have a sensible approach to complaining, and you should get whatever you want in life.

Grammar folder

Unit 1
Conditionals

Conditional sentences are usually grouped into four main types.

- The zero conditional is used to talk about common states or events (form = if/when + present simple + present simple).
  *If she **knows** you well, she **is** more talkative.*
  *We **say** hello when we **see** each other in the street.*
- The first conditional is used to talk about possible future states or events (form = if/when + present simple/continuous + will / be going to).
  *If you **go** away to study, you'**ll meet** a lot of new people.*
  *I'**m going to** start without him if he **doesn't come** soon.*
- The second conditional is used to talk about unlikely or imaginary states or events in the present or future (form = if + past simple/continuous + would/could/should/might).
  *If she **spoke** Spanish, she **could** apply for the job in Madrid.)*
  *They **would** leave their jobs and travel the world if they **had** the money.*
  With *be* the second conditional uses *were* instead of *was* in formal contexts.
  *If I **were/was** good at languages, I'd learn Japanese.*
- The third conditional is used to talk about imaginary states or events in the past (form = if + past perfect + would/could/should/might + have + past participle).
  *If we **had studied** other cultures at school, we **might have been** more confident about travelling.*
  *If you **had arrived** in Japan three months ago, you **would have seen** the cherry blossom.*
- Notice that when the *if* clause is first in the sentence, it is followed by a comma. There is no comma when the main clause comes first.

Mixed conditionals

Different conditional forms are sometimes mixed, particularly second and third conditionals.

- A third conditional cause is sometimes linked to a second conditional result to show the imaginary present result of an imaginary past event or situation.

Third conditional cause	Second conditional result
If my parents had never met,	I wouldn't be here now!

- A second conditional cause is sometimes linked to a third conditional result to show how an ongoing situation produced an effect in the past.

Second conditional cause	Third conditional result
If I knew about computers,	I would have applied for that IT job.

Other conditionals

There are a number of other conditional sentences formed with different patterns of tenses.

- if/when + present simple + imperative (this is used to make suggestions or to give advice or instructions).
  *If you **need** a translator, please **let** me know.*
  ***Get off** the train when you **get** to the third station.*
- if/when + present simple/present perfect + can/could/would/should/might (this is often used with suggestions or advice).
  *She **could** give Martin the message if she **sees** him later.*
  *If you'**ve studied** English, you **should** try to speak it.*
- We can use *will* after *if* in polite requests.
  *If you **will** just wait a moment, I'll tell Mr Jackson you're here.*
- To make the request more polite, we can use *would.*
  *If you **would** take a seat for a moment, I'll let Mr Jackson know you're here.*
- We can replace *if* with *should* at the beginning of the clause, particularly in very formal or literary English.
  ***Should** you wish to extend your stay, please inform reception.*
- We can use *If it was/were not for* or *had not been for* to say that one situation is dependent on another situation or person.
  *I'd go out **if it wasn't for** this rain.*
  ***If it hadn't been for** the tour guide, we would never have seen those carvings in the caves.*
- We can use *if + was/were + to + infinitive* to talk about imaginary future situations.
  ***If** the technology **were to become** available, we would be able to travel across the world in just a couple of hours.*
- We can use *if so, given, otherwise* and *provided* instead of *if*. We can use *unless* instead of *if … not.*
  ***Given** the increase in social-networking sites, it's easy to make new friends from around the world.*
  *I don't want to go **unless** you come with me.*

Unit 2
Dependent prepositions

A preposition is usually a word that expresses the relation between two events, things or people. They can be used to talk about time, space, or other relations.
*She is **in** Tokyo. (place)*
*She is having lunch **at** 2 o'clock. (time)*
*Paris is the capital **of** France. (possession)*
However, some verbs which take an object are often followed by a **dependent preposition.** We need to use this preposition between the verb and the object, and usually, there is no choice about what preposition to use. We need to think of this verb + preposition combination as one phrase. We need to learn each verb + preposition individually. It is helpful to group verbs according to the preposition they take.

Verbs with *for*
Thank you **for** your email.
I apologise **for** the delay.
I opted **for** extra English lessons.

Verbs with *in*
Meals are included **in** the price.
I don't believe **in** lying.
I took part **in** a marathon last year.

Verbs with *to*
I look forward **to** meeting you.

Verbs with *on*
I drew **on** my experiences to write the essay.

Verbs with *with*
I was provided **with** lots of information.

Verbs with *of*
She reminded me **of** my mother.

Unit 3
Wishes and regrets

wish and *if only*

- *wish* / *if only* + past simple is used to express a wish or regret about a general state that exists in the present, or a usual or regular event or habit.
  He wishes he was a photographer instead of an actor.
  If only we had longer holidays.

- *wish* / *if only* + *would* is also used to express a wish or regret about a usual or regular event or habit. We use *would* when the person or thing doing the action could change their behaviour if they chose to. It is often used to complain about someone's behaviour.
  If only the children **would** be quiet.
  I wish you would look for a job.

- *wish* / *if only* + past perfect is used to express a wish or regret about the past by saying how we would like the past to be different.
  I wish I had trained as a doctor instead of as a teacher.

- *wish* + infinitive with *to* is used in more formal situations to mean *want* + infinitive. It can be used to talk about the past, present or future.
  Napoleon **wished to keep** his battle plans a secret until the very last moment.

- Note that when people talk about their wishes for the future, the verb *hope* is more often used.
  I hope you enjoy your stay in our town.
  She **hopes** to get a job in television.

would rather / would prefer

- *would rather* + infinitive without *to* is used to express a preference about a general situation or event, or about a possible future situation or event.
  I'd rather work days than nights.

- *would prefer* + infinitive with *to* is also used to express a preference about a general situation or event, or about a possible future situation or event.
  I'd prefer to travel with a group of people.

- *would rather* + subject + present/past simple is used to express a preference for another person (or thing) to do something now or in the future. The use of the past simple expresses the preference more tentatively or politely than the present simple.
  I **would rather she works** than does nothing.
  He**'d rather you didn't tell** anyone about the interview yet.

- *would prefer* + *it if* + object + past simple is used in the same way.
  I**'d prefer it if the interviewer asked** a range of questions.
  I**'d prefer it if they didn't always focus** on the same things

- In formal contexts, the subjunctive is used with *would rather*. Instead of the present simple we use the infinitive without *to*; past subjunctive is the same as past simple except for *be*, where the past subjunctive always uses *were*.
  I**'d rather he go** now.
  I**'d rather she were** happy in her work.

- *would rather* + *have* + past participle is used to express a preference for one situation or outcome in the past over another.
  When he was young, he**'d rather have been** a photographer than an actor.

- *would rather* + subject + past perfect is used to express a wish or preference that actions or events in the past were different.
  I**'d rather you had asked** me before borrowing the car yesterday.
  I**'d rather it hadn't rained** all through the holiday.

It's time …

There are several different structures that can be used with *it's time*. The meanings are very similar – that the time is right for something to happen.

It's time +	
infinitive with *to*	**It's time to go** home now.
object + infinitive	**It's time for us to go** home now.
subject + past simple	**It's time we went** home now.
subject + past continuous	**It's time we were going** home now.

- To say that something should have been done already, *about time* and *high time* can be used. These also use the past simple.
  It's about time we went home.
  It's high time we went home.

Unit 4
Modals and semi-modals (1)

Modal and semi-modal verbs give an indication of a speaker's attitude and of the relationship between the speaker and listener.

Ability

- *can* expresses ability in the present; *could* expresses general ability in the past.
  He's lucky he **can** remember facts very easily.
  When I was a child I **could** speak Welsh but now I've forgotten it completely.

- To talk about an achievement or something that was done with difficulty, we use *was/were able to* + infinitive.
  *She **was able to memorise** all the words before the test.*
- We can also use *was/were able to* to express that someone was successful in doing something on one occasion.
  ***Were you able to** get his autograph after the concert?*

Permission

- *can* is often used to express permission; *can't* is often used to express prohibition in the present and in general time; *could* and *couldn't* are used to express permission and prohibition in the past.
  *You **can** leave whenever you want.* (permission)
  *In the UK, children **can't** leave school until they are 16.* (prohibition)
  *In the 1950s, children in the UK **could** leave school at 14.* (permission)
  *In the 1950s in the UK, young adults **couldn't** vote until they were 21.* (prohibition)
- *may* is sometimes used to express permission and prohibition in the present. It is more formal than *can*.
  *Members **may not** wear jeans or T-shirts at formal ceremonies.*

Requests, suggestions and polite orders

- *can* and *could* are both used to make offers and requests and to give polite orders and suggestions: *can* is informal; *could* is neutral.
  ***Can/Could** I help you with that?* (offer)
  ***Can/Could** you test me on these words?* (request)
  *You **can/could** check the recipe and find the ingredients while I wash up.* (polite order/suggestion)
- *might* is sometimes used to request permission, but only in very formal situations.
  ***Might** I be allowed to give an opinion on this matter?*
  ***Might** I suggest that we take a vote on this proposal?*

Possibility and probability

- *may/might/could* are used to speculate about the present and future: *might* indicates a lower probability or more uncertainty than *may* or *could*; *couldn't* indicates almost total certainty, much greater than *may not* or *might not*.
  *They **could** decide to take the train.* (possible)
  *She **may** get here on time if she catches the early train.* (possible)
  *She **might** get here on time if she catches the later train.* (less probable)
  *She **couldn't** arrive before 10 – it's impossible.* (certain)
- *may/might/could have* + past participle are used to speculate about the past.
  *They're late. They **may have been** held up in the rush hour traffic.*
  *I left a message at their hotel but they **might not have got** it yet.*
  *They **couldn't have met** by coincidence in London – it's too big.*

- *may/might/could* + *have* + past participle are used to talk about possibilities in the past that we know didn't actually happen. The context has to be examined to decide whether the structure has this meaning or whether it expresses speculation about something that did actually happen.
  *Didn't you use a map? You **might have got lost**.* (But you didn't.)
  *She was very intelligent and **could have gone** to university.* (But she didn't.)
- *can't* is used to express negative certainty about the present based on evidence.
  *This bill **can't** be right. We've only had two coffees!*
- *can't* + *have* + past participle is used to express negative certainty about the past based on evidence.
  *This doesn't taste right. They **can't have followed** the recipe.*
- *can/could* are used to talk about theoretical possibility; *could* indicates less confidence than *can*.
  *The school **can** take 1,000 pupils – it usually does.*
  *The school **could** take 1,000 pupils but it would be difficult in terms of space.*
- *may/might/could* + *be* + verb + *-ing* are used to speculate about events and situations in the immediate present and in the future.
  *Where's Sam? He **might be studying** in his room.*
  *Fiona **could be managing** her own company a year from now.*

Obligation

- *must / have to* are used to say what you think is necessary, or to recommend someone else to do something.
  *You **must** remember to email Jelena.*
- *have to* (not *must*) is used to say what someone else has told you to do. The speaker is not giving their own opinion.
  *I **have to** write 500 words for my project.*

Necessity

- *need to / don't need to* + infinitive are used to say what is necessary.
  *You **need to** make three copies of this.*
  *You **needn't** hurry.*
- *didn't need to* is used to say that it wasn't necessary to do something, so you didn't.
  *I **didn't need to** go to the bank.* (So I didn't.)
- *needn't have* + past participle is used to say you did something but it wasn't necessary.
  *I **needn't have gone** to the bank.* (I went to the bank but it wasn't necessary.)

Unit 5
Relative clauses

Defining relative clauses

- Defining relative clauses give essential information so that we can identify who or what is being talked about. The relative clause follows immediately after the noun referring to the person(s) or thing(s) we are talking about.
  ***The woman who showed the most determination** got the job.*

- We do not put commas at the beginning or end of a defining relative clause.
- We can sometimes omit the relative pronoun. The relative pronoun must be used when it is the subject of the following verb.
  *She showed me photos of the gorillas (**which/that**) she had studied.*
  *She showed me photos of the gorillas **which/that** lived nearby.* (The relative pronoun must be used here because it is the subject of *lived*.)

Non-defining relative clauses

- Non-defining relative clauses give non-essential, extra information about something or someone.
  *Her CV, **which made a big impression on the interviewers**, helped her get the job.*
- We use a comma before and immediately after the clause.
- We cannot omit the relative pronoun in non-defining relative clauses.

Relative pronouns

Many relative clauses are introduced by a relative pronoun.

- *which* and *that* refer to things but *that* is not used in non-defining relative clauses.
  *The study **that** she published last month is remarkable.*
  *Her most recent study, **which** she's just published, is her best yet.*
- *who* refers to people.
  *Dian, **who** has been working in the IT department for two years, has been promoted.*
- *whom* refers to people if they are the object of the clause. It is formal and not common in modern English.
  *Professor West, **with whom** I worked recently, has won the Nobel Prize.*
- *whose* can be used with things or people and expresses possession or belonging.
  *She is a scientist **whose** work is world famous.*
- *when* refers to time.
  *She described the moment **when** she first saw her baby daughter.*
- *where* refers to place.
  *She spent many years in China, **where** she worked in a bank.*

Prepositions in relative clauses

- Prepositions can be placed at the end of the sentence in neutral and informal English. Formal sentences are often constructed to place the preposition earlier in the sentence.

That was the story **which** the film was based **on**.	That was the story **on which** the film was based.

- When the preposition is placed earlier in the sentence, *that* cannot be used.

That's the research **that/which** she received the award **for**.	That is the research **for which** she received the award.

- When the preposition is placed earlier in the sentence, *whom* must be used as the relative pronoun when the object is a person.

She spoke to a professor **that/who** she is friendly **with**.	She spoke to a professor **with whom** she is friendly.

Unit 6
Phrasal verbs (1)

Phrasal verbs are verbs + particles (a preposition or an adverb).

- An adverb modifies an action. It gives extra information about the time, place, manner, frequency, etc. of an event or process.
  *Please sit **down**.* (*down* shows the direction of the action *sit*)
  *She followed **out** the instructions.* (*out* gives the meaning of something being done until it is finished)
  *The coach broke **down** on the way to the concert.* (*down* gives the meaning of something being damaged or destroyed)
- Phrasal verbs can be used with or without an object.
  *He **went in**.* (*go in* is not used with an object)
  *He **went in** the house.* (*go in* is used with an object)
  *Are we going to **go for** the salmon or the beef?* (*go for* is used with an object)
  NOT *I am going to go for.* (*go for* cannot be used without an object)
- With some phrasal verbs, the position of the object can vary.
  *She followed **out** the instructions.*
  NOT *She followed the instructions **out**.*
- With some phrasal verbs, the verb and the particle cannot be separated.
  *Are we going to **go for** the salmon or the beef?*
  NOT *Are we going to go the salmon or the beef for?*
- Three-word verbs can consist of a phrasal verb + preposition.
  *I **look forward to** meeting you.*
  *I've always **looked up to** her.*
- With phrasal verbs, it is not always possible to work out the meaning by looking at its parts.
  go in = enter
  go for = choose
  look up to = admire

There are many phrasal verbs in English and they are most frequently, though not exclusively, used in spoken English and in more informal writing. They are made up of more than one part: verbs with prepositional or adverbial particles. Their meanings are not always obvious from the meaning of its components. It is best to learn them as individual items. There is often a single word with the same meaning which is preferred in more formal writing.

The football match has been **put off** until next week.	The football match has been **postponed** until next week.
The price of petrol has **gone up** three times already this year.	The price of petrol has **increased** three times already this year.

- Many phrasal verbs have more than one meaning, and more than one form.

He asked her to stop singing as it was **putting** him **off**.	= distract (can be separated by an object)
The football match has been **put off** until next week.	= postpone (cannot be separated by an object)
Don't be **put off** if you can't do it straight away.	= disappointed (cannot be separated by an object)

- Some can have their object before or after the particle.
  *We **did** our bathroom **up** last year.*
  *We **did up** our bathroom last year.*
- If the object is a pronoun, it must go between the two parts of the verb.
  *We **did** it **up** by ourselves.*

Unit 7
Reason, result and purpose

Conjunctions and adverbs
The following conjunctions and adverbs show relationships between cause and effect.
*She got to the top in her career **because** she spoke to all the right people.*
*He is ambitious, **so** he doesn't mind staying late at work most evenings.*
*She decided to do an evening course in book-keeping **so as to** be better able to help her brother with his new business.*

Prepositions
The following prepositions introduce cause.
*Rosie got the job **because of** her pleasant manner.*
***Owing to** the storms, all trains have been cancelled.*
*I couldn't sleep **for** worrying.*

Verbs and verb phrases
- The following verbs introduce effect (= consequences or results).
  *Summer clubs for school students in the UK **have led to** a decrease in the crime rate.*
  *A poor diet **will result in** health problems.*
- The following verbs introduce cause.
  *Her attitude **stems from** her background.*
  *The success of the company **is based on** the employees' hard work and enthusiasm.*
- Participle clauses can also express cause and effect.
  ***Having done** extensive market research, the company was confident its new product would succeed.*
  ***Having studied** Spanish and Portuguese, Anna is keen to go to South America.*

Nouns and noun phrases
- The following nouns can refer to cause and effect: *aim, basis, consequence, explanation, motive, outcome, purpose, reason, result.*
  ***The aim of** the programme was to give students work experience.*
  *His laziness is **the reason why** he is not as successful as he could be.*
  *Jack's business venture could be said to have benefited **as a result of** being in the right place at the right time.*
  *Pauline did very well in her final accountancy exams **with the result that** she was easily able to find work with a good company.*

Unit 8
Modals and semi-modals (2)

must
- *must* can be used to express obligation; *mustn't* expresses prohibition. The past form of *must* used to express obligation is *had to*.
  *You **must** do exactly what the exam questions ask you to do.*
  *You **mustn't** talk during the exam.*
  *We **had to** write two compositions in last week's exam.*
- *must* can also be used to make deductions from evidence and expresses certainty. The past form of *must* for deduction is *must + have + past participle*. We use *must be going to + infinitive* to make deductions about the future. The negative of *must* for this meaning is *can't* (see Unit 4).
  *That **must** be John coming up the steps – I recognise his footsteps!*
  *The train is late – the heavy snow **must have caused** delays.*
  *They bought lots of paint – they **must be going to decorate**.*
- *must* and *mustn't* are used to give strong advice.
  *You **mustn't** give up hope.*
- *must* and *mustn't* are used to make recommendations.
  *You **must** see his new film – it's brilliant!*
- *must* and *mustn't* are used to talk about strong necessity.
  *We **must** go or we'll miss the train.*

ought to and *should*
- *ought to* or *should* are used to say the following (*should* is more common and less formal).

something seems likely because it is logical or normal	*It's 6 o'clock. He **ought to/ should** be home soon.*
give advice or suggest that something would be a good idea	*You **ought to/should** tell her how you feel.*
talk about duty and express weak obligation	*People **ought to/should** wait in the queue and not push in.*
criticise actions or attitudes	*People **ought to/should** show more respect for old people.*
talk about the importance of doing something	*We **ought to/should** get back before the sun goes down.*
to talk about necessity	*Sports clothes **ought to/ should** be light and allow you to move easily.*

- The past forms are *ought to/should + have + past participle.*
  *You **ought to have/should have told** us you were coming.*

will and *would*
- *will* and *would* are used to make polite invitations and requests. *Would* is more polite.
  ***Will/Would** you sit here, please?*
- *will* and *won't* are used to describe habits and characteristic behaviour in the present and in general. If *will* is stressed, it indicates the speaker's irritation with or negative opinion of the habit.
  *He **will**/'**ll** watch TV all evening. Sometimes he **won't** talk for hours.*
  *He **will** play golf every weekend, instead of helping me in the garden.*

- *would* and *wouldn't* are used to talk about past habits and characteristics. If *would* is stressed, it indicates the speaker's irritation with or negative opinion of the habit.
  *Every evening she **would**/'**d** sit in the garden reading her newspaper. She **wouldn't** stop until she'd read every page.*
  *He **would** insist on smoking, even if he knew if was bad for him.*

- *will* is used to express demands, insist that something happens in the future, or express determination.
  *You **will** do as I say immediately!*
  *I **will**/'**ll** go where I want and don't try to stop me!*

Unit 9
Future forms

will

- *will* is used to talk about a future action or event at the point of decision.
  *I**'ll** come to the cinema with you tonight, I think.*

- It is used to make predictions about the future.
  *You **will** meet a tall, dark stranger.*

- It is used to make promises.
  *I**'ll** buy you a car for your birthday.*

going to

- *going to* is used to talk about intentions. Sometimes it is used to talk about plans and arrangements based on intentions (but the present continuous is more commonly used for talking about arrangements).
  *We're **going to** visit our friends in New Zealand next winter.*

- *going to* is also used to talk about future events and actions based on present evidence, especially when we can see that the event is imminent.
  *The way Brazil are playing at the moment, they're **going to** win the match.*
  *Watch out! We're **going to** hit that tree!*

Present continuous form

- The present continuous form is used to talk about plans and arrangements for the future. A time reference often makes the future meaning clear.
  *What **are you doing tonight**?*
  *We're **meeting** early **tomorrow** morning.*

Present simple form

- The present simple form is used to talk about timetables and schedules.
  *Our train **leaves** at 6.30 tomorrow morning.*

- It is used with future references in subordinate clauses after time conjunctions such as *when, before, until, as soon as.*
  *We'll reply **when** we **hear** from you.*
  *I hope you'll write to us **as soon as** you **get** home.*

be + infinitive

- *be* + infinitive is formal. It is used in rules or instructions, or to talk about official plans. It is particularly common in news reports.
  *Staff **are not to use** company telephones for personal calls.*
  *The Prime Minister **is to visit** South America next month.*

Future continuous

- The future continuous focuses on an action or event in progress at a specific time in the future.
  *This time next week I**'ll be lying** on a beach in the sun.*

Future perfect

- The future perfect looks forward to a future time and then looks back from that point.
  *By the end of next year we**'ll have finished** the project.*

Future in the past

- The form *was/were going to* or *would* + verb is used to look back to a past time and talk about the future as it was at that past time.
  *By the time I left school I knew I **was going to become** a doctor.*
  *I thought it **would be** cold today, but it isn't.*

Unit 10
Participle clauses

There are different participle forms.

Present active	washing
Present passive	being washed
Past	washed
Perfect active	having washed
Perfect passive	having been washed

- Participle clauses with a present participle can be used adjectivally.
  *Look at that man **sitting** in the corner.* (= who is sitting)
  *What's the name of the girl **being interviewed** by the journalist?* (= who is being interviewed)

- All participle clauses can be used adverbially.
  ***Feeling exhausted** after the flight, I went to bed as soon as I got to the hotel.* (= Because I felt exhausted)
  ***Washed** by hand, this jersey will keep its shape for years.* (= If it is washed by hand)

- Perfect participle clauses are often adverbial clauses showing when or why something happened.
  ***Having made** your decision, it is not possible to change your mind.* (= When you have made)
  ***Having spent** happy holidays in Spain as a child, she was keen to return there with her own family.* (= Because she had spent)

- The subject of the participle clause is usually the same as that of the main clause. However, it is possible to have participle clauses with a different subject.
  ***There being no money left**, we had to start making our way home.* (= Because there was no money left)
  ***It being too late** to get a bus, we took a taxi.* (= Because it was too late)

- When the participle clause describes a situation, a different subject can be introduced using *with.*
  *I was beginning to get a headache **with** the children all talking at the same time.*
  ***With** it / It being Sunday in New Zealand, we couldn't find any shops open.*

Unit 11
Reported speech

Grammatical changes

Some features of grammar in direct speech must be changed in reported speech.

- When we report what someone said, we tend to change the verb tense, which is called 'backshift'. Personal pronouns, demonstratives and other references to the 'here and now' may also change.

'I've seen a bank clerk wearing a nose ring.'	→ *She said that she'd seen a bank clerk wearing a nose ring.*
'I'll be arriving at your house at 10 tomorrow.'	→ *She said that she would be arriving at my house at 10 the next day.*

- Most modal verbs do not usually change, but *can* changes to *could* and *will* changes to *would*.

'You must dress professionally at all times.'	→ *He told us we must dress professionally at all times.*
'You should have a dress code.'	→ *She suggested that we should have a dress code.*
'I can pay cash.'	→ *He said he could pay cash.*
'I'll pay by credit card.'	→ *He said he'd pay by credit card.*

- When something is reported that is a general truth, or if the situation hasn't changed yet, there is often no tense change.

'Darker clothes look smarter.'	→ *She said that darker clothes look smarter.*
'I want to be a dress designer when I grow up.'	→ *My neighbour's four-year-old told me she wants to be a dress designer when she grows up.*

- In reported questions, the subject usually comes before the verb. The auxiliaries *do*, *does* and *did* are only used in negative reported questions. *Yes/No* questions are reported with *if* or *whether*. Question marks are not used in reported questions.

'Which suit do you prefer?'	→ *She asked (me) which suit I preferred.*
'Why don't you like shopping?'	→ *He asked (me) why I didn't like shopping.*
'Could you help me choose some new shoes?'	→ *She asked (me) if/whether I could help her choose some new shoes.*

Reporting verbs

We can use a wide variety of verbs to introduce reported information. Different verbs are followed by different structures.

Note: *that* may be omitted after many reporting verbs.

advise + object + *to* + infinitive	She **advised** us to check the contract carefully.
agree (+ *that*) *agree* + *to* + infinitive	He **agreed** (that) our money would be refunded. He **agreed** to refund our money.
ask + *if/whether* *ask* + *to* + infinitive	We **asked** if we could have more training. We **asked** to have more training.
complain + *that*	We **complained** that the service was very slow.

deny (+ *that*) *deny* + *-ing*	She **denied** (that) she had taken the credit card. She **denied** taking the credit card.
insist (+ *that*) *insist* + *on* + *-ing*	He **insisted** (that) we stay at his house. He **insisted** on our staying at his house.
invite + object + *to* + infinitive	She **invited** us to visit any time.
offer + *to* + infinitive	They have **offered** to help.
promise (+ *that*) *promise* + *to* + infinitive	The management has **promised** (that) training will be provided. The management has **promised** to provide training.
recommend (+ *that*) *recommend* + *-ing*	I **recommend** (that) you book well in advance. I **recommend** booking well in advance.
regret (+ *that*) *regret* + *-ing*	He **regrets** (that) he won't be able to attend the ceremony. He **regrets** not being able to attend the ceremony.
say (+ *that*)	The manager **said** (that) we should arrange an appointment.
suggest + object (+ *that*) *suggest* + *-ing*	She **suggested** (that) I (should) buy the black jeans. She **suggested** buying the black jeans.
tell + object (+ *that*) *tell* + object + *to* + infinitive	His sister **told** him (that) he should get a job. His sister **told** him to get a job.
threaten (+ *that*) *threaten* + *to* + infinitive	The bank manager **threatened** (that) she would take away my credit card. The bank manager **threatened** to take away my credit card.
warn + object (+ *that*) *warn* + object + *to* + infinitive *warn* + object + *about* + *-ing*	She **warned** me (that) credit cards were expensive. She **warned** me not to use credit cards. She **warned** me about using credit cards.

Unit 12
-ing forms

With verbs

- The *-ing* form can be the subject or the object of a verb.
 Travelling broadens *the mind.* (subject)
 I dislike ***travelling*** *by ship.* (object)
- Common verbs which are followed by an *-ing* form include: *admit, avoid, consider, delay, deny, dislike, enjoy, imagine, mind, miss, practise, resent, risk, suggest.*
- Some verbs can also be followed by an infinitive with no change in meaning: *begin, hate, like, love, prefer, start.*
 She began ***to feel*** *sleepy. / She* began ***feeling*** *sleepy.*
- Some verbs can also be followed by an infinitive, but the meaning is different: *forget, regret, remember, stop, try.*
 He tried ***to do*** *it in a different way.* (he attempted it, but we don't know if he did it)
 He tried ***doing*** *it in a different way.* (he actually tested a different method, but we don't know if the new method was any better or worse)

- Verbs which are followed by the *-ing* form can also be used in the passive (*being* + past participle).
  She <u>enjoys</u> **being looked after**.
- The verbs *need*, *want* and *require* can be followed by *-ing*, but they have a passive meaning.
  The machine <u>needs</u>/<u>wants</u>/<u>requires</u> **servicing**. (The machine needs to be serviced.)

After prepositions
- The *-ing* form can be the object of a preposition. The *-ing* form (rather than the infinitive) always follows a preposition.
  He isn't interested <u>in</u> **listening** to stories.
  They apologised <u>for</u> **being** late.

After common phrases
The *-ing* form follows some common phrases.
<u>It's worth</u> **getting** a book about the country before you go.
I play the guitar <u>as well as</u> **playing** the saxophone.
<u>It's no good/use</u> **crying**. It won't change anything.
<u>There's no point</u> **waiting** because he's not coming.
Let's take the car <u>instead of</u> **walking** in the rain.
I <u>can't help</u> **laughing** whenever I see that film.
After a few years of travelling by tube, I'm <u>used to</u> people **ignoring** each other.

After determiners
- The *-ing* form can be used after determiners in more formal English to show the possessive.
  Does <u>my</u> **listening** to the radio bother you?

Unit 13
Past tenses and the present perfect

Past time can be expressed in many different ways in English.

Past simple
- The past simple is used to talk about a completed action, event or situation at a particular time or over a particular time in the past.
  The train **left** at 8.30 am.

- It is used to talk about repeated actions in the past.
  He **read** a chapter of the book every night before going to sleep.
  We **went** to the beach at weekends in the summer.

Past continuous
- The past continuous cannot be used with stative verbs (*be, know, love*, etc.), which describe a state rather than an action. With stative verbs, the past simple is used.
- It is used to talk about a situation or action in progress around a point in time in the past.
  I **was living** in London when Prince William married Kate Middleton.

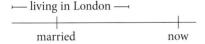

- It is used to talk about a situation or action in progress that is interrupted by another event.
  While I **was thinking** about the problem, I suddenly had the most amazing idea.
  The plane **was coming** in to land when it was struck by lightning.
- It is used to emphasise that two situations or events were happening simultaneously.
  While I **was trying** to phone her, she **was trying** to phone me!
- It is used with *always* and *forever* to talk about repeated actions or behaviour.
  They **were forever asking** for favours, but they never did anything for anyone else.
  She **was always offering** to babysit so that my husband and I could go out.

Present perfect simple
The present perfect simple is used to talk about past events or situations in a time period that extends from the past up to the present. It is often used to talk about experience. The specific time is unknown or unimportant and we do not use it with words which mark the specific moment when the event happened (e.g. *yesterday, last year*). It is also used to say how many times something has happened in that period.
I'**ve been** to Russia three times since 2003. I went last in 2013.

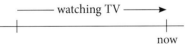

- It is used to talk about an event in the past that has a result in the present. The focus is on the effect or importance of the past event at the present moment. The event is often, but not always, in the recent past. The specific time is unknown or unimportant. We do not use words which mark specific points in time like *yesterday* or *last year*.
  Cancel the skiing trip – I'**ve broken** my leg.
- It is used to talk about the duration of an event or situation which started in the past and extends up to the present. The specific starting point or the length of the period is given.
  I'**ve lived** here since I was four.

Present perfect continuous
The present perfect continuous cannot be used with stative verbs (*be, know, love*, etc.), which describe a state rather than an action. With stative verbs, the present perfect simple is used.
- It is used to talk about past events which continue up to the present or up to a time in the recent past.
  I'**ve been watching** this film on TV but I'm going to turn it off if something doesn't happen soon.

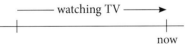

She's **been helping** me with the housework but now she's got bored with it.
- It is used to talk about repeated past events in a time period that extends up to the present.
  The car **has been breaking down** a lot recently.

- It is used to talk about an event, action or behaviour in the recent past that has a result in the present. The action may be finished or unfinished. In this use, the focus is on the present evidence for the past event. The specific time is unknown or unimportant and we do not use words which mark specific points in time.
  It's been raining. (The rain has stopped but the streets are wet.)
  *You look exhausted. **Have you been working** hard?*
- It is used to talk about the duration of an event or situation which started in the past and extends up to the present. The specific starting point or the length of the period is given.
  Has she been writing *her novel for a long time?*
  She's been working *on it for about six years.*

Past perfect simple
The past perfect simple can be used in similar ways to the present perfect simple, but instead of referring to actions or events up to the present, it refers to actions or events before a particular time (or before another event or action at a particular time) in the past.
*I'd only just **sat down** at my desk when my boss started asking me where the letters were.*

I sat down	boss started	now

*Before I was 18, I **hadn't been** outside my home town.* (experience)
*When I got home, I realised I **had left** my key at the office, so I couldn't get into my flat.* (cause)
*I'd **lived** in the house since I was a child and was sorry to leave.* (duration)

- Unlike the present perfect, the past perfect can refer to specific times in the past.
  *We already felt like old friends even though we **had** only **met** that morning.*
  *He asked me when exactly I **had** first **heard** about the problem.*

Past perfect continuous
The past perfect continuous cannot be used with stative verbs (*be, know, love*, etc.), which describe a state rather than an action. With stative verbs, the past perfect simple is used.

- It can be used in similar ways to the present perfect continuous, but instead of referring to actions or events up to the present, it refers to actions or events up to a particular time (or up to another event or action at a particular time) in the past.
  *They **had been planning** their expedition for months before I joined their team.* (duration)

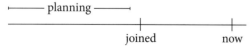

*The government **had been watching** the situation closely and were considering whether to intervene.* (continuous action)
*She'd **been helping** at a charity soup kitchen on and off for a few months.* (repeated action)

- Unlike the present perfect continuous, the past perfect continuous can refer to specific past times.
  *At breakfast I wondered why I felt so tired, then I remembered that at 2 o'clock, I'd **been listening** to my neighbours arguing again.*

Unit 14
The passive

When to use the passive
- We use the passive when the action is more important than the person or thing doing the action (the agent).
- We often use the passive when the agent is unknown.
- The passive is often used in more formal situations, such as lectures, academic writing and news reports.

How to form the passive
- The passive is usually formed by moving the object to the front of the sentence. Because of this, usually only transitive verbs (verbs which have an object) can become passive. We cannot say ~~It has been happened~~ because *happen* is intransitive.
- Some intransitive phrasal verbs can also be passives.
  He woke up because of the noise. (active)
  *He **was woken up** by the noise.* (passive)
- Passives use the verb *to be* + past participle.

	active	passive
present continuous	Someone is doing it.	It **is being done.**
present perfect	Someone has done it.	It **has been done.**
past simple	Someone did it.	It **was done.**
past continuous	Someone was doing it.	It **was being done.**
past perfect simple	Someone had done it.	It **had been done.**
modal verbs	Someone will do it.	It **will be done.**
past modal verbs	Someone might have done it.	It **might have been done.**

- When a verb has two objects, either object can be the subject of a passive clause. The object that is more important to the message of the sentence is generally the subject.
  *Jill **gave** her brother the money.*
  → *Her brother **was given** the money.*
  → *The money **was given** to her brother.*
- We can use passive verb + *by* + agent, when the agent is important to the message.
  *Her portrait **was painted by Picasso.***
  *She's **been awarded** a medal **by the Queen.***

Reporting information

We can use the passive form of reporting verbs to give ideas or opinions without saying exactly where the ideas come from.

- Verbs typically used in the passive for this purpose include: *assume, believe, claim, consider, feel, hope, report, say, think.* We can use *it* + passive (+ *that*) + active clause, where *it* is an impersonal pronoun that does not refer to a real subject (like in *It's raining.*).
  It is said (that) most computer users are women.
  It is thought (that) there are 2.5 billion internet users in the world.
- We can use passive + *to* + infinitive.
- We can use *there* + passive + *to* + infinitive (usually *be*).
  There is reported to be an increasing threat to our ecosystem.
  There are believed to be more than 600 species of trees per hectare in tropical rain forests.
- We can use passive + perfect infinitive, which indicates that the event has already occurred.
  People **are said to have begun** writing 6,000 years ago.
  Language **is thought to have emerged** 50,000 years ago.
  There is more information about the passive *-ing* form in the Grammar folder for Unit 12.

have/get something *done*

- We use the construction subject + *have/get* + object + past participle to say that the subject arranges for something to be done by someone else. The same construction is used to say that something is done to a person or thing belonging to the subject of *have/get.*
  I'm going to have/get my hair cut.
  She's going to have/get her portrait painted.
  There are some differences in meaning when using *have/get.*
- We use *have something done* to imply that the subject of the sentence is not responsible for, or has little control over what happens. However, *get* can also be used in sentences like these in informal spoken English. We also tend to use *have* to focus on the result of an action (rather than the action itself).
  I **had/got my passport stolen** while I was away.
  She **had/got her wisdom teeth taken out** last year.
  I'll **have/get the report finished** by tomorrow morning.
- We use *get something done* to imply that the subject of the sentence causes something to happen (perhaps accidentally) or they are to blame for it.
  I'll **get the letters sent** to you today.
  I never **get** invited to parties.

won't have

- *won't have* + object + present participle / past participle. This can be used to say that we will not allow someone to do something, or something to happen.
  I **won't have you watching** TV all day.
  She **won't have her holiday ruined** by them.

want something done

- *want* + object + past participle. This can be used to say that we would like someone to do something or we would like something to happen.
  I **want the report finished** by next Monday.
  Put your car in my garage. We **don't want it damaged** in the street.

Unit 15
The infinitive

The infinitive in English is the base form of the verb. It is called the full infinitive when *to* is used before the verb and the bare infinitive when there is no *to.*
*I want **to watch** the film tonight. (full infinitive with *to*)
*Let me **see** the newspaper. (bare infinitive without *to*)

The full infinitive is used:

- after certain verbs. Common examples include *afford, agree, appear, ask, choose, expect, help, hope, intend, prefer, pretend, promise, seem, want.*
  I <u>asked</u> **to see** the head teacher.
  We <u>expect</u> **to arrive** by eight.
- after impersonal *it* + *be* + adjective where the adjective describes the event that follows.
  <u>It was good</u> **to see** her again.
  <u>It's always interesting</u> **to hear** your views on life.
- after *have* + noun.
  I <u>have no wish</u> **to be** difficult.
  We <u>have plans</u> **to get** married.
- after certain verbs in the pattern verb + someone + *to do* something. Common examples include *allow, ask, beg, encouraged, force, persuade, teach.*
  My mother <u>persuaded me</u> **to buy** a computer.
- after the verbs above when we use them in the passive.
  I <u>was persuaded</u> **to buy** a computer.
- after *be* with the meaning of a formal instruction or information about the future.
  You <u>are</u> **to report** here at 8 tomorrow morning.
- to express purpose.
  She's saving her money **to go on holiday**.

The bare infinitive is used:

- after verbs which follow the pattern verb + someone + *do* something. Common examples include *have, let, make.*
  I'll <u>have the waiter</u> **bring** us more water.
  His father <u>lets him</u> **play** football.
- after modal verbs (but remember that some semi-modals contain *to: have to do, ought to do* and *need to do*).
  We <u>might</u> **go** to Italy on holiday this year.
  We <u>should</u> **get** some brochures.

Unit 16
Inversion

For emphasis, certain adverbs and adverbial phrases can be put at the beginning of a sentence or clause with an inversion of the following verb; the position of the subject and verb is the same as in question forms. These structures are often used in literary or formal contexts. The adverbials are referred to as *broad negatives* and have negative or restricted meanings.

Forms of inversion

- When the verb is used in a form with an auxiliary, the structure is adverbial + auxiliary + subject + main verb.
  Hardly had I started speaking when he interrupted me.

- When the verb is used in a form with more than one auxiliary, the structure is adverbial + first auxiliary + subject + other auxiliaries + main verb.
  Never have I been introduced to so many people in a single night.
- With present/past simple, the structure is adverbial + *do/did* + subject + main verb.
  Never did he consider he might be discovered.
- With the simple form of *be*, the main verb is placed before the subject.
  Rarely was he at home.
- Common examples of adverbials used in these structures are shown below.
  Little <u>did I</u> ever imagine that I would one day be working here myself.
  Never <u>have I</u> seen anything more remarkable.
  No sooner <u>had she</u> walked in the room than everyone fell silent.
  Not only <u>did he</u> cook dinner for everyone **but** he **also** tidied the kitchen after everyone had gone home.
  On no account <u>am I</u> going to tell him what I think of him.
  Seldom <u>have I</u> encountered such rudeness!
  Under no circumstances <u>could we</u> ever agree to such an arrangement.

There are other adverbials which are followed by different patterns of inversion.
So alarmed <u>was he</u> **that** he fell from his horse.
Only after this project is completed <u>could we</u> contemplate taking on something new.
Not until you convince me that you are committed <u>will I</u> give you my agreement.

Unit 17
Articles

There are many different rules about the use of articles in English. Here are some of the points which cause difficulty for advanced learners of English.

- No article is used before uncountable and plural nouns when used in a general sense.
  I like music.
  She's interested in animals and wants to be a vet.
- When there is a following phrase or clause specifying exactly what is being talked about, the definite article is required before uncountable and plural nouns.
  *I like **the** music they play at the jazz club in town.*
  *Are **the** animals in the rainforest safe in their environment?*
- *a* or *an* is used the first time a singular countable noun is mentioned, but after this *the* is used since the reader or listener is clear about what is being referred to.
  ***A** bird was trapped in the room and Anna called for her brother to help her free **the** poor creature.*
- Singular countable nouns must always have an article or some other determiner (like *each, my, this*) except for a few fixed expressions like *by car, in hospital,* etc.
- *The* is not used with the names of most countries. It is, however, used with plural names or names of countries which contain a common noun.

***The** Philippines* (plural), ***The** United Kingdom* (*kingdom* = common noun), ***The** United States* (plural and state = common noun)
(Note that these nouns behave like singular nouns with verbs: ***The** United States is a huge country.*)

- *The* is used with playing instruments but no article is used with playing games.
  *Mary's hobby is playing **the** guitar and mine is playing chess.*
- *The* can often be used before *car, train, bus, plane, ferry* or *boat* when talking about the use of different types of transport in general, even when the mode of transport has not previously been referred to. *A* is also used.
  *Are you going to take **the** train / **a** train or **the** bus / **a** bus to London tomorrow?*
- Parts of the body are usually preceded by a possessive pronoun rather than an article when they are talked about in the context of their relation to a specific body or bodies. When parts of the body are talked about in general, *the* is normally used.
  *Sally has sprained **her** ankle.*
  ***The** liver is the largest organ in the body.*
- The word *own* must be preceded by a possessive pronoun rather than *the* or *a*.
  *When did you first get **your** own car?*
- When we talk about the units in which commodities are generally bought or sold, we often use *by + the*. When we talk about price, we usually use *a /an*.
  *Her parents used to buy coal **by the** ton.*
  *Those chocolates are nearly $100 **a** kilo.*
- If we miss out *a* before *few* and *little,* the meaning is changed to mean *not many / not much.*
  *She had **a** few friends.* (some)
  She had few friends. (less than you would expect)
- We use *a/an* when describing someone or something in a way that applies to others.
  *Kim is **an** interesting character.* (There are other interesting characters in the world.)

Unit 18
Emphasis

Cleft sentences
Cleft sentences create emphasis by using a relative clause. They often use *the thing / something* or *the person / someone,* etc. For more emphasis, *one thing / person,* etc. is used.
***The thing (that) I like about him** is his honesty.*
***One person (who) I can't understand** is the Prime Minister.*
- We can use *the only* or *all* to emphasise that we're excluding everything else.
  *The **only** thing that interests me is your happiness.*
  ***All** (that) I want is your happiness.*
- *The thing that* is often replaced with *what* (making a nominal relative clause).
  ***What** I really liked was the climate.*
  *The climate was **what** I really liked.*

- When we want to talk about actions in the main clause of cleft sentences, we use *be* + infinitive clause.
  *What we often do on cold, dark winter nights **is light a big fire**.*
- Cleft sentences are often formed with impersonal *it* + *be*.
  ***It was** you that created this problem, not me.*
- Cleft sentences can be used to emphasise the subject or the object of a sentence.

| My brother cut down the apple tree. | *It was my brother who cut down the apple tree.* (not someone else) |
| | *It was the apple tree that my brother cut down.* (not another tree) |

Auxiliary verbs

Auxiliary verbs in spoken English are not usually stressed (except for modal auxiliaries), and are usually contracted, e.g. *I am* becomes *I'm*. If we stress auxiliary verbs, it adds emphasis to the sentence. This emphasis is used in various ways, e.g. to show determination, to convince someone or to contradict someone.
*I **will** finish this race, or I'll die trying.*
*I **am** going to tell him. I promise.*
– I don't think she's coming.
*– She **is** coming. I know for a fact.*

- In present and past simple forms, *do* and *did* are used as stressed auxiliaries before the main verb to give emphasis.
  *I **do** enjoy a good detective novel!*
  *You **did** get permission for this, didn't you?*

Other ways of emphasising
*It's **so** good to see you.* (*so* and *such*)
*He's **such** a nice man!*
*We're **starving**!* (exaggerated vocabulary)
*She's **absolutely** wonderful.* (intensifying adverbs)
*It's **as cold as ice**!* (simile)
*Why **on Earth** did you say that?* (*on Earth*)

Unit 19
Language of persuasion

Listed below are some of the structures that can be useful for persuading people to do things. There are many other different expressions which could be added to each set. However, the lists provide an indication of the variety of language that is available.
While language used for persuasion is very sensitive to register and context, there is overlap between the lists. Some more informal phrases may be used in formal situations and vice versa. Tone of voice, for example, can also help to make something more or less formal.

Formal writing (e.g. discursive essay, business letter)
- More formal persuasive language tends to be less personal, often using passive constructions rather than *I* or *we*.
  It goes without saying that ...
  One of the most successful ways of ... is ....
  Most experts in the field agree that ...
  It cannot be denied that ...
  There is every reason to believe that ...
  The advantages of ... strongly outweigh the disadvantages.

- If the first person (*I* or *we*) is used in persuasive writing then it is likely to be supported by an objectively presented reason or example:
  ***My opinion is borne out of** research.*
  ***The point I am making** can be effectively illustrated by an example.*
  ***There are three reasons why** I hold this view.*

Formal speech
- Modals are often used to make persuasive language sound more tentative and polite.
  *How **can** I persuade you to ...*
  ***Can't** I persuade you to ...*
  ***Couldn't** you be persuaded to ...*
  *I think you **might** regret it later if you didn't ...*
  *I really think it **would** be a pity if we didn't ...*
- Questions and adverbs also can soften persuasive language to make it feel more tentative and polite.
  *But **really** the best course of action would be to ...*
  ***Possibly** the most sensible thing would be to ...*
  *But **surely** it's in our own interests to ...*
  ***Are you quite sure** you won't reconsider?*
  ***Do you think** you've taken everything into account?*

Informal and neutral speech
- Short, simple structures – often imperatives or questions – are typical in less formal persuasion.
  Come on!, Go on!, Don't be like that!, Please!, Go for it!, Please let me ..., It won't (hurt / take long / cost much)!, Do it for my sake!, Won't you ..., please?, Why don't you ...?, You're not going to let me down, are you?
- Structures that are often used in giving advice can be used for persuading in neutral speech.
  I really think you should ...
  You'd be well advised to ...

Unit 20
Hypothesising

Listed below are some of the structures that can be useful for signalling a hypothesis or a proposition. There are many other expressions which could be added to each set, but the lists provide an indication of the variety of language that is available. While language used for hypothesising is sensitive to register and context, there is overlap between the lists. Some more informal phrases may be used in formal situations and vice versa. Tone of voice, for example, can also help to make something more or less formal.

Formal writing and formal speech
- Notice the use of participle phrases to start the following sentences.
  ***Allowing for the fact (that)** eating a lot of fruit and vegetables is known to be healthy, what else might there be about these people's lifestyle that could explain their longevity?*
  ***Given that** he has been a heavy smoker since he was a teenager, it is not surprising that he is having respiratory problems now.*
  ***Speculating for a moment**, I would like to consider what might happen if we encouraged garlic as part of everyone's everyday diet.*

- Notice the use of inversion in the following sentences.
  Were we to go more deeply into this subject, we should probably come to the conclusion that people in the past became immune to many of the germs that would have a devastating effect on the pampered modern body.
  Had we access to the documents that we now know were destroyed in the fire a hundred years ago, we could be much better informed about how things really were at that time.
  If we were to go back to medieval times, we would probably be rather shocked at the level of hygiene we found.
- *Let* often introduces a hypothesis in formal speech.
  Let me describe a hypothetical case: two twins are separated at birth and are brought up in two very different homes, one in which a healthy and varied diet is the norm and the other in which the child is fed almost exclusively on junk food.
  Let us imagine/consider/suppose/assume that this house once belonged to a rich merchant, his wife and their four young children.
  Let us imagine/consider what life must have been like for women in the past.

Neutral speech and informal writing

Neutral and informal phrases tend to be shorter and simpler than those used in more formal situations.

If we had more examples of women's writing from that period, we would be much more able to comment with confidence on how things really were for them then.

I wonder if people were basically more or less stressed in past times.

Suppose you had the opportunity to go back to any period in the past, when would you choose?

What if we could be transported back to Ancient Greece? Wouldn't it be wonderful!

Just imagine having the opportunity to listen to Socrates or Plato!

If only we could know more about how ordinary people felt in the past!

Unit 21
Range of grammatical structures

- Making grammatical choices is more than simply a matter of choosing between correct and incorrect structures; you also choose from a range of structures, all of which are correct. In written English especially, too much repetition should be avoided for the sake of style, and variety is important in holding a reader's (or listener's) attention. In an exam situation, variety also allows the examiner to appreciate the breadth of knowledge the student has, but structures must be used in appropriate contexts and without errors.
- The intended meaning is the starting point of any communication. Before we can phrase our ideas, we must have a clear idea of the meaning we wish to express. Only then can we select a grammatical form that is appropriate to convey that meaning. Consider particular features of the situation you have in mind that may require the use of a particular form. For example, does it involve a relationship in time between two events, and, if so, should a perfect form be used? Or is it an event still in progress at that point,

calling for the use of a continuous form? Is there some sort of cause and effect relationship that could be described using a participle clause? Using appropriate vocabulary is essential, of course, but the choice of suitable grammatical forms is equally important.

- Bear in mind that in addition to meaning, aspects of register such as formality also need to be considered when putting an idea into words. Other features, like emphasis, may be important too.
- When a grammatical form has been selected, it is then necessary to pay close attention to how the form is constructed so as to avoid inaccuracies. It is here that small details, such as correct auxiliary verbs or choice of *-ing* forms versus infinitive, become important as they may change the apparent meaning entirely in unintended ways.

Unit 22
Interpreting and comparing

- We use *however* to indicate that one fact or idea contrasts with another, which is usually in the preceding sentence(s). As a linking device, *however* must have punctuation before and after it.

Some people feel low in energy when the light levels fall.	**However**, it is believed that low light levels make people more creative.
	It is believed, **however**, that low light levels make people more creative.

- *However* tends to be less common in neutral English, where sentences with *but* are more commonly used.
  *Some people feel low in energy when the light levels fall, **but** it is believed that low light levels make people more creative.*
- We use *because* to indicate the cause of an event or situation. It is used to link two clauses together within a single sentence. We need a comma between the clauses only if the sentence begins with *because*, not when *because* is in the second clause. We can use *Because* to start an answer to a preceding question.
  *Many animals sleep through winter **because** the temperature and light levels are so low.*
  ***Because** the temperature and light levels are so low, many animals sleep through winter.*
- Where the cause is a noun or noun phrase, we use *because of*.
  *Many animals sleep through winter **because of** the low temperature and light levels.*
  ***Because of** the low temperature and light levels, many animals sleep through winter.*
- We use *on the one hand* and *on the other hand* together to contrast or compare two facts or ideas. They are usually used in different sentences and can be several sentences apart. Used in this way, they must have punctuation before and after. Occasionally, they occur together in the same sentence with a conjunction.

*On the one hand, tanned skin can look very attractive. **On the other hand**, tanned skin tends to age faster.*	*On the one hand, tanned skin can look very attractive, **but on the other hand**, it tends to age faster.*

- We can use *on the other hand* on its own to contrast or compare a fact or idea with something that was said previously.
  There would be lots of advantages to living somewhere that was hot all year round. **On the other hand,** *I think I'd miss watching the seasons change.*
- We use *contrary to* to reject an idea in favour of another one. *Contrary to* is followed by a noun or noun phrase. It is often used in fixed expressions like *contrary to common belief/opinion …* .

Contrary to common belief, the world already produces enough food for everyone.	The world, **contrary to** common belief, already produces enough food for everyone.

- We can use *whereas* and *while* to indicate that a fact or idea contrasts with another in the same sentence. We often use it to talk about small differences between things that are quite similar. A clause with *whereas/while* is put first and is then followed by a contrast.

Whereas/While the hole in the ozone layer is largely the result of CFCs, global warming is caused mainly by CO2.	Global warming is caused mainly by CO2 **whereas/while** the hole in the ozone layer is largely the result of CFCs.

- We can use *indeed*, followed by a comma, to introduce information that reinforces or extends a point just made. It is used in more formal language.
  Cold temperatures can be harmful to health. **Indeed,** *they can be fatal.*
- We can use *in conclusion* to indicate the beginning of the final point or summary of what is being said.
  In conclusion, *it can be said that unless the population as a whole pays more attention to atmospheric pollution, our grandchildren may face a very uncertain future.*
- We can use *on the whole* to indicate that we are speaking generally without taking account of unusual cases.
  On the whole, *the industry is trying to bring carbon emissions under control.*
- We can use *therefore* to indicate that something follows logically from what has been said, or to introduce a result of it. Note its position in these sentences, and the use of punctuation.

The climatic problem is immense. **Therefore,** we should encourage all countries to cooperate on this issue.	We should **therefore** encourage all countries to cooperate on this issue.	We should encourage, **therefore,** all countries to cooperate on this issue.

- We can use *given this* to indicate that if we accept something is true, then what we are about to say follows logically from it. It is used at the start of a sentence.
  We know that overexposure to sunlight can cause skin damage. **Given this,** *the government should promote the use of sun creams.*

Unit 23
Phrasal verbs (2)

Verb + preposition
- These verbs need an object, which is always placed after the preposition.
  I could **look at** *that picture for hours.*

Phrasal verbs
- Some phrasal verbs have no object.
  The school is **gearing up** *for sports day.*
  If you **go ahead,** *I'll see you later in the café.*
  I'll be there at 8 unless something **crops up.**
- Some phrasal verbs need an object. If the object is a noun, it can be placed before or after the adverb. If the object is a pronoun, it must be placed before the particle.

He's picking his friend up at the airport.	He's picking up his friend at the airport.
I'm **picking** *him* up from the airport tomorrow.	~~I'm **picking up** him from the airport tomorrow.~~

- Some phrasal verbs have a very limited set of objects or are fixed expressions. The noun comes after the adverb and we do not use pronouns.
  You must **pluck up** *courage and face the situation.*
  We might get the contract, but I don't **hold out** *much hope.*

Phrasal verb + preposition
- Some of these phrasal verbs need an object, which is always placed after the preposition.
  I must **get on with** *some work.*
  You should always **stick up for** *your friends.*
- Some of these phrasal verbs need two objects. The first one is always placed after the verb and the other after the preposition.
  He didn't want to come, but I **talked** *him* **into** *it.*

Unit 24
Connecting words

- We can use *despite + -ing* or *the fact that* to give the same idea as an *although* clause.

Despite *being* a keen runner, John has no desire to enter a marathon.	**Although** he is a keen runner, John has no desire to enter a marathon.
Despite *the fact that* he is a keen runner, John has no desire to enter a marathon.	

- *Even* is often used before *though*. It gives the idea of *although* but makes the statement more emphatic. **Even though** *he's very fit, Mark didn't manage to finish the marathon.*
- We can begin a sentence with *No sooner* + an inverted form of the verb and subject to convey the idea that something happened immediately or as soon as something else happened. The following clause begins with *than*.
  No sooner *had the marathon started* **than** *Sarah began to ask herself why she had decided to enter it.*

- We can use *even if* to mean *whether or not*.
  Even if *you start training now you're unlikely to be ready in time for the marathon in June.*
- We can use *as* to begin a subordinate clause to indicate that an event or situation happens or exists at the same time as another. In this use, *as* is a conjunction joining two clauses in the same sentence. A comma is needed if the subordinate clause comes before the main clause.

I saw my friends waving to me **as** I finished the marathon.	**As** I finished the marathon, I saw my friends waving to me.

- We use *by then* to say that something happens before that point in time.
  I arrived late. **By then**, *everyone had left and the place was deserted.*
- We can begin subordinate clauses with *provided* to say that something is conditional. A comma is needed if the subordinate clause comes before the main clause.

Provided (that) it doesn't rain, the Fun Run should be a good day out.	The Fun Run should be a good day out, **provided** (that) it doesn't rain.

- We use *result in* + noun to express effect.
  The rain may **result in** <u>the race</u> *being cancelled.*
- We can use *so* as a conjunction to talk about the consequence of an event, and as an adverb to indicate a conclusion or realisation that is a consequence of previous events or information.
  I saw you **so** *I know you were there.* (conjunction)
  There's Lucy! **So** *she did come!* (adverb)
- We use *what is more* (*what's more* is informal) to add emphasis to a point which supports or extends a previous statement.
  She finished in record time. **What's more**, *she didn't seem tired.*
- We can use *in all* to express that something is the final event in a sequence that is already becoming difficult to endure. It can begin a sentence or occur in the middle of one. It is an informal idiom.
  It was crowded, I couldn't see the runners, there were no hot dog vans about and, **in all**, *it started raining.*
- We use *then* to mean *next*.
  I'm going to enter the London marathon this spring and **then** *in the autumn I'll try the New York one*
  It can also mean *in addition*.
  These trainers are popular with serious athletes, **then** *there are these ones which are also excellent.*
  It also can be used to mean *with the result that*.
  If you do enough training, **then** *you should be able to win the race.*

Unit 25
Complex sentences and adverbial clauses

Complex sentences have at least two clauses: a main clause and at least one subordinate clause. Adverbial clauses are subordinate clauses which give information about the main clause, such as time, place, manner, reason, condition, concession, etc.

- Adverbial clauses of time are usually placed just after the main clause. They can be placed before the main clause, followed by a comma. They use conjunctions including: *after, as, as soon as, before, every time, since, until, when* and *while*.

We used to eat baskets of strawberries **every time we visited the farm in summer**.	**Every time we visited the farm in summer**, we used to eat baskets of strawberries.

- Adverbial clauses of place tell us where something happens.
  You can park your car **where I usually put mine**.
  Wherever he goes, *he makes friends with people.*
- Adverbial clauses of manner tell us how something happens.
  He made his living **by/from painting pictures of the rich and famous**.
- Adverbial clauses of reason tell us why something happens. If they come before the main clause, they are followed by a comma. They often use *because* but they can also use the conjunctions *as, for* and *since* (with the same meaning as *because*).
  She was advised to move **as she was told her health would benefit from the sea air**.
  Because you're being promoted, *you'll be given a higher salary.*
- We use adverbial clauses of condition to talk about possible situations and their consequences. When placed before the main clause, they are followed by a comma. These clauses usually use *if* or *unless*.
  If you look at the website, *you will find all the information you need.*
  You won't find the information **unless you check the website**.
- We use adverbial clauses of concession to talk about information that contrasts with information in the main clause, or seems surprising in some way in relation to the main clause. These use conjunctions including *though, although* and *even though* (which is stronger). When placed before the main clause, they are followed by a comma.
  Although we felt we were being too ambitious, *we all agreed to get the report finished by Friday.*

Answer key and scripts

The following pages contain all of the answer keys to exercises and the recording scripts.

The *Map of Objective Advanced Student's Book* on pages 3–5 gives full details of the language and exam skills covered in each unit.

The *Content of Cambridge English: Advanced* on pages 7–9 provides information about the exam, with links to the relevant Exam folder.

Unit 1 pages 10–13

Vocabulary

1

> **Suggested answers**
> 1 conscientious
> 2 competent / knowledgeable
> 3 decisive
> 4 courageous
> 5 down-to-earth
> 6 outgoing
> 7 unconventional
> 8 narrow-minded
> 9 persuasive
> 10 competent / knowledgeable

2

> conscientious
> narrow-minded
> courageous
> unconventional
> competent
> down-to-earth
> outgoing
> decisive
> knowledgeable
> persuasive

Conditionals

1

> *If she's an international lawyer, then she needs to be very knowledgeable in her job.*
> This sentence is an example of the zero conditional. We can form this kind of sentence by using present simple verbs in both clauses. It is used to talk about things which are generally true.
> *What would be your ideal way to spend a weekend?*
> This sentence is an example of the second conditional. We can form this kind of sentence by using *would* in one clause, and past simple verbs in the other. It is used to talk about hypothetical situations – to imagine and speculate about things which probably won't happen.

2

Type	*if* clause	Main clause	Use for …
zero	present simple or continuous	present simple or continuous	common states or events
first	present simple or continuous	*will /* *to be /* *going to /* present simple or continuous	possible states or events
second	past simple or continuous	*would +* infinitive without *to*	hypothetical or very unlikely situations
third	past perfect	*would have* + past participle	the past and say that now it is impossible to do anything about it

3

> **Possible answers**
> 1 If you experience any problems, I'll be available to help.
> 2 If it hadn't been for Jane, the manager would have got the wrong impression of me and my work.
> 3 If it makes the situation easier, I'll keep my real opinion to myself.

4 The words here are all alternatives for *if* in conditional clauses.

> 1 If so   2 otherwise   3 Given   4 unless   5 Provided

Reading

2

> 1 Some cultural differences are easy to see; they are 'on the surface'. This is the *tip of the iceberg*. However, below the surface are many deeper differences, beliefs and attitudes, which are more difficult to understand. This is the larger part of the 'iceberg' which is under the surface.
> 2 Find out as much as you can before going, and then try to make contact with real people.

Vocabulary

1

> *culture shock* = noun–noun
> *make a decision* = verb–noun
> *incredibly exciting* = adverb–adjective
> *acceptable behaviour* = adjective–noun

2

> 1 (gain) insight, experience, confidence
> 2 way of life, ways of behaving, in a very natural way
> 3 sense of humour, self-deprecating humour
> 4 made the decision, make friends
> 5 deeply held (values and beliefs)

Listening

1

> 1 D   2 E   3 B   4 A   5 C

2

> 1 E   2 C   3 F   4 A   5 D

The underlined parts of the script confirm the answers.

Recording script 1 02

Speaker 1: We went to this incredible place, a place which has one of the largest mosques in the whole of North Africa. We went in and then some boys came and they wanted to show us around. Well, we weren't so sure, but they did anyway. After that, they asked us to come to a carpet museum, and they said, really, you have to see – it's wonderful, there are old Tunisian carpets. So we decided to go with them. <u>And guess what! The museum turned out to be a carpet shop, owned by the father of one of the boys. And of course, he wanted to sell us a carpet.</u> We actually didn't want to buy one because we didn't have enough space in our backpacks, but finally he managed to persuade us to buy one. So my friend, yeah, she bought one. To thank us for that, the boys guided us around the town and we ended up going down these <u>really narrow alleyways, and we had no idea where we were because this whole city was like a maze.</u> Then we came to a house and we realised it was the house of one of the boys and we were invited in by his family and <u>we had tea, coffee, nice biscuits, and it was a really, really good experience.</u>

Speaker 2: My story is actually a bit bizarre. I was going to Florida and <u>during the flight</u>, I had to go to the bathroom. And in front of me there was a woman, she was about, maybe 50, who went into the bathroom, but she didn't lock the door, it was still on the er, ... it wasn't completely locked. And I thought that maybe I should knock on the door and tell her that the door wasn't completely closed, but I didn't. And I also had a funny feeling that this wouldn't turn out well. And I was right because a little later the door flew open and <u>there she was, and she gave out a loud shriek</u> and me and the rest of the line just stood there in disbelief, totally in shock.

Speaker 3: Four years ago I was in <u>Indonesia</u>. First, I went to Sumatra and er, there I met a man who wanted to show us his village. So we went off with him. <u>The village was very small</u>, perhaps 500 inhabitants, maybe less. It was very special because the people there had never seen tourists before. So they acted like they treated us like very special people, which we aren't, of course. <u>They were a bit shy at first but then somehow we managed to communicate, and what I realised is that people, good people, are the same perhaps the world over.</u>

Speaker 4: Well, it was supposed to be a weekend trip with the rowing club. It was in the middle of winter. When we got there we couldn't even get out on the water, it was way too cold and we were in this <u>big, er, shed</u>, the size of a football pitch. There was no heating, the water was coming through the roof. The whole time it was windy and terrible. We went there by bike and it took us about three hours to get there, I think. And we just, you know, went on automatic pilot and went on and on and on. And in this shed we couldn't get warm and people <u>started getting really irritable and we started fighting over stupid, stupid things, for example, who has to cook dinner, and who has to do the dishes, and we were really nasty to each other.</u> And we had to sleep all together in one corner otherwise we'd freeze to death. There were about 25 of us all huddled together, <u>trying to sleep and hating each other.</u>

Speaker 5: Whenever people talk about dolphins, they always say they're very intelligent creatures but I never really grasped the idea of how intelligent they are until recently. There's this place in Zanzibar, off Africa, where it's possible to <u>go swimming with dolphins</u>. When you go there, you can meet up with people and you <u>go on a boat with</u> them, <u>and even before you've seen anything, their enjoyment really rubs off on you. They're laughing all the time and when they find some dolphins, they're really proud of themselves because they've found some dolphins and they know that you're really going to love it.</u> What you have to do then is, you have to jump in the water, when the boat stops you jump in the water, and if you're lucky, the dolphins come straight at you, and then they dive really deep in the water so you can't see them any more. They hide themselves and then they come back. And when you see the look in their eyes, you see they're just making fun of you! And for me, that's proof of how smart dolphins really are.

Exam folder 1 pages 14–15

Paper 1 Part 1

There is a full description of the exam on pages 7–9.

The Advanced Reading and Use of English test has eight parts. The test focus in Reading and Use of English Part 1 is vocabulary. The general area of vocabulary can be subdivided into categories such as phrasal verbs, collocations and idioms and the exam tests a range of different vocabulary areas.

1

> 1 A (*reveal* = to show what was previously hidden)
> 2 B (*gain* collocates with *insight*)
> 3 D (*research* needs the dependent preposition *into*)
> 4 B (*rich* collocates with *source*)
> 5 C (*complex* is used when we talk about things with many parts, such as a *network*)
> 6 A (*solely* = not involving anything else)
> 7 C (*consistent* needs the dependent preposition *with*)
> 8 B (*find* collocates with *evidence*)

Unit 2 pages 16–19

Speaking

2

> 1 Ms Bryant seems to be in charge of running tennis courses. Amanda is writing to ask about what the course includes, and whether certain equipment is available.
> 2 The email is written in a formal tone (*Dear …*; *in which you confirm*; *I apologise for the delay in replying*; *I very much look forward to …*; *Yours sincerely*.)

Writing

1

> **Suggested answers**
> 1 beginnings: *To whom it may concern*, *For the attention of …*; endings: *Yours faithfully, …*; *Regards …*; *Best wishes …* .
> 2 The vocabulary does not resemble spoken English, and is much more formal. For example, *I apologise for* rather than *I'm sorry for*; *I am delighted* rather than *I'm happy*.
> 3 Contractions are used less in formal English. Using contractions would give the letter a tone which would resemble spoken English.
> 4 In formal styles, there is less 'personal' language. For example, less use of the word 'I', and more use of passive forms. There are fewer phrasal verbs used. Ideas are expressed more indirectly, for example: *Can I assume that …* rather than *Will you give me … ?*
> 5 Paragraph 1: Thanking for the previous email.
> Paragraph 2: Explaining a delay.
> Paragraph 3: Expressing pleasure at taking part in the course.
> Paragraph 4: Introducing the questions.
> Paragraph 5: Asking about equipment.

2

> **Suggested answers**
> The email is currently too informal. It is bad style to write like this to someone you don't know well.

3

> 1 As part of my Management course …
> 2 The course covers such subjects as …
> 3 Customer care is an area that particularly interests me.
> 4 I hope to be able to develop my understanding of …
> 5 I have some experience of working as a waitress.

Dependent prepositions

1

> Thank you for your email in which you confirm my place on the Tennis Coaching course starting 5th July.
> I apologise for the delay in replying but I have been sitting my final exams in Sports Psychology at university. As soon as my results are available, I will forward them to you. I am sure I will be able to draw on the knowledge that I have acquired at university during my coaching course.
> I am delighted that I have been assigned to the group specialising in coaching 11 to 18-year-olds as this is the age range I am particularly interested in. I believe in the importance of encouraging participation in sports especially for teenagers because this is a period in their lives when they opt for what I consider to be life choices. If a person engages in sport as a young person, they are more likely to continue to lead a healthy life in adulthood.
> I wonder if I could ask a couple of questions. Is breakfast included in the fee we pay for campus accommodation? Can I assume that as you have asked me to bring two tennis rackets and my sports kit, I will be provided with any extra equipment necessary for the course, such as a tennis ball cannon?
> I very much look forward to taking part in the course.

2

> 1 on
> 2 in
> 3 for
> 4 to
> 5 to
> 6 in
> 7 in
> 8 with
> 9 in
> 10 in

Corpus spot

1 She is recovering **from** a bad illness.
2 I'm doing research **into** children's behaviour.
3 I like reading, so I have very good background knowledge **of** history and geography.
4 I wish I could travel back **in** time.
5 We put a lot of effort **into** organising the party.
6 I have the pleasure **of** inviting you to our presentation in July.

Reading

1

Suggested answers
The internet helps us get information quickly, and enables us to keep in contact with more people in more places. However, many people are spending more time in front of a screen, and may feel lonely as a result. Also, we are spending more time working than doing other things.

2

1 on
2 with
3 in
4 to
5 in / among
6 for
7 to
8 for
9 in
10 of
11 to
12 between
13 with
14 with
15 from
16 for

Vocabulary

1

1 in
2 By
3 at
4 on
5 by
6 for

Listening

2

Yolanda
Where are you from?
Spain, 50km north of Madrid
What languages have you studied?
Russian, difficult – gave up

Martin
Where are you from?
Germany, now lives in France
What languages have you studied?
French and Italian
Spanish when he went to Spain on holiday

3

Yolanda
hobbies
concerts and cinema
not much time for hobbies
likes thrillers/suspense because you can get lost in a good plot
future hopes
travel to Australia
recommended by a friend – good lifestyle, can do sporty things
living or working abroad permanently
not sure, likes living in Spain because of the weather in summer, relaxed lifestyle
earliest memories of school
school report, opened it instead of parents, parents pleased with report

Martin
hobbies
watching DVDs
wants to take up karate
invite friend round and watch DVDs together
doesn't go to cinema – too expensive, there isn't one nearby
karate trains the body and the mind

future hopes and dreams
finish studies, get a job, have a family, job in large multinational so that he can travel

living or working abroad permanently
yes, Northern Europeans live to work, people in Mediterranean countries work to live

earliest memories of school
a maths task
wasn't doing task, others went to watch TV, then he completed the task quickly – made him a good student

Recording script 1 03

Yolanda: Hi, I'm Yolanda. I'm from Spain.

Martin: Hi, nice to meet you. I'm originally from Germany, but I live in France now because my dad works there.

Yolanda: Wow, that's interesting. I've lived about 50 kilometres north of Madrid all my life.

Martin: Your English is pretty good.

Yolanda: Thanks, that's what I'm studying at the moment. I studied Russian for a while but I found it very difficult and gave up.

Martin: I did French and Italian at school and then I learned a little bit of Spanish when I went on holiday in Spain.

Recording script 1 04

Martin: What do you do in your free time?

Yolanda: Mm. My hobby is going to concerts and going to the cinema. I know it's not much but I don't really have a lot of time for hobbies. Do you like going to the cinema?

Martin: Well, I don't go to the cinema that often, partly because it's quite expensive and partly because there isn't one close to where I live. But what I like doing is getting a DVD and then inviting friends round to watch it with me. What sort of films do you like watching?

Yolanda: I like thrillers, suspense, that kind of thing. I like it when you get totally involved with a good plot. What else do you do in your free time?

Martin: I've just taken up karate because I think it trains both your body and your mind.

Yolanda: I think that's a good aim. What other aims have you got for the future?

Martin: Well for the short-term future I'm going to finish my studies and then the idea is to get a job in a large multinational company where I'll have the opportunity to travel for my job. I sometimes wonder if that doesn't match my other more long-term ambition, which is to settle down and have a family. Would you like to travel?

Yolanda: Absolutely, I'd love to go to Australia because I have a friend who went on holiday there and she said the lifestyle is great. People are really into sport and the climate's perfect for lots of outdoor things. But I don't know how I'd feel about living or working abroad permanently. Could you do that?

Martin: Yeah, I can see myself ending up in a foreign country for a long time. But I think in England, Germany and all of northern Europe, people like, work all the time, and people, especially in Mediterranean countries, people work to live and we live to work and we need to get back to that same kind of philosophy that they have.

Yolanda: I don't know if I could live abroad permanently and I must admit I like living in Spain with its warm, sunny summers. And I think you're right, the people are more relaxed. Like you say, you can get stressed out if you're studying or working, but then when you've finished, you know, you've got a good few hours of sunshine left and you can go outside. I remember when I was at primary school, I loved going home to play in the garden in summer.

Martin: Wow, you've got a good memory if you can remember being at primary school. What's your earliest memory of school?

Yolanda: My earliest memory is when I was in primary school, and every term you got a report to take home. And I remember the teacher saying, whatever you do, you must not open this report, it must go home to your parents. And I remember I was dying to open it but I was scared of disobeying the teacher. Anyway, when I gave it to my parents, they were pleased because it was a good report.

Martin: Actually, I think my earliest memory is in primary school as well. And I was supposed to be doing this maths task but I was being lazy and couldn't be bothered to start it. And everyone else had gone off to watch this TV programme that we were allowed to watch once a week. And the teacher said, you've got to stay here and finish this. And I thought, right then, and I did the maths problem in about 10 seconds. And I remember thinking, I should have just done my work in the first place. Perhaps realising that at an early age turned me into a good student!

Speaking

1

> **Suggested answers**
> A good communicator asks questions, takes turns, listens, develops answers and uses appropriate body language.

2

> **Suggested answers**
> 1 talk about the size of the city, its facilities/amenities
> 2 pleasure, future job, studies
> 3 places visited/cinema/theatre/concert – why it was interesting
> 4 work, study, family, travel, ambitions

Writing folder 1 pages 20–21

Informal and formal writing

1

A informal, a friend writing to a friend – giving news about holiday plans – promising to tell him/her about the holiday when he/she returns

B formal, a college writing to a course applicant – apologising for the delay in replying and confirming the applicant's place on the course and that information will be sent out soon

C informal, a friend writing to a friend – regretting the fact that the friend could not go to a party as he/she was ill – giving news about who was at the party and hoping the friend will get better soon

D formal, a film club confirming receipt of a member's application form and information that a receipt will be sent once the membership fee has been paid

2

2 opening sentence, referring back to a previous letter (formal)
3 apologising for delay in replying (informal)
4 apologising for delay in replying (formal)
5 thanking for a previous last letter (informal)
6 thanking for a party invitation (formal)
7 thanking for a wedding invitation (informal)
8 finishing a letter (formal)

3

Refusing an invitation
Oh no! I'm sorry I can't come to your party because I'll be on holiday. (informal)
I'm afraid I am unable to attend due to a prior arrangement. (formal)
Congratulating
Wow, well done you – you passed your driving test first time! (informal)
Congratulations on passing your examination. (formal)
Giving your opinion
I think … (informal)
In my opinion … (formal)
Giving advice
Why don't you … (informal)
I think you should … (formal)

4

1 would, grateful, could, further
2 acknowledge, receipt
3 attached
4 would, appreciate, response
5 forward, hearing, earliest, convenience

Corpus spot

1 ? (totally disinterested) might sound a little strong in some situations
2 ✗ (it is not good to call people 'stupid')
3 ✗ (the language is too critical and should be softened)
4 ✓
5 ✗ (the writer could request a refund in a more polite way)
6 ✓
7 ✓
8 ? (the language is a little too direct, and could be seen as being critical)

Unit 3 pages 22–25

Reading

3

1 A   2 B   3 A   4 B

4

1 To change things in society you need to work hard and have concrete ideas not just emotion. Nothing will get done, or expectations may be unrealistic, if we get too emotional.
2 The leader is a person too. People have to change at an individual level if they want to bring about changes in society.

Wishes and regrets

1

1 had met
2 had / could have
3 to inform
4 were / was
5 would give / had given
6 wouldn't ask / hadn't asked
7 had known

2

A: Would you prefer to watch an interview with someone, or read it in a magazine?
B: Well, I think I'd prefer to see the person, because when they're asked an awkward question, you can see if they'd prefer not to answer it.
A: I don't like it when people are asked awkward questions. For example, why did this interview ask so many questions about Michelle Obama's personal life?
B: You mean you'd prefer it if she'd focused more on questions about politics?

3

1 to start
2 started

4

1. had / would have
2. read
3. woke up
4. had been born
5. to do

Listening

1

school life, a person who helped him, fans, his working relationship with a director, his marriage, his daughter

Recording script 1 05

Interviewer: With me today in the studio is David Burns, who freely admits that he's had a troubled past. And when I read through this biography – a difficult childhood, married to a fellow soap-opera star, a relationship with a famous actress, an 11-year-old daughter from a subsequent relationship – all I can say, David, is that your life has been a roller coaster. It's no wonder you're constantly in the public eye. Do you think it all started in your teenage years?

David: I think it all stemmed from when I was at school. When I was about 14, I was picked on by a bully. One day, he went too far, saying something about my mother. I snapped. I really laid into him.

Interviewer: What happened?

David: Oh, there was a big fuss at school and I was branded a troublemaker. My mum began to think she couldn't cope with me. Things went from bad to worse. I started avoiding lessons.

Interviewer: And how did you get out of that downward spiral?

David: I was lucky. A drama teacher we had really understood me. She said I could choose to go in whichever direction I wanted. I could continue getting into trouble or I could make something of myself. She was the one who recognised that I had talent.

Interviewer: I wonder if directors see that tough upbringing, because the irony is that you've specialised in playing villains ...

David: I've always been an edgy person. I can bring that out if the part demands it. I've got a dark side. People say they can see an element of that in my eyes.

Interviewer: Does that mean people think they don't like you as a person, because you always tend to play bad people?

David: Er, I get a very mixed reception. There are fans that write very complimentary letters, saying I'm good-looking and that sort of thing, but then there are those who can't seem to tell fiction from reality, and it can turn nasty.

Interviewer: What do you mean?

David: Well, for example, one fan became obsessed, sort of jealous, and she caused me a lot of problems. She didn't like anyone in the TV series getting near me. She'd send 50 letters every week and pictures from the show with everyone cut out except me. Then she wrote to another cast member saying she knew I had a daughter. That's when I went to my producer who contacted the police.

Interviewer: Tell us about your experience in *Joseph And The Amazing Technicolor Dreamcoat* ...

David: I played the lead role. I did it for two years – and then I got sacked. The director saw I was getting a lot of attention. I think it was thought I was hogging the limelight. It may have been internal politics, but I wasn't even given the chance to give my final performance.

Interviewer: And tell us about your marriage to your fellow soap-opera star Julia Watts. Do you wish things had worked out better between you?

David: Looking back, I don't think we were destined to spend all our lives together. We just didn't know it at the time. But she's a great actress. She could be in the soap for another 20 years. She's brilliant in it. I've been offered a lot of money to tell my story, but I'm not interested. It's just a pity she's said all those bad things about me in interviews. But if she wants to do that, well, that's her business.

Interviewer: And what about your daughter, Sarah?

David: She's 11 and she's very beautiful and she's talented, too. Her mother, Carol, was a model. When we separated, we always said we'd put Sarah first. She lives with Carol and I see her every other weekend.

Interviewer: Will you ever marry again?

David: I'm in a relationship with someone right now. She's not in show business. But my lips are sealed. I do believe in marriage, but that's all I'll say on the subject.

Vocabulary

1

1. d
2. a
3. f
4. b
5. c
6. e

2

1. put the record straight
2. addressing the issue
3. to face the music
4. to tell the difference

4

1 c 2 e 3 a 4 d 5 b

Exam folder 2 pages 26–27

Paper 1 Part 2

1 & 2

1 other
2 as
3 around / round
4 whereas / while / but
5 every
6 which / that
7 if / whether
8 its
9 out
10 is

3

Suggested answers

Many famous people find themselves in the public eye as soon as they step out of their front door.

However, most celebrities have their own way of dealing with the paparazzi. One strategy can be to adopt a reserved personality. Some actors in particular say that this helps them ignore the photographers. Another strategy is to take on a victim mentality and simply to accept that there is nothing that can be done about the unwanted attention, so it is pointless getting upset about it. It should be seen as a part of the job.

However, some people who are related to famous people – members of the celebrity's family – may well have problems with having attention from the press. It may take years for them to get used to it. If they have a group of photographers following them around when they are trying to carry on with their normal daily life, it can be hard to block it out and pretend it is not happening.

6 & 7

1 makes
2 they
3 its / their
4 out
5 for
6 whether
7 from
8 being

Unit 4 pages 28–31

Listening

2

It's a supervisor giving instructions to candidates at the beginning of an exam.

Recording script 1 06

Come into the room quietly and put your bags at the front of the room here. If you have a mobile phone or any other electronic device, please switch if off and leave it in your bag. Only take your pens and pencils to your seat. Can you look for your candidate number on the desk and sit there? That's your place. Good.

Now, I'm going to hand out this form along with the papers. Would you mind filling it in? It's the candidate information sheet. Please ask if there's anything you don't understand.

Right. Could I ask for silence now, because I'm going to hand out the papers?

4

Suggested answers

Put your bags at the front of the room.
If you have …, please switch it off and leave it in your bag.
Only take …
Would you mind filling in … ?
Please ask if there's …
Could I ask for … ?
Imperative verbs (like *Put* …) sound more direct. Other structures (like *If* …, *Would you mind* …?) sound more polite.

Reading

3

1, 2, 3, 6

Modals and semi-modals (1)

1

1 *might* is used when making a tentative suggestion – the speaker doesn't want to be too direct or assertive, and wants to give the listener more choice about what to do.
2 *could* is used to show that the speaker is requesting action. It shows that the listener has some choice about whether to act in the way the speaker wants.
3 *must* is used here to describe an ideal or desired situation. It is stronger than *should* and shows that the listener has less choice about what to do.

2

1 ability
2 offer
3 negative certainty
4 request
5 instruction
6 theoretical possibility
7 permission

3

1 a The use of *could* suggests a general or physical ability – the person could get into the house by climbing through the window.
  b The use of *was able to* suggests that the person is referring to one specific achievement/occasion.
2 a *may* is used for possibility
  b *may* is used for asking for permission (formal)
3 a *might* is used for possibility (smaller possibility than *may*)
  b *might* is used for making a suggestion, or tentatively offering advice (formal)
4 a *must* is used for an obligation which comes from the speaker (internal obligation)
  b *have to* is used for an obligation which is imposed on us by someone else (external obligation)
5 a *need* is used to express the idea that it is necessary to do something
  b *didn't need to* is used when someone has done something, but it wasn't necessary to do it
6 a *needn't have* is used to tell someone that an action they did wasn't necessary
  b *don't need to* is used to say that an action is not necessary

5

Suggested answers
B She might have fallen over.
C They might have just had an accident.
D She might be doing her homework.
E They might have got lost.

Listening

2

1 press 1 followed by the hash (#) key
2 press 3
3 press 001
4 bring a passport or a driving licence
5 enter the last three digits of the code
6 press 4

Recording script 1 07

1 Hello and welcome to H4 mobile pay and go, top up, tariff and bolt-on service.
  If you want to top up your credit, press 1 followed by the hash key and have your credit or debit card handy. If you want to check your call time, remaining tariff or bolt-on balance, press 2. If you want to change your tariff, add or cancel a bolt on, press 3.
  And to hear more about what H4 mobile can offer you, press 4.
2 Thank you for calling Riverside dental practice. The practice is now closed. Our phone lines are open from 8 a.m. to 12.30 p.m. and from 1.30 p.m. to 6.30 p.m.

If you would like to make an appointment for a dental check-up, please press double oh one now.
  Remember that if you are a new patient, you will need to bring proof of identity to your first appointment. This must have your photo on it so a passport or driving licence would be ideal. We will also need proof of your address and ask you to bring a utility bill with this information on it.
3 Thank you for calling Dexter Bank. Please listen carefully to the following options so that we can provide you with the service you require. If you already have an account with Dexter Bank, please enter your account number. Thank you. Now, please enter the last three digits of your security code. Thank you. Please select from the following options: to open a new account, press 1, to change an existing account, press 2, to enquire about interest rates, press 3, to check your balance on any of your accounts with us, press 4. For any other questions, please hold the line and one of our advisors will speak to you as soon as possible.

Vocabulary

1

dis: disappear, discontinue, distrust
non: non-smoker
il: illogical, illiterate
mis: mislead, mistrust
im: immature, impersonal, impolite
un: unavoidable, unconventional, unjustified
in: inaccessible, insensitive, inconclusive
ir: irresistible, irregular

2

1 *im*
2 *il*
3 *ir*

3

(The words in bold show where the spelling of the original word has changed.)
able: photocopiable, countable, employable, **arguable**, recommendable, respectable, **reliable**
ation: exploration, **dramatisation**, recommendation
ency: **efficiency**, **frequency**, tendency
ful: deceitful, careful, respectful
ly: timely, rudely, frequently, calmly
less: countless, timeless, speechless, careless, pointless
ment: judg(e)ment, employment, **argument**
ness: rudeness, awareness

Writing folder 2 pages 32–33

Formal writing

1

Suggested answers

Give us a ring soon is informal English, probably spoken and used with someone who the speaker knows well. *We look forward to hearing from you at your earliest convenience* is formal English, almost certainly written and probably used with someone who the speaker does not know well.

3

Suggested answers

1 It is not usually appropriate to use verb contractions in formal writing.
2 Try to avoid phrasal verbs in formal writing, although sometimes there is no alternative or the alternative would sound too stilted to be appropriate.
3 Avoid slang or colloquial expressions in formal writing – if they are included, it will be done for some special effect.
4 Layout is more fixed in formal contexts.
5 Structure is always important, but because you are more likely to be writing formally to someone whom you do not know and with whom you do not have so much shared knowledge, clarity of structure is particularly important.
6 Again, this is important in all kinds of writing but may perhaps be particularly so in formal writing (as one way of clarifying structure).

4

Suggested answers

1 Moreover, we are content with your staff. Having kind and helpful personnel is important – people expect this ~~kind of stuff~~ level of service.
2 Lastly, I would like to say that the discount seems ~~a bit~~ rather/slightly smaller than the ten per cent originally promised.
3 I am writing this letter to your newspaper because I think ~~you guys made~~ there was a mistake in your Thursday edition ~~the other day~~.
4 Interviewees' responses depended on ~~how old they were, whether they were male or female,~~ their age, gender, occupation and educational background.
5 ~~And some more things~~ With regard to other matters, I would like to make a few suggestions, which I hope you can take into consideration.

5

1 Firstly
2 Secondly
3 Moreover
4 Finally
5 although
6 So that
7 However
8 Consequently
9 then
10 Firstly
11 when
12 Gradually
13 After that
14 especially
15 because
16 Finally

Unit 5 pages 34–37

Speaking

2

A a pilot or flight attendant (getting on the course was harder than expected)
B a surgeon (it is still exciting to see people getting better)
C a writer (the financial insecurity prevents this person from working effectively)

Reading

1

For. The writer says *you can achieve your dream job … you must never give up.*

2

1 B
2 C
3 A

3

Suggested answers

You need a (short-term and long-term) plan. Find out as much as you can about the job.

4

Suggested answers

- Don't be disappointed by the inevitable rejections.
- You will get your dream job if you're determined.
- Accept that you may have to work long hours without getting a promotion.
- It's an advantage to learn a job from the bottom up.
- You probably won't earn a lot at first.
- The best jobs will be challenging.

Writing

1

1 Caretaker of the Islands of the Great Barrier Reef; Hamilton Island, part of the Great Barrier Reef in Australia
2 A$150,000, that's $103,000, or £70,000 for six months and a rent-free three-bedroom villa, complete with pool.

Recording script 1 08

Leo: Look at this advert.

Silvia: What is it?

Leo: They want someone to be the 'Caretaker of the Islands of the Great Barrier Reef'. It's a completely new job.

Silvia: What would you have to do?

Leo: Just live on a beautiful island for six months and watch the fish swim by!

Silvia: I can't believe that's for real. It sounds like a holiday!

Leo: Well, there's more to it than that. The Great Barrier Reef is a World Heritage Listed natural wonder – and the islands of the Great Barrier Reef have, it says here, an 'abundance' of wildlife so it's an important site for naturalists. This sounds just my thing. It says the Island Caretaker will be based on Hamilton Island – that's the largest inhabited island in the region.

Silvia: So if that's off the coast of Queensland, it'll be warm all year round and then there'll be the blue skies, crystal-clear waters and … What's the catch?

Leo: No formal qualifications needed but ideal candidate must be able to swim, snorkel, dive, sail … I can do all that. The successful applicant will receive a salary of A$150,000 – not bad – for six months and get to live rent-free in a three-bedroom villa, complete with pool. Wow!

Silvia: What are you waiting for? Who do you have to write to?

Vocabulary

1

Possible answers
1 I have successfully completed a first-aid course …
2 I can speak English fluently. (Or indicate the correct level or course attended.)
3 I am able to attend an interview at your earliest convenience.
4 I am willing to work shifts.
5 I have excellent communication skills.

2

1 experience (*experienced* = having skill or knowledge; *wise* = having the ability to make good judgements – usually older people are *wise*)
2 challenges (*challenge* has a more positive connotation than *problem*)
3 new (*novel* = new and original, unlike anything seen before)
4 competitive (*competitive* has a more positive connotation than *aggressive*)
5 flexible (*easy-going* suggests something too relaxed to be appropriate in a business-related environment)

3

1 eliminate
2 exceed
3 funds
4 my predecessor
5 therefore
6 install
7 delayed
8 repeat
9 out of order
10 in addition

4

1 in response
2 appeared
3 attaching
4 provides
5 similar business
6 enjoyed enormously
7 am available
8 convenient to

Relative clauses

1

Suggested answers
1 There was only one advert and it appeared on Jobline yesterday. (defining relative clause)
2 There were several adverts and the person is writing about the one which appeared yesterday. (non-defining relative clause)

2

Suggested answers
1 The company gave the job to the person who showed determination.
2 The applicant, who graduated from Bologna University, has a degree in biology.
3 The Head Office, which is in New York, employs 2,000 people.
4 The manager who interviewed me was kind and helpful.

3

> We can leave out the relative pronoun when it is the object of its clause.

4

> 1 I worked in a building which had no air conditioning.
> 2 The clothes ~~that~~ she wore to the office were too scruffy.
> 3 The place ~~where~~ she works has a gym for staff.
> 4 The place ~~that~~ I worked in last summer was great.
> 5 He has an inspirational quality which defies analysis.
> 6 Her colleagues are also the people ~~that~~ she socialises with.

5

> Sentences 1a and 2b are more formal.

> **Corpus spot**
> 1 This is the area of research on which he is working.
> 2 Here are some new statistics in which you can have confidence.
> 3 This is a theory for which there is little support.
> 4 Is this the person with whom you spoke? / Is this the person who you spoke to?
> 5 Unfortunately, the conference in which you enrolled has been cancelled.

Listening

2 & 3

> 1 coach
> 2 a camera crew
> 3 calm
> 4 sixth
> 5 petrol
> 6 sponsors
> 7 boat
> 8 jobs

Recording script 1 09

Interviewer: The darkness refuses to lift over the racetrack and the rain is beating against the windows of the motor home. A tiny race suit is hanging in the corner, but the young man sat back on the sofa is not ready for it yet as he rubs his eyes and comes to terms with the fact that he could still be snuggled up in bed instead of putting himself on display – yet again – at such an unearthly hour. Cesar, how did you get yourself into this business?

Cesar: Well, it's all down to my coach. He took a calculated risk with me when I was completely unknown. And then, as you know, it was a rapid change for me as I suddenly became famous.

Interviewer: How has your family coped with your fame and, I suppose, their fame too?

Cesar: Well the fame thing doesn't bother me, most people don't disturb me when they see me eating in a restaurant or something like that but I think my mother finds it a bit disturbing, you know, having to deal with a camera crew every time she comes out of the house. And in fact, my sisters now, they don't come down to the track to see me race, they watch me on TV at home.

Interviewer: Your father has shown great faith in you, hasn't he?

Cesar: Well, I think both of us have had many doubts at times about my talent but he reckons it's being calm which makes the difference between champions and the rest. He's amazing too – he's become really hardened to the constant attention. And he's the one who has to watch from the sidelines. I think that must be a lot worse than doing the race.

Interviewer: Yes, you had a scary moment in Australia, didn't you?

Cesar: Yeah, I'd qualified 21st and in the race got up to sixth position before my car gave out. It was real scary. You've only got split seconds to make life and death decisions. In an instant I knew something had gone wrong with the car and then you've got to get off the track and out of the way of the other drivers as fast as you can.

Interviewer: And you did it. But from an early age you proved that you've got what it takes.

Cesar: Oh, I don't know. When I left school as a teenager it was just hard work. I went from track to track. And, yeah, I suppose when I had to live in Italy and Belgium on my own it was a bit tough, but my dad was a great support. I remember he had to borrow money so that I could afford petrol money, just to get to a race once. And that's only a couple of years ago.

Interviewer: Things are very different now – you've got sponsors queuing up to take you on and make you a millionaire.

Cesar: And I've already got more money than I'd ever dreamed of. but I'm trying to be sensible with the money.

Interviewer: I've heard about the Ferrari in the garage and the BMW sports car. What's next on the list?

Cesar: I'm not irresponsible, even though to many people it must seem like I am. But it's strange what money and fame can do to you. I mean it just seems normal to me now to have all those things and, in fact, if I had to say, I would like a boat. I'd love that, to have it somewhere hot.

Interviewer: Does this mean that you have nothing or little in common with your old friends back home?

Cesar: When I go back home I still meet up with my old friends but lots of them have moved on too, they're living different places, or they have new family lives, so I don't get to see them so often. I suppose at our age, people are moving around a lot and doing different things. I don't think my situation is any different. It's just that I've changed jobs. But when we meet up we still talk about the same things. Like we never changed.

Interviewer: He might not have changed among his friends, but on Sunday he will be the new young star of Formula One, driving in front of five hundred million TV viewers.

Units 1–5 Revision

pages 38–39

2

1	could
2	hadn't
3	get / be
4	were / was
5	thought
6	had

3

1	D
2	B
3	C
4	D
5	C
6	A
7	B
8	C

4

1	came to
2	take on
3	totally
4	set off
5	incredibly
6	shock

5

1	misled
2	waterproof
3	judgment
4	tendency
5	efficiency
6	justified
7	impolite

6

Possible answers

1	she received a reply/response
2	at your convenience
3	I look forward to
4	however
5	a similar job
6	I am writing regarding / in connection with …
7	I am punctual
8	I would welcome the opportunity

7

1	to
2	when
3	which
4	across
5	like
6	up
7	for
8	but / though / although

Unit 6 pages 40–43

Speaking

2

Suggested answers

1 Her boyfriend had decided he had got tired of her and wanted to end their relationship.
2 She dialled an automatic recorded message from his phone while he was away for a month and then left the phone off the hook.
3 Students' own answers.

Recording script 1 10

Oh, talking of revenge, I read about a great one once. There was this girl, she'd been dumped by her boyfriend, 'cos he'd decided he'd gone off her and he told her to move her things out of his flat before he got back from a business trip. I think he was going to the States for a month or something. Anyway, she moves her stuff out straightaway but before she leaves, she picks up the phone and dials the speaking clock. Then she leaves the phone off the hook while the clock goes on telling the time to an empty flat. 'At the third stroke, it'll be 10:25 and 30 seconds …' So the boyfriend finds it when he returns four weeks later. You can imagine what the bill was like after a solid month of this. Huge! That must have been really satisfying for the dumped girl!

Phrasal verbs (1)

1

> 1 **For:** Andy
> **From:** Eddie
> **Number:** 07930 245 908
> **Message:** What website? Please call back before two.
> 2 **For:** Michael Removals
> **From:** Robert Smith
> **Number:** 0207 562 495
> **Message:** Recommended by Richard Johnstone. Wants to know charges for moving a few things on 21st or 22nd. Is moving beds, chests of drawers, fridge, washing machine, etc. out of house (moving about one mile). Also could you fix in the washing machine for him?
> 3 **For:** Nicky
> **From:** Leila
> **Number:** not given
> **Message:** Just wants a gossip. (Jo's resigned – wants to tell you why!)
> 4 **For:** Nicola
> **From:** Olga
> **Number:** not given
> **Message:** Calling from Omsk. Not back till 19th (has to do extra workshop). Will get bus home from airport – flight gets in 10.15 so should be home after midday. May try calling again later.
> 5 **For:** Piotr
> **From:** Jens
> **Number:** not given
> **Message:** Leaving party tonight meeting in the King's Pub next to the station, 6.30 NOT 7.30.
> 6 **For:** Matt
> **From:** Alex
> **Number:** not given
> **Message:** Has new game. Do you want to go round and play it?

Recording script 1 11

Speaker 1: Hi, Andy. I wanted to know about our homework. This history project. What was that website you said I should look up? Can you ring me back? Oh, this is Eddie by the way, I don't think I said. In case my number isn't showing up on your phone, it's 07930 245 908. I've got my seminar at two, so if you can call back before then, great. Bye.

Speaker 2: Hello, is that Michael Removals? Richard Johnstone gave me your number and suggested I contact you. I was wondering if you could move some stuff on the 21st or 22nd. It's just some beds and chests of drawers and bits and pieces into a house. I'm only moving about a mile away. Oh yes, and there's a fridge, and a washing machine too. Would you be able to fix those in for me as well, to the new place? Could you get back to me and let me know your charges? My name's Robert Smith, on 0207 562 495.

Speaker 3: Hi Nicky, it's Leila. Just ringing for a bit of a catch up of the latest gossip. There's some news you might be interested in. Jo's decided to resign. And wait until you hear why. There'll soon be nobody left at all here. Anyway, give me a ring when you can and I'll fill you in on all the details. Bye.

Speaker 4: Hi Nicola, it's Olga. I'm calling from Omsk, and it's taken me ages to get through to you. Are you OK? I tried ringing you at work a couple of times but kept getting cut off before they could put me through to you. Anyway, I just wanted to let you know that I won't be back till the 19th. They want me to do an extra workshop on the 18th and they've managed to rearrange my flights for me. Don't worry about meeting me. I'll just catch the bus home from the airport. The flight gets in at 10.15, so I'll probably be home after midday. OK, I'm going to try calling again later. Bye.

Speaker 5: Hi Piotr, it's Jens. I left my mobile at home so I'm calling from the street. Haven't used one of these for ages so hope I can tell you everything before my coins run out. OK. So we're meeting for the leaving party at 6.30 tonight not 7.30. Hang on a moment. I'll just find the address. Yes, here it is. It's the King's Pub next to the station. OK, see you there later. Bye

Speaker 6: Matt? This is Alex. I've downloaded version two. The graphics are just amazing. Do you want to come round and play it? I've got to get my homework done first but that'll only take ten minutes. I'll …
Oh – I think I'm breaking up. I'm going to hang up. I'll text you.

2

> 1 look up; ring me back; showing up; call back; fix those in; get back; catch up; give me a ring; fill you in; get through; cut off; put me through; gets in; run out; hang on; come round; breaking up; hang up
> 2 when a phone signal starts to go bad during a call – break up
> connect a caller with someone else – put through
> wait – hang on
> end a phone call – hang up
> achieve a phone connection – get through
> lose a phone connection – cut off

3

> 1 your battery runs out
> 2 get through
> 3 them to speak up
> 4 put you through
> 5 Hang on a moment
> 6 pass you over

Speaking

1

| **b** 1 | **c** 6 | **d** 7 | **e** 4 | **f** 10 | **g** 9 | **h** 3 | **i** 8 | **j** 5 |

Vocabulary

1

make / take / have a phone call
take / have a bath
make a cake
take / have a chance
have a go
make a mistake
have a party
take a photo
have / take a shower
make an effort
make an excuse
have / make dinner (note that *take dinner* sounds quite old-fashioned and is rarely used)
have / make fun
take hold of
take part in
do the cooking
do someone a favour
do your best
take someone seriously
take an exam
take a course
take someone's word for it
do work
make sure

Corpus spot

1 course I recently ~~had~~ **took**
2 ~~have~~ **take** a driving test
3 ~~take~~ **have** a light breakfast
4 jobs mainly ~~made~~ **done** by men
5 ~~make~~ **take** some pictures
6 ~~do~~ **take** a decision
7 ~~make~~ **do** business with us
8 ~~do~~ **make** some changes
9 correct some **mistakes** you have ~~done~~ **made**

Reading

1

1 A – the writer feels that the best way to communicate is to talk to someone directly.
2 satirical

2

1 texting
2 texting for long periods
3 a Museum of Texting
4 the invention of the 'Immobile Phone'
5 person-to-person conversation
6 phone-free conversation

3

come out (*wrong*) = were typed inaccurately
came out (*right*) = were typed accurately
leave out (*all the vowels*) = omit
texted back = responded
(*message had*) *got through* = reached its destination
drawn out = extended
dress up = wear fancy dress
came up with (*the bright idea*) = had
(*battery*) *running down* = losing its charge
walking around = walking (the around is not strictly necessary)
switch off = unwind
come up with (*a way / solution*) = devised
(*PFC has*) *taken off* = become a great success

4

take time
have no way (of knowing)
reach a destination
take place
come up with a (bright) idea
feel the need to (do something)
give (people an) opportunity
make progress
come up with a way of (doing something)
come up with a solution
have no idea

Exam folder 3 pages 44–45

Paper 1 Part 3

1 & 2

1 (adverb) surprisingly
2 (adjective) military
3 (noun) travellers
4 (noun) literature
5 (verb) describes / described (both would be possible – we often use the present simple when talking about the plots of books or films, even if they were made in the past)
6 (adverb) suddenly
7 (verb–past participle) entered
8 (noun) conversation

3

Verbs	Adjectives	Nouns
unwrap	unsafe	disappearance
de-ice	disloyal	insecurity
untie	insane	discomfort
disengage	uncomfortable	unbalance
misunderstand	irresponsible	immobility

Corpus spot

1 dissatisfaction
2 unsatisfactory
3 inadequate
4 disorganised
5 inexpensive

4

1 **law:** lawyer, lawful, unlawful, lawless, law-abiding
2 **hope:** hopeful, hopeless, hopelessness, hopefully
3 **act:** action, actor, react, reaction, enact, enactment
4 **press:** pressure, pressing, depress, oppress, repress, oppression, oppressive, oppressor
5 **centre:** central, centrally, centralise, decentralise, centralisation, concentrate, concentration
6 **head:** heading, header, subhead, behead, heady, big-headed, pig-headed
7 **office:** officer, official, officiate, officious, officially
8 **broad:** breadth, broaden, broadly, broad-minded

5

1 being
2 incoming
3 currently
4 participated
5 steadily
6 reliability
7 inconsiderable
8 introduction

6

1 happily
2 skilled
3 recognition
4 unfamiliar
5 injury
6 discharged
7 fortunately
8 psychologically

Unit 7 pages 46–49

Reading

1

1 13
2 selling scooters
3 family and friends
4 companies were happy to give him advice

2

1 with
2 come
3 one
4 neither / nor
5 if
6 which
7 did, sold
8 in
9 case
10 a
11 them
12 of
13 do, did
14 what

3

1 A
2 B
3 D
4 B

Vocabulary

1

do business
a gap in the market
make a profit
take action
stocks and shares
competitive prices
daily commute
overwhelmed by problems
stuck in traffic

2

1 doing business
2 daily commute; stuck in traffic
3 a gap in the market; make a profit
4 stocks and shares
5 overwhelmed by problems; took action
6 competitive prices

3

1 freedom
2 profitable
3 variety
4 competitors
5 explosive
6 childish

Reason, result and purpose

1

1 be a consequence of …
2 in order to get …
3 because of …

2

1 so
2 because
3 Having had
4 so
5 so as to
6 because
7 As a result of
8 with the result that

Writing

1

The report is generally positive.

2

1 The headings are appropriate and useful in that they state clearly what each paragraph includes. The report is clear and unambiguous and uses headings to inform and guide the reader. The report therefore follows a fairly standard pattern.
2 *Firstly, Secondly, Thirdly, Finally* – listing points
For example – giving an example
In conclusion – drawing a conclusion
However – making a point that contrasts in some way with what has gone before
3 *thanks to, as a result of, Consequently*

Listening and Speaking

2

1 hairdresser
2 private detective
3 stunt woman
4 window cleaner
5 fitness instructor
6 journalist
7 psychologist
8 sports commentator

Recording script 1 12

Speaker 1: When I was at school, I decided I definitely wanted a career and I thought about what I could do working with other people. I got a part-time job in a salon, and it was only until I got an apprenticeship that I really thought this is what I want to do. I love the work because you meet different people every day. You can be creative, which is important to me. If there is any downside, it's that you're on your feet all day, but at the end of the day, it's something I really love doing.

Speaker 2: Well this job found me, really. A friend recommended me and so I did a job for someone and it seemed to work out OK. I never fancied doing a run-of-the-mill job, nine-to-five, and I quite like the secrecy of what I'm doing now. There is a lot of boring paper work – it's not as dramatic as you see in the films – but the best part is when I'm out on the street. I'm a private man by nature, so it sort of suits me.

Speaker 3: Initially, I wanted to be an actor and then I realised, eventually, that wasn't going to happen. I've always been sporty and I used to go to judo class every week, and then got more and more interested, and sort of started going more often. It was my teacher who sort of suggested I get into it. So he introduced me to someone, and I've been on film sets ever since, really. There's a lot of travel, which sometimes gets me down, but I do get to meet famous people – including the ones I'm supposed to be.

Speaker 4: I got into it by accident really. I needed extra money, and I've always liked, you know, the outdoors and getting out and all that sort of thing, so I just decided to give it a try and keep on going. It's not been bad – lucrative even. You get the cash straight in your hand when you've finished. And it's hard work. It's harder work than you imagine, especially when you're out in the cold. The nice thing is the satisfaction on people's faces, looking at people's faces afterwards when they realise they can actually see outside again.

Speaker 5: I'd always been interested in fitness. I was, actually, a gym champion when I was young. Then I decided what to do when I grew up and, yeah, it was, it was a really good choice in the end because what I really like is helping other people get fit, and to actually bring out the best in them. I can advise them what to do and what not to do, what's best for their muscles and, yeah, it's really worthwhile.

Speaker 6: First of all, well, I did an English degree and then I didn't know what to do really, after that. I wanted to get out and, you know, do a job where you sort of meet a lot of people and so I fell into it, really. It's great, you know, because you meet a lot of interesting people. What I really like about it is you're always breaking a story, so whatever you get involved in is, you know, always going to be interesting. I suppose the thing I don't like is the public's perception of us as being like the paparazzi, never reporting the truth, always up to no good. But I think we do a very important job. If someone's famous, then it's in the public interest to sort of find out as much as possible about them, you know, and that's what I do.

Speaker 7: I think it was clear to my family what I was going to be from an early age. I'm the eldest of five and my brothers and sisters always came to me for advice, and in the end, actually, my mother used to come to me for advice, or she'd talk things over, or as a family, we liked to try and find out why things happened as they did. I didn't really learn anything about it at school, but as part of biology, we did look at the way people behaved and why they do what they do. It was a long training, but something that's absolutely worthwhile. My belief and commitment in people, I suppose, is what made me choose this career. If there's anything I find disappointing, it's that if I've helped someone, I can't necessarily see the changes in their everyday lives.

Speaker 8: Yes, I was an only child, no brothers or sisters. My mother left my father when I was about seven so every holiday, I went to be with my father. I used to follow him everywhere and his job was a sports commentator. He travelled all over the place, following the races, and I went with him. It must have had a huge effect on me. I met all the famous drivers and the smell of the track, the noise from the cars and everything was a very powerful thing that led me into this profession. Now I'm actually doing it myself, I feel under pressure. I don't see enough of my own family, I'm travelling all over the world. So it's not the dream I thought it would be.

Writing folder 3 pages 50–51

Essays

1

1 Between 220 and 260.
2 the impact of technology on employment opportunities
3 The opinions in inverted commas comment on the topics in the bullet points.
4 two
5 You have to explain which is more significant, giving reasons.
6 You can use the opinions, but you should express them in your own words.

2

1 four
2 (paragraph 1) to introduce the essay's theme
(paragraph 2) to describe one of the arguments in the bullet point in the task
(paragraph 3) to describe an alternative argument
(paragraph 4) to conclude the essay, giving the writer's own opinion

3

ever since – to explain a time relationship
while – to indicate a contrast
others – to avoid repeating *some people*
the former group of people – to refer back to the people who think technology will have a negative impact
as – to explain a reason
these prophets of doom – to refer back to the people who think technology will have a negative impact
as a result – to explain a reason
on the other hand – to indicate a contrast
when – to explain a time relationship
because – to explain a reason
although – to indicate a contrast
my opinion is – to explain a reason
than ever before – to explain a time relationship

Unit 8 pages 52–55

Speaking

1

1 wristwatch (1904)
2 electric dishwasher (1914)
3 sliced bread (1928)
4 the toaster (1937)
5 the biro (1938)
6 video recorder (1956)
7 ring-pull can (1962)
8 personal stereo (1979)
9 computer mouse (1984)
10 wi-fi (1985)

Reading

3

Suggested answers

1 *courting* = the early stages of a romantic relationship
contours = shape
suction pad = piece of rubber that fixes itself to a smooth surface using suction
treadmill = wide wheel turned by people climbing on steps around its edge (used in the past to provide power for machines or as punishment)
mop = stick with material on one end for washing floors
pivotable = can be moved about a fixed point
2 *mini-* = small (e.g. *minimal, mini-series, miniskirt*)
3 *-able* = can or able to be (e.g. *disposable, regrettable, comparable*)
-less = without (e.g. *hopeless, thoughtless, careless*)
4 *common* ≠ separate
flexible ≠ inflexible, rigid
inner ≠ outer
drives ≠ halts, stops
mess up ≠ keep tidy
stowed ≠ unfolded

Vocabulary

1

1 breathtaking
2 hideous
3 ingenious
4 hackneyed
5 stunning
6 appalling
7 ridiculous; delightful

2

Positive	Negative
absorbing	grotesque
breathtaking	hackneyed
brilliant	hideous
delightful	ill-conceived
enchanting	impractical
engrossing	monstrous
ingenious	pointless
inspired	repulsive
ravishing	ridiculous
stunning	trivial

Listening

1

Suggested answers
A: they're indispensable; a brilliant invention
B: it's just so convenient
C: brilliant for getting from A to B
D: great design
E: an inspired design; ingenious
F: makes it so easy to find information; make contact easily with people all over the world

2

Positive: brilliant, stunning, inspired, ingenious, indispensable, extraordinary
Negative: vain, hideous

Recording script 1 13

Simon: OK, so the question is 'What couldn't you live without?' Is there anything that you just couldn't imagine life without?

Caroline: Yes, that's easy. Though it's something I used to think was a waste of money before I actually got one.

Ben: Don't tell me – it's your car. You spend most of your time driving.

Caroline: Nearly. It's my SatNav. We got it last year. It was just brilliant for getting from A to B. When we went on holiday last year, we programmed it to avoid the main roads and it took us on all sorts of back roads through the countryside. It's much better than stopping all the time, looking at the map, discovering you're lost and arguing. It took us to some stunning places we wouldn't have found otherwise. The air-conditioning in the car is useful but I wouldn't say I couldn't live without that. Just open the window if it gets hot. What about you?

Annie: Well, because of the kids, the one thing I really couldn't do without is my washing machine, especially because we've got so much laundry to do. Nappies, as well, because we use washable nappies, which are more eco-friendly than the disposable ones.

Caroline: Oh yes. That's something most of us take for granted.

Annie: And ours is an inspired design, because it's got lots of features like the half-load button, for example, and it's ingenious the way it can do that. And the other thing I really couldn't do without is my hair-dryer. Oh I love my hair-dryer! I think that's another piece of great design. Yeah, those are the things I really couldn't cope without.

Simon: I think I could easily do without mine.

Ben: That's only because you're getting a bit bald on top! I couldn't live without contact lenses. They're indispensable. Apart from being a brilliant invention, they – well, I couldn't see without them. I don't like wearing glasses – I'm quite vain – so I do need them. I mean, I think they're an absolutely extraordinary and inspired invention. But the other thing that I couldn't possibly live without is my microwave. The one I've got – it's a big hideous thing in the corner – is great because it can heat things up at the last minute. Cold cups of coffee suddenly become hot again, so … without those two, with those two things, I'm fine. Without them, I'd be lost. But what about you?

Simon: Me? Well, the first would have to be my mobile, of course. It's got lots of features – though I still mainly use it for phoning and texting and taking the odd photo if I don't have an actual camera to hand. It's just so convenient when you have to change arrangements at the last minute or when you want to keep in touch with people who aren't at home much. I wish its battery lasted longer – but apart from that, I've no complaints. My second thing would be the internet. Does that count?

Ben: As an invention? Why not?

Simon: OK, so that's what I'd go for then. It just makes it so easy to find information, to buy things – I get most of my books online and download most of my music, and movies. You can also make contact easily with people all over the world. I've done some great online courses, studying and meeting people who I'll probably never see face-to-face. I love it!

Modals and semi-modals (2)

1

1 Someone really <u>ought to</u> invent a machine to do the ironing for you. (suggesting something would be a good idea)
2 This key ring bleeps when you whistle – that <u>should</u> help you next time you lose your keys. (suggesting something is likely)
3 You <u>must</u> get yourself a mobile phone – everyone else has got one. (giving advice)
4 My hair dryer's missing – my flatmate <u>must have</u> borrowed it again. (making a deduction)
5 You <u>should have</u> kept the instructions for the DVD recorder! (disapproval)
6 He submitted his request for a patent ages ago – he <u>must</u> be going to hear from the department soon. (probability)
7 You <u>shouldn't have</u> pressed that button before switching the power off. (he thinks the person did do something wrong)
8 The design has been approved and we <u>should</u> be starting production next week. (probability)
9 Even when he was still at school, he <u>would</u> spend hours in the shed designing weird and wonderful inventions. (frequently)
10 You <u>will</u> accept this design or else. (no choice)
11 We <u>must</u> light a fire somehow but no one's brought any matches – what <u>shall</u> we do? (suggestions)

2

1 must (obligation)
2 should / ought to (advice)
3 should have; must have (deduction)
4 would (past habit)
5 mustn't (prohibition)
6 should / ought to (advice)
7 Will (willingness)
8 shouldn't have (criticism)

Corpus spot

1 would
2 should
3 would
4 would
5 should
6 could

Speaking

1

expressing agreement: 1, 9
expressing admiration: 2, 7
expressing surprise or disbelief: 3, 5, 8, 11, 12, 14
expressing sympathy: 4, 6, 10, 13

2

Suggested answers

1 Brilliant!
2 Poor you!
3 You must be joking!
4 Oh dear!
5 Fantastic!
6 Surely not!
7 Me too!
8 What a shame!

Recording script 1.14 (possible answers in brackets)

1 The safety pin was invented in 1849. (No, really?)
2 I've had toothache since Tuesday. I haven't slept at all. (Poor you!)
3 When Mrs Lincoln, the wife of President Lincoln, had her photograph taken after her husband had been assassinated, the photograph included a ghostly image of the President. (That's interesting.)
4 You have been selected to advise the government on the problems of education in this country. (You're joking!)
5 My grandfather, my mother, my sister and I were all born on the same date – 6th of June! (What a coincidence!)
6 There are 400 billion stars in the Milky Way. (That's incredible!)
7 From 13th June 1948 to 1st June 1949, one person in Los Angeles hiccuped 160 million times! 60,000 suggestions for cures were received before he eventually stopped. (You must be joking!)
8 King Gustav II of Sweden thought that coffee was poisonous. He once sentenced a man to death by ordering him to drink coffee every day. The condemned man in fact lived to be very old! (That's interesting.)
9 The first alarm clock was invented by Leonardo da Vinci. It woke the sleeper by gently rubbing the soles of his feet. (Fantastic!)
10 The common housefly may be the biggest threat to human health. It carries 30 different diseases which can be passed to humans. (No, really?)

Exam folder 4 pages 56–57

Paper 1 Part 4

1

1 Sam's essay <u>made an impression on</u> his tutor.
2 He <u>insisted on (only) speaking</u> English with the visitors.
3 There was a <u>sharp increase in</u> the price of petrol last month.
4 I <u>caught sight of</u> the postman for a second as he passed by.

2

1 The phrasal verb is to *hand something down to someone* – *to* is missing.
The secret recipe <u>is handed down to</u> each new generation.

2 The given word is in the past tense and cannot be changed.
The present <u>came as a complete surprise</u> to me.

3 The wrong preposition is used.
The child's mother <u>was overcome with emotion</u> when he was found.

4 The idiom for *to help someone* is *to give someone a hand*.
Could you possibly <u>give me a hand</u> with this suitcase?

3

1 b
2 e
3 a
4 f
5 c
6 d

4

1 in
2 of
3 from
4 in
5 with
6 in

5

1 If we don't get the 8 o'clock train, <u>it will mean</u> missing lunch.

2 Italian football players are <u>said to get the highest</u> salaries.

3 The tour operator <u>apologised for not</u> emailing the details earlier.

4 Your accountant <u>should have given you</u> better advice.

6

1 A medical certificate <u>isn't required for</u> a US visa.
2 The island <u>is rich in</u> natural resources.
3 Gina <u>does nothing but</u> complain.
4 The candidate <u>gave honest answers to</u> the questions.
5 If the tennis court hadn't been so wet, the match <u>wouldn't have been called</u> off.
6 I'd <u>be on your side</u> even if you weren't my friend.
7 Sam <u>flatly refused to give me a</u> hand.
8 Would you mind <u>getting some milk on your way</u> home?

Unit 9 pages 58–61

Speaking and Reading

2

1 g
2 f
3 c
4 a
5 h
6 d
7 e
8 b

3 & 4

Suggested notes

1 Streets did not have to be so wide. Pollution from traffic fumes was less of a problem.

2 They have a lot to offer because they have a lot of vitality and energy but they leave much to be desired because they also have many problems – inadequate housing, traffic problems, crime.

3 history; cultural life; prosperity; exciting physical features; at least one comfortable season; well-managed; clean; no congestion; can get around easily.

4 Because people do not know their neighbours in the way they do in smaller places and because the stresses of life in a mega-city makes it harder for people to pay attention to other people. (Students may well come up with other good answers than these.)

5 Because the speed and scale of developments mean that there are plenty of exciting opportunities there.

6 transport

7 The way cities have developed in the past has shown us that we need greater awareness of environmental issues, especially in connection with energy use.
We can also learn from the negative results of allowing market forces to determine how cities develop as well as from our greater awareness of how a beautiful location may have been spoilt by uncontrolled development.

8 economic prosperity, a just society, a thriving cultural life and government support

Vocabulary

1

1 h
2 g
3 f
4 b
5 a
6 e
7 c
8 d

2

1 hustle and bustle
2 traffic congestion
3 unique character
4 standards of living
5 beyond all recognition
6 environmental concerns
7 modern amenities
8 rich in history

Listening

Recording script 1 15

Speaker 1: I'm originally from Sri Lanka but I've been living in Dubai for almost … oh three years? I'm working for a British company here. I come from a small town in Sri Lanka called Negombo – it's near the capital. So living in Dubai is a rather different experience for me. But it still feels pretty comfortable here. There are lots of other Sri Lankan families here, although I don't often mix with them. Most of my colleagues are from the UK. What's interesting is that my kids, who are still quite young, are growing up speaking English, because that's what they hear around them all the time. I think it's the same for a lot of the other expat families living here. So, this will create a new generation of English-speaking foreign workers living here, I suppose. Dubai, I have to say, has a very good infrastructure. The airport is very easy to get to, and it connects with many other cities. There are taxis everywhere, and of course the shopping is first-class. It's actually not as bustling as Colombo, the Sri Lankan capital, but it does have a similar energy. So, I do like living here, yes.

Speaker 2: I've been in Kuala Lumpur for about ten years now. It's incredible how much the city has changed. There are many parts of the city that have been completely developed, or modernised. It's all been given a make-over. There are new skyscrapers, shopping malls, transportation systems, everything. And this has solved a lot of problems, actually. It's much easier to get around, and the air does feel cleaner. I would say, however, that I do miss some of the old Kuala Lumpur – the city I knew when I first came here. When you could have a snack on the street in a little market, or see a real old Chinese bakery with old gentlemen chatting inside. Those places still exist, although they are sometimes hard to find.

Speaker 3: I was born in New York, but I've spent a lot of time here in Delhi. I think it's been about 15 years since I first arrived. My wife and kids live here, too. And I have seen a lot of development here. Many things have improved. But there's also a lot of congestion. Luckily, we live in one of the greener parts of the city, but when I have to get around, it can be slow and difficult. But I love it here. We adore the food – we can't get enough of it. The variety is incredible. That's always been the case, though. The best thing, I think, is the people here. It's a big, crowded city, but it's also very human. And it's great to belong to a city like that.

Speaker 4: When did I first come to Bangkok? It must have been ten years ago. I currently work in an English school here, but I also do a lot in my spare time. I'm still trying to learn Thai, but not with very much success. Things have changed a lot since I first came. There are more modern, air-conditioned buildings now. More hotels. Certainly, there are more tourists, especially coming from China. I think that's possibly one reason why the prices have gone up. But another thing that's changed is that the city has got cleaner. There are still lots of cars everywhere, but you don't see as many tuk tuks as you use to – the little three-wheeled vehicles people use as taxis. This means that there is far less pollution. And the older buildings and canals are really being cleaned up, too. Most people are surprised that there are canals in Bangkok – but there are! And this means that a lot of the traditions have come back, like the floating markets, where people sell fruit, flowers, and so on, on boats. It's amazing.

3

Speaker	1	2	3	4
City	Dubai	Kuala Lumpur	Delhi	Bangkok
Length of time there	3 years	10 years	15 years	10 years
Change(s) mentioned	new generation of English-speaking foreign workers	new skyscrapers, shopping malls, transportation systems	a lot of development; congestion	more modern buildings, hotels, tourists; prices have gone up; cleaner
Favourite aspect of the city	good infrastructure; airport is easy to get to; taxis everywhere; shopping is first-class	easier to get around; air feels cleaner	the food; the people	traditions, like the floating markets

Future forms

1

1. e
2. a
3. f
4. d, f
5. e
6. i
7. g
8. c
9. j
10. b

2

1. I'm going
2. get
3. we'll be lying
4. he'd leave
5. to get
6. leaves / is leaving
7. are, are going to spend
8. gets, she's going to study
9. will have set foot

Writing folder 4 pages 62–63

Reports

1

1. F. They begin with a title and (usually) a statement of their purpose.
2. T
3. F. This is not essential but it is a good idea to do this as you probably would when writing a report in 'real life'.
4. F. The aim of a report is more to inform than to interest.
5. T
6. F. Both reports and proposals are likely to have these.
7. F. Reports do not always make recommendations but they often do.
8. F. They will usually be written in neutral or formal language.
9. T
10. F. It is important for any task to spend time planning what you are going to write.

2

Your college has asked students to <u>report</u> on the <u>sports facilities which students can use in their leisure time</u>. Write a report for the <u>college principal</u>, commenting on the extent to which the <u>facilities meet students' needs</u>. You should also <u>make recommendations about what you think the college should do to improve the facilities</u>.

3

1. The principal of a college where you are studying.
2. Neutral or formal.
3. Information about leisure (sports and music) facilities at the college.
4. A report.

4

Suggested answers

Both answers are in accurate English. However, B would get an excellent mark while A would not. The problems with A are that:
- its language is too informal.
- it is a letter and not a report.
- it is not organised into paragraphs.
- it introduces irrelevant material (e.g. about the library, which is not a leisure facility).

Unit 10 pages 64–67

Reading

2

1. D
2. C
3. A
4. B

3

1. B
2. C
3. D
4. B

4

looks for – seeks
main – primary
choose – opt for
replied – responded
views – perspectives
develop – acquire
do – accomplish
methods – strategies
before – prior to
given – administered

5

1 acquire
2 strategies
3 administered
4 primary
5 responses
6 seeks
7 prior to
8 perspectives
9 opt for

Vocabulary

1

Verb	Noun	Adjective
accept	acceptance	accepted
assume	assumption	assumptuous
attend	attention / attendance	attentive
compete	competition	competitive
conclude	conclusion	conclusive
contribute	contribution	x
determine	determination	determined
establish	establishment	established
opt	option	x
signify	significance	significant

2

1 The results of the survey are not conclusive.
2 In my opinion the research made certain false assumptions.
3 The idea was initially controversial but it rapidly became accepted / but people rapidly accepted it.
4 There is a lot of competition for places at this university.
5 The government's inadequate response to the economic crisis was a contributory factor in their election defeat.
6 Attendance at the last lecture of the course was poor.
7 The party's aim was to establish a fairer distribution of wealth in society.
8 I admire this student because of her determination to succeed.

Participle clauses

2

2 were concerned about the lack of cultural awareness of their staff
3 we had administered a questionnaire

3

Possible answers
1 Because he hoped to encourage people to respond, the researcher offered the chance to win a prize …
2 Since it was a Sunday, most of the shops were shut.
3 Charles I, who was generally considered a weak king, was eventually beheaded.
4 Although Charlton's work was ignored until recently by many scholars, it is at last getting the recognition it deserves.
5 If it is seen from a distance, the castle looks like something out of a fairy tale.
6 As Picton had previously learned their language, he was able to communicate with the tribe.

4

Suggested answers
1 Walking round the exhibition, I caught sight of an old school friend at the far end of the gallery.
2 Having made so many mistakes in her homework, Marti had to do it all over again.
3 Being only a child, she can't understand what is happening.
4 Not knowing anyone in the town to spend the evening with, Jack decided to have an early night.
5 Looked at from a sociological point of view, the problem can be seen as one of tension between social classes.

5

Possible answers
1 Having studied English for some years now, I feel quite confident about using the language.
2 Having spent a lot of time trying to master the piano, I've accepted that I'll never be a great player.
3 It being a sunny day today, I think we should go to the beach.
4 Not wanting to appear boastful, I must tell you that my English pronunciation has often been praised.
5 Knowing what I know now about Mary, I wish I'd trusted her more.

Speaking

2 The words which are stressed are underlined in the script.

Recording script 1 16

1 **A:** Did you go to the cinema last night?
  B: No, but I went to the <u>theatre</u>.

2 **A:** Did you go by bike to the theatre last night?
  B: No, <u>Marco</u> was using my bike last night.

3 **A:** Did you go to the theatre by bus last night?
  B: No, I went to the theatre by <u>taxi</u> last night.

4 **A:** Did you go home by taxi last night?
  B: No, I went home by taxi <u>two</u> nights ago.

5 **A:** Anna's wearing a lovely green dress.
  B: It's a green <u>blouse</u> and <u>skirt</u>, actually.

6 **A:** Did you have a good time at the party last night?
  B: Yes, we had a <u>brilliant</u> time.

7 **A:** Are you hungry yet?
  B: I'm not <u>hungry</u>, I'm <u>starving</u>.

8 **A:** Are you hungry yet?
  B: <u>I'm</u> not hungry but <u>Tina</u> is.

Units 6–10 Revision

pages 68–69

6

1 C
2 A
3 D
4 C
5 B
6 C
7 B
8 D

7

1 inventive
2 recognition
3 executive
4 pointless
5 appallingly
6 complaints
7 satisfaction
8 insignificant
9 assumptions
10 conclusive

8

1 out
2 grow
3 to
4 of
5 symbol / sign
6 all
7 in
8 than

Unit 11 pages 70–73

Reading

2

1 C
2 F
3 A
4 E
5 D
6 G

4

1 ran (several) trials
2 over
3 the end of
4 good value for
5 allergic to
6 in mind
7 further
8 into

5

to suit someone: 7
designer labels: 8
to fit someone: 3
a rack: 6
out of fashion: 4
a look: 2
a changing room: 5
item of clothing: 1
fabric: 10
stylish: 9

Listening

3

1 reception
2 a tie and a dark suit
3 accountants
4 dress-down Friday
5 (a) training day(s)
6 a nose ring
7 civil liberties
8 Human Resources

Recording script 1 17

Now, it's been brought to my attention that certain members of staff have been flouting the dress code. So I want to make it crystal clear to everyone just exactly what's expected. Those of you who work at the reception must be – how shall I put it – business-like at all times. That's the look we want to achieve. You are the first person that visitors see when they enter the building. Whether they then go on to the Managing Director or the canteen is irrelevant. You create the first impression of the company, and as we all know, first and last impressions count. Now, for men that means wearing a tie and a dark suit. For women, a suit, that can be a tailored trouser suit, or a smart dress or skirt and jacket. Blouses must be short- or long-sleeved, not sleeveless. It goes without saying that hair and so on needs to be neat and tidy.

Now, as for accountants … You never know when a client may come in to see you. You may think you're not in the public relations business but in a way, you are. And I know most of the time people make appointments, but there are occasions when someone just happens to be in the area and decides to drop in. In this case, you represent us. This is a firm with a good reputation. Clients expect their accountant to reflect this, not only in their work but also in the way they present themselves. Don't forget, in many people's eyes, sloppy clothes means sloppy work, and I must say, I tend to agree.

The only possible exception to this is dress-down Friday. Now, this doesn't mean that you can turn up wearing whatever you like – no shorts and sandals, please! It's got to be 'smart-casual'. That's what it says here. But you can wear smart jeans and a jacket or even a sweater.

Now, something's come to my attention that I'm not at all happy about – training days. It seems as though some of you have got the idea into your head that when you're on a training day, that means you can dress like a student. It does not. You're still a representative of this company. When you go out to Business College, you're judged there too. I've heard remarks about a certain man who turned up there wearing a nose ring. This is not acceptable; it's all in the company's dress code, which you've all had a copy of. What I want to emphasise is that it's a matter of professional pride, the way you dress.

I know some people start complaining about civil liberties and all that, but I'm sorry, as I see it, we're all here to do a job. We are employees of a company, and we have to toe the line, and not only in what we do and how we do our job, but also in the way we dress.

If anyone feels particularly aggrieved by any of this, all I can suggest is that you take it up with the Human Resources Department.

But really, I hope I won't have to refer to this again and I expect to see a dramatic improvement in personal presentation.

Reported speech

1

1 exactly what was/is expected.
2 those of us who work/worked on reception must/had to be business-like at all times.
3 us that in many people's eyes, sloppy clothes meant/means sloppy work.
4 she was/is not at all happy about the way some people dressed/dress for training days.
5 it seemed/seems as though some of us had/have got the idea into our head that when we were/are on a training day we could/can dress like a student.
6 had turned up wearing a nose ring.
7 it was/is a matter of professional pride, the way we dress.
8 we had/have to toe the line.
9 if anyone felt/feels particularly aggrieved by any of that/this, all she could say was/is that we should take it up with the Human Resources department.
10 she wouldn't/won't have to refer to this/that again.

2

1 He promised to do it
2 She suggested doing it / that I (should) do it
3 We agreed to do it / that I (should) do it
4 They told me (not) to do it
5 She asked to do it / me (not) to do it
6 He offered to do it
7 She advised doing it / me (not) to do it
8 He recommended doing it / that I (should) do it
9 He denied doing it
10 She invited me (not) to do it
11 They warned me (not) to do it
12 I insisted that I (should) do it
13 He threatened to do it
14 I regretted doing it

3

Corpus spot
1 It is **recommended** to book in advance.
2 I would recommend **asking / that you ask** for further information.
3 **We were told that** the problems **would be solved / were going to be solved**.
4 It has been suggested **that we have** a film club once a month.
5 He suggested **asking Colin / that you ask Colin** to make the opening speech.
6 She regrets **not having** enough time to play an instrument.
7 We promised **(that) there** would be 35 stalls at the charity day.

Speaking

1

Suggested answers
Talking about similarities
is similar to the other (picture) in that ...
shows the same kind of ...
like the second (picture), ...
is much the same as ...
Talking about differences
However,
although
on the one hand,
on the other hand,
while

2

1 *but, and, in contrast* (and students' own answers)
2 flamboyant
3 a teacher

Recording script 1 18

Examiner: In this part of the test, I'm going to give each of you some pictures. I'd like you to talk about them on your own for about a minute and also to answer a question briefly about your partner's pictures. Angela, it's your turn first. Here are your pictures, A and B. These show people wearing different types of clothes. I'd like you to compare these pictures, and say why these people may have chosen to wear these clothes, and what clothes might tell us about the wearer. All right?

Angela: OK, in photos A and B, they are both pictures of men but they are wearing very different clothes. In picture A, we can see a man wearing a suit and in fact the stripes are quite prominent; it's not a subtle sort of stripe that the typical businessman wears. And there's another interesting thing about the suit; it's shiny – that's quite flamboyant. Then this man is wearing a tie – sort of pink with deeper stripes. Again, that's outrageous, some might say. This leads me to think that perhaps he's not a businessman who works in a bank or insurance company but perhaps he's something to do with the arts or in advertising. It's got to be a profession which allows him to express his slightly extrovert personality. In contrast, in photo B, there's a man wearing casual clothes. He's wearing some sort of brown top with a zip and then over that he's got another blue jacket which is undone. It looks as if it's made of that fleece material. He's got a scarf tucked into his top. His trousers have got large pockets on the sides of the legs – quite fashionable, I think. I'm not absolutely sure but perhaps they might be made of corduroy. And then he's wearing walking boots. Looking at this picture, I would say this man is enjoying some time at the weekend, out in the country – he's a man who loves being out in nature and he's quite a free thinker. I can't imagine him working in a bank either – look at his hair. He could be a teacher.

Examiner: Thank you. Now, Luciano, which picture shows the clothes that you would be most comfortable wearing?

Luciano: Oh, definitely picture B. I feel much better when I'm wearing casual clothes and I would certainly never wear a suit like that!

Examiner: Thank you.

Exam folder 5 pages 74–75

Paper 1 Part 5

1

1 D   2 D   3 C   4 A   5 B   6 C

2

1 former
2 If something is *mainstream*, then it is accepted by the majority of the population – it is not unusual.
3 principles and viewpoints
4 By breaking up the word to find the root, *lie* and the prefix *under*. It means 'real but not immediately obvious'.
5 It means the things that you do to make your appearance tidy and pleasant, for example brushing your hair. In this paragraph its meaning may be extended to include a person's concern to look fashionable.
6 implication

Unit 12 pages 76–79

Reading and Writing

1

> **Suggested answers**
> 1 Student's own answers.
> 2 (Paragraph 1) We rarely make rational decisions. Most people think it's best to choose the most expensive thing.
> (Paragraph 2) Our decision-making process is easily influenced by the power of suggestion.
> (Paragraph 3) Our decisions are influenced by external and internal/personal factors.
> (Paragraph 4) Our attempts to make rational decisions often fail.
> 3 Decision-making is irrational; it's an instinct or gut feeling.

2

> **Suggested answers**
> 1 neutral / formal
> 2 an opening salutation (or greeting) and a reason for writing

Vocabulary

1 Students complete the exercise alone, and then check their answers in pairs.

> 1 e
> 2 c
> 3 h
> 4 g
> 5 f
> 6 a
> 7 b
> 8 d

2

> 1 gut feeling
> 2 wide range
> 3 follow
> 4 favourable opinion
> 5 expectations; raised
> 6 playing tricks
> 7 as a result
> 8 positive outcome

Listening

Recording script 1·19

Good morning everyone. My name's Jane Hurley and I work for Gradbiz Recruiters where I've been matching job seekers to vacancies for over ten years. I'd like to share some of my experience and insights with you today and hope that it may help you find the right job.

The first things you have to think about are your CV, or resume, and your letter of application. These are what count when employers make their initial decisions about you. As you can imagine, companies' vacancies attract a huge number of candidates for top jobs. And while, of course your CV is important, it's your letter of application that the employer will look at first. That's where you'll be able to show how you're different from the other 10 candidates who also have a top class degree in Business Studies, or whatever the relevant degree may be. Try getting a friend to read it to check that it's got real impact.

Interestingly, while we're on the subject of degrees, I know there've been a lot of articles in the papers saying how hard it is for arts graduates to get jobs in the UK. But actually, over the last ten months I've filled numerous vacancies in marketing with arts graduates. Before that, many were going into publishing, for example; jobs which might seem more immediately suitable for arts graduates. So don't decide to only apply for jobs in statistics because that's what you've studied.

I know I've just referred to the UK but don't forget that you should think internationally. Don't limit yourself to looking for jobs in or near your home town, or in the UK. Globalisation means that many companies work on an international level. And as English is often the company language, you may not need to speak another language fluently, although obviously it's an advantage. What will be expected though is for you to be very conscious of issues of culture in this cosmopolitan environment.

Another area I'd like you to be alerted to, and this concerns me greatly, is the high standard of technical skills that lots of companies are demanding in their job adverts. This is given a more prominent position even than communication skills, which personally, I've always seen as very useful. It means being prepared for some searching questions on this area that they're now hot on at interview.

As new graduates, you'll have your paper qualifications but you may not have very much experience. If possible, I'd suggest you do a work placement during your course. I'm sure many of you have that built into the structure of your course. Once a company knows you and sees that you work well and can learn on the job, if they have a vacancy, you might well be offered it. Working as a volunteer is also a possibility but doesn't always give you relevant experience.

It's worth getting the job description for the role you're applying for. Some companies specify very particular skills for particular roles; it could be giving presentations or in the case of one engineering firm I was recently in touch with, they saw teamwork as key to most of the activities their workers were involved in.

As you can imagine, I deal with a whole range of sectors from the hospitality industry to manufacturing, and what I've seen over my years in recruitment is that rather than vague skills like the ability to take the initiative it's the more concrete ability of being able to meet deadlines that is needed in all sectors. An employee will need to show they can do that, otherwise a company may lose their reputation and orders.

3

1	letter of application / application letter
2	marketing
3	culture
4	technical skills
5	(work) placement
6	teamwork
7	deadlines

4

2	job
3	job
4	work
5	work
6	job
7	job
8	work
9	job
10	job

-ing forms

1

1	to share
2	being
3	help
4	to read
5	getting
6	to show

2

1	c
2	e
3	f
4	a
5	d
6	g
7	b and e

Corpus spot

1 Some people would probably burst out **laughing**.
2 Our generation has grown up in a society which is used to **having** greater access to information.
3 **Having** a break to do something different is the best way to solve the problem.
4 I am looking forward to **seeing** you again.
5 ✓
6 It was my fault **not telling** you about our plans. You must have been very puzzled.
7 ✓

Writing folder 5 pages 80–81

Letters / emails

2

Suggested answers
1 The letter is for the editor of a festival (probably the festival's magazine or newsletter).
The purpose is to apply to be a host for guests coming to the festival. Potential hosts are required to explain what aspects of their culture they find interesting, and how they can explain or show it to guests.
2 The letter is to a college principal. Writers need to explain why they will be late coming back to college, and ask for permission to do so.
3 The letter is to an events agency. The writer needs to write a letter of complaint, explaining why a recent dinner and concert failed to meet expectations.

3

> **It answers task 3.**
> Dear Sir/Madam
> I am writing regarding my trip to the Vivaldi concert in Chesterton on 14th March, which I booked through your events agency. Travel by coach from Linton to the venue in Chesterton and dinner before the concert were included in the cost of the ticket, £150. This was a significant amount of money especially as the concert ticket itself was only £42 but I was happy to pay this for a special occasion.
> However, I would like to draw your attention to the aspects of the trip that did not live up to my expectations. Firstly, what was described as a dinner in your promotional material was no more than a light snack consisting of salad, bread and a drink. I had been looking forward to at least a two-course hot meal. Secondly, an even greater disappointment was my seat. There was a column between me and the stage which meant I was unable to see the orchestra and fully enjoy the event. Finally, after the concert had finished the coach driver had arranged to pick us up at 11pm but the coach did not arrive until 11.30. We were left waiting outside and no apology was offered by the driver.
> The quality of these aspects of the trip did not reflect the price paid or indeed the information sent out prior to the trip. As a result, I expect a refund. I feel that your agency should offer this as a gesture of goodwill and to do something to redeem your reputation.
> I look forward to your prompt reply.
> Yours faithfully
> Astrid Pett

4

> **Suggested answers**
> The letter should start with a paragraph stating the reason for writing (in this case, that you have some ideas for a TV programme about decision-making). The body of the letter should contain two ideas (preferably different) and explanations of why these might be interesting for viewers. The concluding paragraph could summarise the ideas, and explain how the programme might help viewers make decisions more effectively.

Unit 13 pages 82–85

Listening

2

> **Suggested answers**
> 1 There will be five sections.
> 2 Student's own answers.

3

> 1 red means stop, green means go
> 2 80
> 3 familiar
> 4 white = marriage in Western societies; but it symbolises death in China. Yellow is sacred to the Chinese, but it signifies sadness in Greece, and jealousy in France.
> 5 tropics – shades of orange; northern countries – blues
> 6 medieval European bridges were green
> 7 heart rate and blood pressure rises
> 8 feeling tired
> 9 they want customers to eat and leave quickly
> 10 soft

Recording script 2 01

All retailers, from the corner store to big multinational supermarket chains can gain major psychological influence by making use of colour. Some of the top stores pay huge amounts of money for the advice of design consultants and they are right to do so. Colour can be everything to a successful store, if the palettes work well across the whole shop and complement other elements such as product displays and lighting. The point, according to retail designers, isn't about creating the most beautiful shop, but one that has unity.

Colour is central to our lives because we react instinctively to it. Red means 'stop' and green means 'go.' Our brains are hot-wired to respond to colour and, for modern retailers, the trick to using colour is to understand both its psychological and physiological influences. So, let's start with the psychological influences.

We react at a very fundamental level to colours because they help us make sense of our surroundings; in fact, about 80 per cent of information reaches our brains via our eyes. It means that we're naturally more comfortable when colours remind us of something familiar – for example, a soft shade of blue triggers associations with the sky – an image that we've had almost since birth – and a psychological sense of calm. Prisons and hospitals have started to use colour to influence the behaviour of inmates and patients.

In children, by contrast, those colour associations haven't yet been formed, which is why youngsters respond best to primary colours. As children, we didn't instinctively go for a delicate shade of pink, we chose the bright red. That's why those bold colours are the colours of most toys, clothes and children's books – and the colour schemes of the most successful kids' retailers or sections in supermarkets.

Although we all share similar responses to colour, some cultural variations exist. For example, white is the colour of marriage in Western societies but it's the colour of death in China. Yellow is sacred to the Chinese, but signifies sadness in Greece and jealousy in France. You'll probably have noticed that people from tropical countries respond most favourably to shades of orange whereas people from northern climates prefer blues. What's more, attitudes to colour change over time too. If you look at paintings of Medieval European brides, they sometimes wore green wedding dresses.

Now, turning to physiological influences, it has been demonstrated that when we look at intense reds, our heart rate and blood pressure rise. Conversely, by looking at large areas of bright whites or greys we can become tired. In a retail environment, understanding those responses can be crucial to enticing customers inside, and then persuading them to open their wallet or purse.

Colour association also extends into food retailing. For example, most fast-food restaurants are decorated in vivid reds and oranges. These are colours that encourage us to eat quickly and leave – exactly what the fast-food operator wants us to do. Luxurious brands, on the other hand, favour soft colours that appear more sophisticated. In classier restaurants, those are the colours that encourage us to linger – and to order another drink, another coffee.

By recognising how colour influences us, retailers are better able to induce feelings of warmth, intimacy or serenity – or, by using more vibrant palettes, to excite or stimulate. It's about understanding target markets and making sure the product lines appeal to them, and identifying the kind of brand the retailer wants to be known for.

Vocabulary

1

> bath – bathe
> belief – believe
> licence – license
> relief – relieve
> proof – prove
> loss – lose
> life – live
> practice – practise
> effect – affect

2

> The following pairs have the same pronunciation.
> licence – license
> practice – practise

3

> **1 a** complement = match, go with
> **b** compliment = something nice you say to another person
> **2 a** council = an organisation which governs an area
> **b** counsel = to give support and advice
> **3 a** affect = (verb) to change something as a result of something else
> **b** effect = (noun) the change that happens as a result of something else
> **4 a** principle = an idea or concept
> **b** principal = main, most important

Past tenses and the present perfect

1

> I'd got all the ingredients listed in the recipe from the market and I was assured they were really fresh. I had to trust the stall holder because quite honestly, the red peppers, carrots, broccoli and other vegetables I'd bought all looked an unappealing shade of dull green. And I must admit at that point, I was beginning to doubt the wisdom of my offer to cook dinner.

2   See the Grammar Folder on page 169.

3

> **1** **I'd read** several recipes before I **decided** to cook a stir fry.
> **2** I decided that this week I **would invite** her round to my flat and cook her a meal.
> **3** Kate bought a new computer because she **had been accepted** on an Interior Design course.
> **4** ✓
> **5** My neighbour **owned** an interesting collection of antiques.
> **6** ✓
> **7** I **finished** painting the kitchen just as Karen came in from work.
> **8** ✓
> **9** The first paragraph of the blog **seemed** very interesting, that's why I read all of it.
> **10** Are you sure Martin cooked the dinner? I thought it **was** Emma.

4

> **Suggested answers**
> **B** She has just hit the ball.
> **C** She's had her hair cut. / She's been to the salon.
> **D** He's done something wrong.
> **E** They've been running for three hours. / They've finished the race.
> **F** He's forgotten her name.
> **G** It's finished the food. / It's been eating its dinner.
> **H** They have just arrived. / They've been travelling.
> **I** He's been working in a garage. / He's fixed the car.

5

1. has been going out
2. went
3. haven't used
4. has always been
5. have been playing

Vocabulary

1

1. a delicious vegetarian stir fry
2. a beautiful, red silk dress
3. a shabby black suit
4. an extensive, exciting new menu
5. a small, pale face

Exam folder 6 pages 86–87

Paper 1 Part 6

2

Which reviewer:
- has a different opinion from the others about the influence of van Gogh's paintings on sunflowers on the art world? (D)
- shares reviewer C's opinion on the impact of seeing the original works? (A)
- expresses a different view from the others regarding the extent to which the paintings should be seen as a metaphor for life? (B)
- takes a similar view to reviewer B on the quality of the colour in the paintings? (D)

Unit 14 pages 88–91

Speaking and Listening

3

1. A or B
2. B
3. B
4. C

4

1. 6,000
2. 9,000; 1.3 million
3. 1.5 million years
4. 300,000
5. gestures
6. primitive; basic; natural
7. tools; at night (time)

Recording script 2 02

In this lecture on the evolutionary factors of language, I'm going to begin by looking at early language in humans.

Writing began about 6,000 years ago, so it is fair to say that speech preceded that, although estimates of when humans began to speak range from 9,000 years ago to 1.3 million years ago. Primitive tools have been found that date back to 1.5 million years BC – the tools show that our ancestors had at least low level spatial thinking. Later tools, about 300,000 years old, are more advanced, revealing that cognition was on a level that was similar or equal to modern intelligence – tools had been planned in three dimensions, allowing for abstract thought – the cognitive capacity for language was present.

Krantz (1980) argues that language emerged 50,000 years ago because then the fossil records show that significant changes took place. Tools became more sophisticated and specialised, projectiles appeared along with fire and there was a large spread and expansion of the population. According to Krantz, the cause may have been to do with the emergence of full language and a new cognitive competence in humans.

Presumably, initially, people used gestures to communicate, then gestures with vocal communication. Both provided an evolutionary push towards a higher level of cognition, fuelled by a need to communicate effectively and the frustration at not being able to do so. Pettito and Marentette (1991) examined deaf infants, and found that they start to babble, and then because there is no auditory feedback, they stop. Deaf children use manual babbling (an early form of sign language equivalent to the vocalisations of hearing infants), but this manual babbling stage starts earlier than in hearing children and ends sooner. Pettito and Marentette suggest that manual language is therefore more primitive, basic and natural than spoken language, a clue that the first languages were iconic, not spoken.

The emergence of tool use with spoken language is particularly interesting. Possibly, hands were needed to manipulate tools, and humans found it difficult to communicate with sign language and use tools at the same time. Vocal communication, if possible, would allow the hands to do other things. Also, a vocal language would allow humans to communicate at night time, and without having to look at each other.

Reading

1

1. B
2. C
3. A

The passive

1

It is common for the passive to be used in statements like this when the action is more important than the person who carried it out. The passive is also commonly used when we do not know who did something.

2

1 e
2 h
3 b
4 i
5 g
6 d
7 c
8 a
9 f

3

Suggested answers

Three important areas have been revealed recently in the study of the evolutionary factors of language. 90% of humans are right-handed and have language in the left hemisphere of their brain. The second is that humans' hands were freed in order to make and use tools, which meant a method of communication other than sign language had to be found. Thirdly, syntax developed which increased the quality and quantity of the message.
It is said that chimps can be taught to speak but there are several biological factors which make humans more predisposed to speech. It should be noted that the form of the human teeth, lips, tongue and larynx are all important when it comes to speech.

6

1 This webpage is being constructed/built.
2 The case is being investigated.
3 The situation is now being controlled.
4 I was ordered not to tell anyone the company's future plans.
5 The prime minister was attacked for the statements he made.

7 Refer to the Grammar folder on page 170 for the explanations to these questions.

8

1 Have you ever had
2 had our wedding photos taken by
3 to have/get a suitable illustration produced

Vocabulary

1

1 underpractised
2 introductory
3 reference
4 outstanding
5 scientific
6 relatively
7 memorable
8 expertise

Writing folder 6 pages 92–93

Essays (2)

1 & 2

Stage of essay	Content	Purpose
Introduction	General statement	1 To introduce the reader to the topic ✓
	Definition(s) – optional	2 To explain what is understood by some key words/concepts
	Scope of essay	3 To tell the reader what you intend to cover in this essay ✓
Body	Arguments	4 To express important ideas ✓
	Evidence	5 To support ideas with examples ✓
Conclusions	Summary	6 To remind the reader of the key ideas ✓
	Relate the argument to a more general world view	7 To underline the writer's point of view ✓

3

1 *in addition, also, as soon as, therefore, before, however, then, and, in fact, for many (and varied) reasons, in conclusion, secondly*
2 Most of the linkers are formal or neutral.

Unit 15 pages 94–97

Speaking and Reading

1

1	A
2	D
3	B
4	C

2

1	g
2	e
3	f
4	b
5	d
6	a
7	c

5

1	B
2	D
3	C
4	A
5	C

The infinitive

1

Infinitive with *to*: 1, 3
Infinitive without *to*: 2, 4

2

1 I don't want you **to** think I'm complaining, because I am not.
2 ✓
3 I must ~~to~~ **go** home before I miss the last bus.
4 In my opinion parents should not let their daughters ~~to~~ **wear** make-up until they are over 16.
5 ✓
6 ✓
7 ✓
8 It was fantastic **to** see so many young people enter the competition.
9 ✓

Listening

2

1	H
2	E
3	B
4	C
5	G

Claire: Er, sorry, but I can't stand cookery shows. Why would you want to watch someone cooking? On TV? It's not as if we can taste it, or smell how good they say it is. Anyway, there's almost nothing good on TV these days. Just celebrities and cookery, and reality TV.

Karim: Yeah, I wouldn't miss reality TV shows if they completely disappeared.

Stella: I don't like reality shows either. I'm not interested in who the latest pop star's going to be, or whether someone's going to survive another week locked up in a house. But this one now on Saturdays, it's wonderful …

Claire: What, the one with the singing housewives and talking dogs? You can't be serious?

Stella: I'm really starting to get into it! I think it's because they're just ordinary people. Well, I say ordinary, some of them are really gifted. Like the woman they had on last week. She had an amazing singing voice. I want to see if she gets voted off next week.

Claire: I'm shocked …

Stella: No, watch it, it's great! (Laughter)

Karim: No way!

3

1	F
2	G
3	C
4	D
5	A

Units 11–15 Revision

pages 98–99

2

1 C	**2** C	**3** B

3

1	to fetch
2	lying
3	to remain
4	to say
5	to find
6	to stand up
7	to secure
8	complaining

6

1	concentration
2	inability
3	laziness
4	outcome
5	adulthood
6	activity
7	environmental
8	effectively

Unit 16 pages 100–103

Speaking and Reading

2

1	10,000,000,000,000,000 (the number of cells in a human body)
2	billions (the number of cells which die every day)
3	approximately one month (the lifespan of an average cell)
4	several years (the lifetime of a liver cell)
5	every few days (the length of time it takes to renew a liver cell)
6	approximately 100,000,000,000 (the number of brain cells you have when you are born)
7	500 (the number of brain cells you lose every hour)
8	nine years (the time it takes for the body to replace every cell in the body)

Listening

3

1	a cell
2	plants
3	large number
4	30
5	devices
6	secretive

Recording script 2 04

The first person to describe a cell was called Robert Hooke. Hooke achieved many things in his 68 years – he was both an accomplished theoretician and a dab hand at making ingenious and useful instruments – but nothing he did brought him greater admiration than his popular book Micrographia published in 1665. It revealed to an enchanted public the world of the very small that was far more diverse, crowded and finely structured than anyone had ever come close to imagining.

Among the microscopic features first identified by Hooke were little chambers in plants that he called 'cells' because they reminded him of monks' cells. Hooke calculated that a one-inch square of cork would contain 1,259,712,000 of these tiny chambers – the first appearance of such a very large number anywhere in science. Microscopes by this time had been around for a generation or so but what set Hooke's apart were their technical supremacy. They achieved magnifications of 30 times, making them the last word in 17th century optical technology.

So it came as something of a shock when just a decade later Hooke and the other members of London's Royal Society began to receive drawings and reports from an unlettered linen draper in the Dutch city of Delft employing magnification of up to 275 times. The draper's name was Antoni van Leeuwenhoek. Though he had little formal education and no background in science, he was a perceptive and dedicated observer and a technical genius.

To this day it is not known how he got such magnificent magnifications from such simple handheld devices, which were little more than modest wooden dowels with a tiny bubble of glass embedded in them, far more like a magnifying glass than what most of us think of as microscopes, but really not much like either. Leeuwenhoek made a new instrument for every experiment he performed, and was extremely secretive about his techniques, though he did sometimes offer tips to the British on how they might improve their resolutions.

Vocabulary

1

1	toes (H)
2	heart (C)
3	hand (B)
4	ears (G)
5	head (A)
6	feet (F)
7	eye (E)
8	fingers (D)

2

1	e
2	g
3	d
4	a
5	h
6	b
7	c
8	f

3

1	fell head over heels in love
2	to give her a hand
3	has her head in the clouds
4	has set her heart
5	keeps her on her toes
6	was all ears
7	bite his tongue
8	was down in the mouth
9	put his mind at rest
10	to keep my fingers crossed

Inversion

1

1	Living cells rarely last more than a month or so.
2	You shouldn't waste a single moment.

2

1	Never was there any doubt about the results of the experiment.
2	Under no circumstances are credit cards accepted.
3	Not until much later did the public appreciate the significance of this research.
4	Only when he arrived back at the lab did the scientist realise what had happened.
5	Not only did the report included recommendations for this company but also for many other businesses.
6	Only after she died did the press discover her secret.

Corpus spot

1	Never could I have imagined how many arrangements were necessary.
2	Not only were the family kind, but they were also helpful.

Exam folder 7 pages 104–105

Paper 1 Part 7

2

1	F
2	C
3	A
4	G
5	E
6	B

Unit 17 pages 106–109

Reading

1

Suggested answers
A Hostel for backpackers – not clear from the headline it is going to be mainly praising or criticising.
B It is about a film, although that is not clear from the headline. The headline does, however, make it clear that it is praising rather than criticising.
C It is about a computer game – praising.
D A music album – sounds generally positive but headline does not give much away.
E It is about a website, although the headline only makes clear that it is something digital. It sounds generally as if it is praising rather than criticising – it implies that the website is convenient.

2

Review A
a true
b false (the author says it is 'interesting' and 'quirky')
c not given

Review B
a true
b false (it is said to stand up remarkably well)
c not given

Review C
a false (it is the third version)
b false (it is said to be well ahead of previous versions in terms of presentation, structure and accessibility)
c false (the writer says that earlier versions were unforgiving at times, which implies that he or she felt that some improvement would be desirable)

Review D
a true
b not given
c false (it is said to leave the listener with a sense of haunted mystification)

Review E
a true
b not given
c false (the writer says it is easy to explore the site)

Articles

1

Review A
1 No, it couldn't because it is referring to a specific colour which has already been mentioned).
2 No, although it might suggest to the reader that there is another kitchen elsewhere.
3 Yes, it would then appear to be talking about some specific previously mentioned visitors rather than visitors in general.

Review B
1 the great film (it's making a general statement)
2 viewers
3 its themes of sacrifice

Review C
1 through a stroke of luck
2 a bit of time

Review D
1 listeners

Review E
1 No, because *Music, Cinema and TV* are referring to general categories rather than to specific examples of music, cinema and TV.
2 post any comments

Corpus spot

1 **Life** after the revolution was very difficult. (No article is usually used in general statements.)
2 **The** life of an artist or singer is very cruel, full of obstacles and enemies. (The article is used in general statements where the noun has a post-modifying phrase.)
3 My brother is **a** biochemist in London. (The indefinite article is used when saying what people's jobs are.)
4 Jack broke **his** leg skiing. (A possessive adjective is usually used before parts of the body.)
5 He's only 18 but he already has **his** own business. (A possessive adjective is usually used before *own*.)
6 I was on a business trip to **the** People's Republic of China. (*The* is not used with most countries but it is used for countries or places containing a common noun like *Republic*, *Federation* or *Kingdom*.)
7 Since they built the tunnel, no one uses **the** ferry. (*The* is often used with means of transport to refer to the type of transport being used, rather than a specific bus, car or boat, e.g. *I take the bus to work.*)

Listening

2

1 Two films: *The Stalker* and *Shakespeare in Love.*
2 *The Stalker* by Russian director Andrey Tarkovsky, is hard to follow, has an interesting use of camera, music and dialogue.
   Shakespeare in Love is based on the life of Shakespeare and suggests how he used his own love for Viola in his play *Romeo and Juliet*. We can't be sure how much it reflects reality.
3 *amazing; didn't really understand what was going on; something incredibly beautiful and mysterious about it; stunning camera shot; evocative use of music; thought-provoking piece of dialogue; that's what I like about it; prefer films where I can follow the plot; really loved; gave me an insight; made me look at Romeo and Juliet in a new light; enjoyed it; totally convincing*

Recording script 2 05

Man: What would you say is your favourite film ever?

Woman: Oh dear. I don't know. I've enjoyed lots of different films but I'd have to give it a lot more thought before singling out one. So, what's yours then?

Man: Well, I just loved *The Stalker*. You know, that amazing film by the Russian director Andrey Tarkovsky.

Woman: Oh, yes, I remember seeing that once. I didn't really understand what was going on, though.

Man: I'm not sure that I do either, even though I've seen it loads of times – but there's just something incredibly beautiful and mysterious about it. Each time I watch it, I notice something I haven't paid any attention to before – whether it's a stunning camera shot, a piece of music or a piece of dialogue – and I think that's what I like about it.

Woman: Well, I think I prefer films where I can follow the plot. I'm obviously much more low-brow than you. I really loved *Shakespeare in Love*, for example. I felt it really gave me an insight into life at that time and it made me look at the play *Romeo and Juliet* in a fresh light. Maybe it was based on Shakespeare's own love life.

Man: Yes, I enjoyed it too. But no one knows if there's any truth in it, do they? We don't know enough about Shakespeare's own private life.

Woman: Maybe. But I found it totally convincing. I believe it's true.

Vocabulary

1

1	buffs
2	gave
3	attention
4	crystal
5	stands
6	experienced
7	ring
8	provoking
9	light
10	follow

3

1	Why don't we
2	I might as well
3	am I right in saying
4	In other words
5	mainly a matter of
6	I'm not entirely convinced
7	I agree with you on the whole; take you up on
8	I'm in two minds as to whether

Writing folder 7 pages 110–111

Reviews

2

Suggested answers

Facts about the film and its plot

The name of the film is *Avatar*. It was directed by James Cameron. It used new 3D technology. The story is set a hundred years in the future.

Actor Stephen Lang plays the role of Colonel Miles Quaritch, Sigourney Weaver plays the part of Dr Grace Augustine and Sam Worthington plays pilot Jake Sully.

Phrases that convey the writer's opinion of the film

among the greats; super-sleek 3D; eminently watchable and hugely entertaining sci-fi spectacular; unable to decide if …; The digitally created world meshes pretty much seamlessly with …; undoubtedly impressive; The effects of Avatar are certainly something to see … But it's difficult to tell if cinema as a genre has really been changed or not; a truly fascinating story; What a great idea it is – and that is what makes it an experience.

Things included to interest and entertain the reader

the inclusion of super-sleek new-tech 3D; the 'quirky-scary CGI animals'; the planet's aboriginal inhabitants … hugely tall blue quasi-humanoids called the Na'vi, who have pointy ears, flat noses, ethnic dreadlocks and beads; the exotic, subtitled language of the Na'vi; the love story; the battle scenes

4

1	unfolds;	character
2	shot;	location
3	lacks;	special
4	lead;	romantic
5	set;	turbulent
6	gave;	stunning
7	storm;	winning
8	fell;	thunderous

Unit 18 pages 112–115

Reading

1

Suggested answers

It is about various psychology studies into lying and how it might be possible to improve people's currently poor ability to know whether someone is telling the truth or not.

2

Suggested answers

1	often
2	hard
3	incorrect
4	ask

3

Suggested answers
1 to create a good impression; to obtain an advantage; to avoid punishment
2 not making eye contact; blinking; fidgeting
3 criminal justice (e.g. establishing whether an alibi is true or not)
intelligence gathering (e.g. is your agent actually a double agent?)
financial situations (e.g. is that person selling you a car telling the truth?)
business situations (e.g. is the job applicant as qualified and experienced as they claim?)

Vocabulary

1

1 interactions
2 currently
3 claimed
4 identify
5 indicate
6 frequency
7 major
8 pose
9 applications
10 consistent

2

1 b
2 e
3 d
4 f
5 a
6 c

3

1 identify
2 frequency
3 leave something up to chance
4 pay close attention
5 currently
6 look me in the eye / make eye contact
7 indicate

Emphasis

2

Possible answers
1 The girl / person (who) Paulo loves is Maria.
2 What happened was that Katya had an accident. / It was Katya that had an accident.
3 What Rolf won / The amount that Rolf won was a million dollars.

3

1 I do believe what you're saying. (auxiliary verb *do* added)
2 He's such a nice man and he's been so kind to us. (Use of *so* and *such*.)
3 Can you open the window? I'm boiling! (Use of exaggerated lexis.)
4 He's intensely jealous of his sister. (Use of intensifying adverb *intensely*.)
5 That joke is as old as the hills! (Use of simile.)
6 Little did he imagine what was going to happen next. (Use of inversion after a restricting adverbial.)
7 Never was so much owed by so many to so few! (Use of inversion after a negative adverbial.)
8 What on Earth is that man doing? (Use of *on Earth*, only used after a question word.)
9 I really like this exercise! (Use of intensifying adverbials such as *really*, etc.)

4

Suggested answers
1 Jake **does** admire her work.
2 I **do** love you.
3 Mary **did** do her very best.
4 I **did** use to be able to dive quite well.
5 They **have** agreed to help us.

6

Suggested answers
1 No, I **am** right.
2 I **did** give you the right information.
3 I **do** help you with the housework.
4 He **didn't** cheat.
5 I **shall/will** be able to!
6 I **haven't** forgotten it!

Listening

Recording script 2 07
1 Have you been enjoying your studies?
2 What interesting things have you done recently?
3 How would you feel about living abroad permanently?
4 How about your social life?
5 What are your plans for the future?
6 Have you always lived in the same place?
7 What would you say has been the most memorable event here so far?
8 Have you made any good friends here?

2

Better answers are given by:
1 Yolanda
2 Martin
3 Yolanda
4 Martin
5 Martin
6 Yolanda
7 Martin
8 Yolanda

Recording script 2 08

Chris: Hello, I hope you're both well. Have you been enjoying your studies?

Martin: Well, actually I'm finding it quite hard. I think first of all the pronunciation of many words is very very different in English, something to do with the spelling maybe. There are very many words, so it's difficult to learn them all and the main thing I think is the verbs, I'm used to putting those at the end of a sentence, not at the beginning or the middle, so that's difficult.

Yolanda: I'm really enjoying it, now that I can speak English so much better, going to see films and understanding exactly what is going on. I also like listening to songs and knowing what they mean.

Chris: What interesting things have you done recently?

Martin: Well, funnily enough last Saturday I went to a football match, which I've never been to before, and that was a great experience, very exciting and it's good to be among so many people. I enjoyed that very very much.

Yolanda: I went to the supermarket. I took a bus around town, I visited some friends and I've also been reading a lot. Not so interesting, actually!

Chris: How would you feel about living abroad permanently?

Martin: Oh, that's something I would really like to do. I think you get a very interesting sense of yourself when you live abroad and you can meet very interesting people.

Yolanda: I have a friend who, a school friend, who went to live in France for a few months and he said that for the first two months it was very good, very exciting but after that he said that he started to miss his friends and his family, and he wanted to get home and it wasn't so good after that.

Chris: OK, and how about your social life?

Yolanda: Well, I don't really enjoy going to parties at all. I haven't got time.

Martin: For me it depends what kind of mood I'm in. Often I like going to parties where you can dance a lot and there's loud music playing and other times I like going to parties where you can talk to people and get to know them, get to meet them and I think most of all I like going to parties that last a long time, you know? They go on all over the weekend maybe, or – not just one evening.

Chris: What are your plans for the future?

Martin: Well, my course lasts another three and a half months and as soon as that finishes, I'd like to do some travelling, around South-east Asia, if I can, because that's a part of the world I'm really interested in, and then after another four months I am going back home to see my family and go back to my studies there.

Yolanda: Well, I don't know really. I haven't made any definite plans at the moment.

Chris: Have you always lived in the same place?

Martin: I've lived in a lot of different places.

Yolanda: Yes, I've always lived in just one place and for me I really enjoy this. It's a great sense of community life and I've known people in my village who have known me all my life and I've known them for as long as I can remember. Whenever I go out, I meet someone that I know. For example, all my friends from school still live in the same village and I, it's something I really really like.

Chris: What would you say has been the most memorable event here so far?

Martin: Er, I think probably last year, I was given my birthday present which was a weekend course in how to, how to jump with a parachute. And a few weeks later I went up in a plane and I actually jumped out of the plane with the parachute, and that was something I will remember forever, for sure.

Chris: Have you made any good friends here?

Yolanda: Yes, but I've kept in touch with my best friend. We talk nearly every day. Her name's Marisol and she has a brilliant sense of humour. She is also a very good gymnast. She is 18 years old and she has short brown hair and I have known her since we were very young and she is very intelligent as well.

Martin: Yes, Gerhard. I've known him since I started here, and he's, he's good, you know.

6

1	B
2	A

Recording script 2 09

Piotr: Oh, Jason, can I introduce Sophie? This is Sophie, she works in our Cologne office. Sophie, this is Jason.

Sophie: Hi, Jason.

Piotr: Jason's the manager of our branch in New York.

Sophie: Yeah, pleased to meet you.

Jason: And you. You're in Cologne, right?

Sophie: Yeah, that's right, yeah.

Jason: Yeah, did we meet before because I was in Cologne a couple of years ago? I don't think we met then, did we?

Sophie: No, I don't think so. I can't remember your face but I've only worked for the company for a couple of months you see, so ...

Jason: Oh, right, OK, so who did you work for before?

Sophie: Oh, well I was with Smith & Goldberg in Philadelphia.

Jason: Oh, really, in Philly? Excellent! I know it well, I grew up there, actually.

Sophie: Oh, really?

Piotr: I spent a year at graduate school there. Great place, isn't it, great place?

Jason: Yeah, yeah, great.

Sophie: Absolutely yeah, oh I loved my time there. I'd have been really happy to stay actually but ...

Piotr: Did you have to come back?

Sophie: Yeah, well, the thing is my husband's German so ...

Jason: Oh, right.

Sophie: Yeah, we really wanted to come home and then we'd be closer to the family because when our little boy was born, we thought it would be nice for him, you know.

Piotr: How many children have you got?

Sophie: Well, now we've got a little boy, Adam, and we've got a little girl as well called Maisie. Little girl, yeah, she's just two.

Piotr: Have you got children, Jason? I can't remember.

Jason: No, no, I don't have any kids right now but you know – never too late! So you know, of course I have to get a wife first but – you know, that could be arranged, I guess!

7

Jason: grew up in Philadelphia, manager of branch in New York, was in Cologne a couple of years ago, grew up in Philadelphia, unmarried, no children

Sophie: works in the Cologne office, has only worked for company for a couple of months, worked previously for Smith and Goldberg in Philadelphia, loved Philadelphia, husband is German, wanted to be closer to home when first child, son called Adam, was born. Also has little girl called Maisie.

Exam folder 8 pages 116–117

Paper 1 Part 8

2

1	B
2	D
3	C
4	D
5	B
6	C
7	D
8	A
9	B
10	D

Unit 19 pages 118–121

Reading

4

1	G	**2**	C	**3**	I
4	E	**5**	B	**6**	H
7	A	**8**	D	**9**	F

Vocabulary

1

1	b, c, d, e, g
2	g
3	f
4	a
5	h
6	b
7	b, d
8	c

2

1	got a degree
2	gave (me) the impression
3	attracts (a lot of) attention
4	get your point across
5	earn (good) salaries
6	resist the temptation
7	fell into the trap
8	overcame (many) obstacles

Language of persuasion

2

1	mother wants toddler to eat his vegetables	encourages, plays games, eats some too, praises
2	employee would like to take some time off work	reassures the employer that everything will be on track before leaving, and that they will always be contactable
3	boss wants workers to do some overtime	explains why it's necessary, shows sympathy with how workers must be feeling
4	girl wants friend to lend her a special dress to wear to a party	explains why she wants it so much, praises the dress, promises to do various favours in return, promises to be careful
5	sales person is trying to sell a fitted kitchen	uses very positive language about the offer, emphasises what a bargain it is, says it will all be very easy for the customer
6	teenager wants to persuade mother to let her stay out	reminds mum that there is no school next day, uses moral blackmail, tries to reassure mum, says all friends are going to be allowed, reminds mum how good she's been
7	wife wants to persuade husband that they should move to a house in the country	emphasises benefits to children, says husband could use commuting time productively and so would be freer when home
8	sales assistant wants to persuade woman to buy dress	flatters, goes into detail about why the dress is good, points out how versatile it is

Recording script 2 10

Speaker 1: Now look, fish fingers and peas and carrots and broccoli. Oh, you like broccoli, don't you? Let me just put that on the fork. There, you have that. Go on, open your mouth. That's a good boy. You chew, that's it. And now a carrot. There you go, in it goes. You take that carrot, that's a good boy. Can I have some, can mummy have some? Oh, that's lovely, thank you. Now you have some, go on. You have that spoon. One for you, one for me. Good boy.

Speaker 2: Excuse me, have you got a moment? I wanted to ask you something, if I'm not disturbing you. The thing is, I'm owed a couple of days holiday and I'd like to use them before the end of the year if possible. I appreciate it's quite a busy time for the department, but I'd really like to take next Thursday and Friday off. My brother's here and I'd like to spend a bit of time with him. We hardly ever manage to meet. Anyway, I'll make sure everything's on track before I leave, and I'll brief the PA so that she can deal with anything. But I don't expect there to be any problems. And you can always contact me, I'll have my phone with me.

Speaker 3: Now, I think you all know why we've had to meet today. I've got the monthly figures back from head office and for the third month running, sales are down and, well, we all know that things are getting tighter. It looks like I'll have to ask you to put in a little bit more overtime. No, no, I know, I know that's not going to be very popular but this is a good chance to make a bit more money. OK? I mean, this is probably just a temporary measure, but thanks for your understanding and all your hard work. Really appreciate it.

Speaker 4: Sorry, no. I don't want that, I don't want the red one. I actually just want to borrow the blue one. I wouldn't ask unless it was for this party. I mean, I just think he's going to be there and I'd just like to look nice and that dress is the most beautiful thing I've ever seen. Look, I won't spill anything on it, I promise, I – I won't even drink anything all night. I won't eat anything either. There'll be no crumbs, nothing, I promise. Look, I'll wash up for a month or take your bike in. I'll do all your washing. Oh, please let me?

Speaker 5: Good morning, I wonder if I could just take a few seconds of your time just to tell you about a special offer we're doing at the moment. We're in your area and we're doing free quotations on brand new kitchen units. Now these units are made to measure, they're marvellous, they're handmade by our craftsmen. Therefore it's very much cheaper making them directly from our workshop than going to the shops and also you don't have to pay at all for anything this year so basically we'll install the kitchen for you and you don't have to pay anything till next year. Now that's a fantastic offer, I'm sure you'll agree.

Speaker 6: All the others are going to be there and there's no school the next day. Do you remember you said that if I started doing better in maths you'd let me stay out? Well, I got good marks, didn't I? And I'll get a taxi home and I'll pay for it, so I'm not asking you to pick me up. Just this time. It's important. Everyone is going to be there.

Speaker 7: The thing is, I know it would be a bit more expensive to live there, and it's further away from work, but it's – I mean, there are so many good sides to it. We'd be closer to my mother, so she could help more looking after the kids. It's greener, everything's less stressful. You could go into work by train. You could work on the train – that'd be OK, wouldn't it? You like trains. That'd mean you could spend more time with the kids in the evening. What do you think?

Speaker 8: Yeah, the mirror's right over here, yeah. Oh, it really looks lovely. Yeah, oh, it's gorgeous on you though, you've got such a lovely figure. What size is that one? Oh, it's a size ten, yeah well there you are, you see. I can only get into size 12. You are lucky. Well, I'll tell you what, though. That dress really looks nice because the way it's cut over your hips, you see if you just turn round there, look, look in the mirror there. It's ever so nice. And the colour's good on you as well because, like, green, green really goes with red hair. Yeah, oh, I think it's really nice, yeah. It's quite good because you can use that dress for all sorts of things, couldn't you? You could go to parties in it and wear it out anywhere, really.

3

1	b	6	d
2	a	7	e
3	f	8	i
4	h	9	g
5	c		

4

1	b
2	a
3	a
4	a
5	b

5

Suggested answers
a Have you got time to check through this report?
b I'd rather you were more flexible.
c You can't lend me some money, can you?
d I'm sure everything will be fine.
e Do you want to come with me?

Writing folder 8 pages 122–123

Proposals

1

1 Types of proposals
academic proposal, e.g. about research with a view to getting some money or a place at university
work proposal, e.g. with a view to introducing some innovation at the workplace
social proposal, e.g. a plan for change that aims to persuade readers of the desirability of such changes
media proposal, e.g. to a publisher about something that you would like to write
political proposal, e.g. to the public saying what your party plans to do
3 It will probably have some or all of the following: a factual title; a clear statement of aims at beginning; facts presented unambiguously; clearly drawn conclusions at the end; headings used frequently to help clarify

5

1 The aim of this proposal is to put forward a piece of academic research that I would like to undertake.
2 This proposal outlines the scope of the new course being recommended, explaining why it would be of benefit to students. It then concludes with some suggestions as to how the course could be implemented most effectively.
3 There are a number of reasons why I wish to put this proposal forward.
4 There are a number of overwhelming arguments in favour of extending the computer centre at the college, rather than the sports facilities.
5 Firstly, the proposed new college magazine would help to create a stronger feeling of community within the student body.
6 Secondly, the proposed extension to the college library would serve the additional useful purpose of attracting more students to apply for courses here.
7 Despite the fact that the suggested programme might be expensive, the additional cost could be justified in terms of the benefits that participants would receive.
8 There are a number of recommendations that I would like to make.
9 Taking all the evidence into account, I recommend that the English Club should make some radical changes to its current programme.
10 I would urge you to give these recommendations serious consideration.
11 Please do not hesitate to contact me if you would like me to expand on anything in this proposal.
12 Having outlined the proposal in general terms, I would now like to discuss three key issues in more detail.

Unit 20 pages 124–127

Reading

1

1 B
2 A
3 D
4 C

2

1 A
2 B
3 C
4 D

3

1 C
2 B
3 A
4 D

Vocabulary

1

1 necessity
2 affluence
3 obesity
4 transmission
5 breeding
6 consumption

2

1 scientifically (adverb)
2 breadth (noun)
3 inconclusive (adjective)
4 leisurely (adjective)
5 clarify (verb)
6 unhygienic (adjective)
7 overeating (verb)
8 tasty (adjective)
9 nutritious (adjective)
10 fattening (adjective)

Hypothesising

1

1 B
2 A

Corpus spot

1 I was wondering if you could make it in July?
2 Imagine you had to live with no central heating …
3 Supposing she took the job in Moscow …
4 The best way to prepare for the driving test is to imagine yourself as a driver.

2

1 a Were there to have been enough food for workers in Russian factories in 1917, there might not have been a revolution that year.

b Had there been enough food for workers in Russian factories in 1917, there might not have been a revolution that year.

2 a If the government had done more about food shortages, it would have been more popular.

b If the government were to have done more about food shortages, it would have been more popular.

3 a Let us imagine the different ways in which food science might help with feeding the growing population of the world.

b Let us consider the different ways in which food science might help with feeding the growing population of the world.

4 a Let us suppose that most people would be prepared to do anything to provide food for their own children.

b Let us assume that most people would be prepared to do anything to provide food for their own children.

Reading

3

I propose that …
If I may speculate for a moment …
Speculating further …
On the assumption that …
Provided that …
Allowing for the fact that …

Units 16–20 Revision

pages 128–129

3

1 eye
2 heart
3 feet
4 hand
5 brains
6 head (over) heels
7 nerve
8 fingers

4

1 what
2 to
3 the
4 (a)round
5 most
6 at
7 long
8 a

5

1 B
2 C
3 A
4 E
5 D
6 F

Unit 21 pages 130–133

Listening

2

the Grand Canyon, the Northern Lights, the Great Barrier Reef, Mount Everest, the Harbour at Rio de Janeiro, Victoria Falls, Paricutin in Mexico

3 The underlined parts of the script confirm the answers.

Recording script 2 11

Located on the <u>northern tip of Australia's East Coast,</u> the tropical city of <u>Cairns is internationally recognised as the gateway to the Great Barrier Reef,</u> one of the seven natural wonders of the world. The city is home to 100,000 people and also <u>boasts the fifth busiest international airport in Australia</u> with many carriers flying direct to Cairns from countries around the world. Cairns has many outdoor restaurants and cafés and great shopping, and also offers a complete range of accommodation options from budget right through to five-star. <u>Great Adventures Cruises have been running trips to the Great Barrier Reef</u> for more than 100 years and, as a result, are recognised as an industry leader. Great Adventures offer day cruises to <u>Green Island, a beautiful 6,000-year-old coral bay.</u> It is perfect for lazing on white sands, swimming, or snorkelling around the surrounding reef or relaxing around the luxurious day-visitor facilities – <u>all just 45 minutes crossing from Cairns.</u> A full range of options on the island include introductory scuba diving, certified scuba diving and guided snorkel tours, as well as a crocodile farm, parasailing and private beach hire. For those wanting the ultimate reef adventure, cruise from Cairns to the luxury of Great Adventures' <u>multi-level pontoon on the Outer Reef.</u> The pontoon features undercover seating and tables where you can enjoy a sumptuous buffet lunch. There's also a sundeck, full bar facilities, an underwater observatory, a semi-submersible coral viewing tour and a swimming enclosure for children. You'll be able to snorkel or dive among the reef's spectacular coral gardens and diverse marine life. <u>A once-in-a-lifetime experience!</u>

4

1 false: it is the fifth busiest international airport in Australia
2 true
3 false: it is 6,000 years old
4 false: it takes 45 minutes by boat
5 false: it is not all under water
6 false: *a once-in-a-lifetime experience* means that it is a very special experience, not that you are only allowed to go there once

Reading

2

Means of travel: car (Landcruiser)
Driver's aim: to keep the car off the ground as much as possible
How Tashi felt about the journey: he seemed to enjoy it
Difficult aspects of the journey: very bumpy
Good aspects of the journey: good visibility and not much other traffic
Scenery: mountains and river
What could be seen on the river: coracles (small boats)

3

village lined with waving Tibetan children
single and double-storey buildings with walled-in courtyards
foothills behind the buildings
solid buildings with walls made of stone up to waist height and mud bricks above
window ledges with marigolds on them
black and white buildings
flags (blue, white, red, green and yellow) on flat roofs standing out against the rich blue sky with pictures of jewelled dragon-horse on them
copse of trees (willows or poplars) but landscape otherwise treeless
each courtyard wall piled high with firewood

4

1 getting materials to burn
2 the men
3 to make it more useful
4 to dry it in the sun

Vocabulary

1

1 f
2 b
3 d
4 e
5 a
6 i
7 g
8 h
9 j
10 c

2

1 off the beaten track
2 hit the road
3 picture-postcard
4 black spot
5 no room to swing a cat

3

Likely: *picture-postcard*, *stone's throw from* (the beach usually), *home from home*.
These emphasise the attractive aspects of places.
Unlikely: *black spot*, *tourist trap*, *no room to swing a cat*.
These emphasise unattractive aspects of places.

Range of grammatical structures

1

Dorje had; which involved keeping; called out; whenever we were; grinning; bracing; would hit; it was hardly surprising that; would have made; is not hindered by; which are; appear; was how hard he could keep his foot pressed down; weighed against; could lead to; setting out; saw me trying to look at them; he shouted; it seems that; to make; are stretched; sewn; made from; are sealed with

2

1 told / had told
2 was cycling / had been cycling
3 arranged / had arranged
4 stayed
5 set
6 was sitting
7 looking
8 thinking

Writing

1

It's a great hotel with loads of character.
The bedrooms get a bit chilly at night and the uncarpeted corridors can be noisy but it's worth putting up with a few minor inconveniences as it has so much atmosphere in other ways.
The food is fantastic and you can stuff yourself at breakfast so you don't need to eat again till the evening.

Exam folder 9 pages 134–135

The Listening test

1

1 four
2 twice
3 sentence completion, multiple choice, multiple matching
4 on the sheet
5 one
6 Spelling is expected to be correct.
7 40 minutes
8 20%

3

1 D
2 B
3 A
4 D
5 C
6 A

Recording script 2 12

Interviewer: With me in the studio today is Julia Crawley, who runs a management consultancy which deals with women in business. Now Julia, if the majority of companies were run by women, what difference do you think it would make? I mean, what did you bring to the company you started?

Julia: Many people had warned me of the difficulties of being a female manager – to begin with, getting people to take you seriously. Male friends of mine in similar management roles always seemed to be worried about how long a woman would stay with a company and whether family commitments would mean she was less loyal than a male manager. I remember when I started as a manager it was natural for me, and I think it is for most women, to want to work with others, to see what they could contribute, and I told them what I was bringing to the table.

Interviewer: Mm. It is important that everyone realises they are important in a company, that every individual is as important as any other, isn't it?

Julia: One of the first female management gurus, Jennifer Alderton, put forward as her 'articles of faith' respect for all staff. She introduced me to the concept of power with rather than power over. Usually when power is discussed, it's taken to mean having power over someone else, getting that person to do what you want him to do, either through actual physical means or through persuasion.

Interviewer: And what do you see as being some of the drawbacks of the traditional male-run business?

Julia: Well, we've had hundreds of years of command control, maybe more, and it kind of works, although days can be lost as disputes are debated and in the meantime, machines are standing idle. And it's a very uncomfortable sort of organisation to work in, isn't it? I think now that people want more from their job; they don't want to be treated as an easily replaceable machine.

Interviewer: Mm. What other concepts that you value might we find in a female-run business?

Julia: Well, it would seek out differences. Say you'd been doing a particular procedure the same way for years and then someone challenged that. By positively encouraging criticism, you'd open up far more creativity and as a result the company would go forward at a faster pace. It's usually the people who have hands-on experience of systems that can see shortcuts.

Interviewer: And at the same time recognising that it's crucial for people to have a balance between their work and home life.

Julia: Yes, this is an issue which has been widely discussed in many countries and there have been some high-profile men and women who have given up highly paid, highly-responsible jobs because of the demand it was making on their time to spend more quality time with friends and family. The fact that these people were in the public eye has moved the debate on no end. I think where we need to go with this now is helping other countries where it is less acceptable for people to say, 'It's 6 o'clock, so I'm off now' to realise that good workers are alert workers who've enjoyed their free time and have slept well.

Interviewer: Is this where you're going to channel your efforts from now on?

Julia: It's tempting, because I can see that with better communication skills the workplace can become a far more attractive place to spend time. However, I'm getting involved in a scheme which backs small businesses which are struggling to get off the ground due to lack of cash. There are some great ideas out there with a demand for the product; but for a small company they've already invested all they had in setting up and getting a working prototype. So that's what appeals to me at the moment.

Interviewer: Well, good luck with that, Julia, and thank you for talking to us today.

4

1 rebellion
2 work clothes
3 (an) organic (product)
4 youthfulness
5 roots/origins
6 presidents
7 brands
8 the knees ripped

Recording script 2 **13**

When youth culture emerged in the early 1950s, jeans were a powerful symbol – a symbol of rebillion. They were frowned upon by parents if you wore them when you went out. That was considered inappropriate because they were seen as work clothes. But, jeans went on to be adopted by young people across the world.

They were saleable across international boundaries because of their fantastic qualities, just as a product in themselves. They are what I'd call an organic product – the more you wear them the better they got. And on top of all that, you have this, this idea of youthfulness.

Remember, culture in the 1950s was all coming from the United States. Rock and roll started in America, that's where its roots were, that's where the roots of jeans are.

Some people wonder if jeans have had their day now. They're not special any more. Some people have suggested that young people are going off jeans because the establishment are wearing them – we've seen presidents wearing them. But it's how you wear them that matters. You can wear them in a very different way to somebody else. Certain brands have that ability, like the Mini car – it can be driven by pop stars or little old grannies. Certain brands go beyond something that's only worn by one group after a period of time and jeans are certainly like that. So now it's the brand you wear, how you wear them, do you wear them loose or tight, washed out, with a crease down them?

The codes become smaller and smaller. And you can still rebel in jeans. If you went somewhere very smart and you wore jeans with the knees ripped, that would be a symbol of rebellion. And all this means jeans are here to stay.

6

List 1	
1	D
2	B
3	C
4	G
5	E

List 2	
6	B
7	C
8	F
9	G
10	A

Recording script 2 🔢

Speaker 1: It's funny how I got to know my closest friend. I mean that doesn't usually happen with clients, but Sara's so outgoing. We got on like a house on fire. We chatted away while we were doing various practical activities on our evening course in photography. I was learning about composition or shutter speeds, or whatever it was and then she started bringing her daughter in too and we'd put the world to rights, giving very honest opinions about everything from politics to family life as we selected the best photos or whatever we were doing. And then one day she said she was having a barbecue and would I like to come along? And that's what I admire in her; that warmth. Not many other people, even my neighbours who come to the salon would do that. And since then we've become good friends.

Speaker 2: I think friendship develops; it isn't an instant thing. For example, at first I thought Tom was a bit bossy, but after a while I realised that it's just his way of getting things done with the minimum amount of fuss and that's what I've come to value in him in all aspects of our friendship. I must say he's great to share an office with. We usually take our breaks together. Last year we started going to the gym together after work on Wednesdays. He's definitely someone I can call a close friend, unlike many other people I've met at the gym, for example. He is as hardworking in the gym as he is in the office.

Speaker 3: It's hard to say what we look for in friends because we don't usually go out and say, OK, I want to meet someone who's sympathetic or who has a sense of fair play. But over time, you become aware of what it is that makes someone a true friend. Interestingly, there is a bit of an age difference between my niece and myself but actually she's the one I turn to for advice. I know she won't just say what she thinks I want to hear – she's always sincere, a great help, and I really welcome that. Recently I told her about a colleague who was being difficult and she gave me some sound advice.

Speaker 4: It seems like I've known her forever. She's really changed, though. You'd never believe it but she used to be quite shy. She'd never speak up in class unless the teacher directly asked her a question. But she was always conscientious, hardworking, and now in retrospect, I can see she was working towards her goal in a very determined way. I really respect that. She always did her homework on time. She'd always wanted to be a novelist. And this year, In year eight, she won a national prize for creative writing and she's confidently giving press interviews; she's even been on a chat show on TV. It's hard to take it in that my best friend's famous! She had been quietly developing into a very clever young woman.

Speaker 5: I think a real friend, in a way, complements you. I mean, they bring out qualities in you that you would either never know you had or that you would never have developed. There's no doubt that Marcela and I became best of friends. She used to work as an accountant in my company but now works for a bank. She was always keen to climb the career ladder. Anyway, she's always coming up with suggestions to go hot-air ballooning or trekking that at first terrify me but that actually turn out to be great fun. Without her keenness to do these exciting things, I know I would never do them. That's why she's my best friend.

Unit 22 pages 136–139

Speaking and Reading

2

A mixture – there are facts about what scientists have discovered and predictions about the future which are educated guesses.

Vocabulary

2

1 e
2 f
3 d
4 a
5 b
6 c
7 i
8 g
9 h

3

1 torrential rain
2 ice cap
3 high tide(s)
4 sea defences
5 below freezing

Interpreting and comparing

1

1 main weather features
2 Rio de Janeiro
3 Stockholm
4 visibility
5 pollution
6 temperatures
7 humidity
8 Buenos Aires

2

1 C
2 A
3 D
4 B

3

1 On the other hand
2 Indeed
3 whereas
4 contrary to
5 However
6 because

Listening

1

Zoltan: floods, global warming, greenhouse-gas emissions, sea level, storms
Kazue: El Niño, floods, droughts, global warming, storms

Recording script 2 15

Zoltan: Some people say, good, it's great if the world's warming up. We'll have better holidays. But if they stopped to think for a second, they'd realise it's serious. I mean, if it gets warmer, it stands to reason that more water will evaporate from the oceans and surely that means more storms somewhere else. There's evidence that there are more storms, hurricanes and so on and that they're more intense. Now that more accurate records are kept we can see that global warming is a fact. Another aspect of global warming is how this will affect the sea level – it'll definitely rise. I read something recently which suggested that the sea might rise by as much as half a metre over this century, you know, because as the ice melts, the oceans expand. Imagine what effect that'll have on low-lying areas around the world. Another thing that gets me is that we know all this and yet we're not reducing our greenhouse-gas emissions anything like fast enough to stop the effects of climate change. We might be able to slow it down a bit but I think that's all.

Kazue: I know it seems as if there are more cases of extreme weather, like floods and droughts, but I wonder if it's only that we hear about them more than before because of the news on TV and the fact that now it's easier to communicate world events to everyone and very quickly. Surely there's always been severe weather. Storms are a natural phenomenon, after all. I admit there is evidence of global warming, but is there evidence to show that that's what's causing severe weather? Maybe we would have had these typhoons and floods anyway. I mean no one even really knows how storms form and the path they'll take. You see, what it is, is that the consequences are much greater these days. The world is more densely populated so in terms of the effect on population and financial loss the results are more devastating. Everybody's heard of El Niño and La Niña, but from what I hear, we still don't know whether it's global warming that's making things worse.

Vocabulary

1

1 increase
2 rise
3 decrease
4 decline
5 reduction
6 fall
7 drop

2

upward change: increase, rise
downward change: decrease, decline, reduction, fall, drop

3

both – it describes something which is changing

4

1 slight, small
2 gradual
3 significant, steep, sharp
4 rapid, sudden

Writing folder 9 pages 140–141

Persuasive writing

2

1 **a** is better as b is far too dismissive for a sensible argument on a serious topic.
2 **b** is better – it gives far more information and is more reasoned.
3 **b** is better as it is using more meaningful vocabulary. It also provides sounder reasons for offering Anna the job.
4 **a** is better as it makes a practical suggestion rather than being rude about people who do not take the approach recommended as rudeness is likely to antagonize readers.
5 **a** is better as it explains things using more interesting vocabulary and structures.
6 **a** is better because it is more polite and is offering a constructive suggestion rather than being negative.

Unit 23 pages 142–145

Reading

2

1 D
2 H
3 F
4 A
5 G
6 C

Phrasal verbs (2)

1

gearing up = get ready for. You can use an object but you need to add *for* (e.g. *gear up for battle*). This phrasal verb is inseparable.
find out = get to know/discover. You can use an object. This phrasal verb is separable.
go ahead = continue/do what you intend to do. You cannot use an object. This phrasal verb is inseparable.
carry out = do for real/execute. You can use an object. This phrasal verb is separable.

2

1 ✓
2 I **looked through the guarantee** but I couldn't find out how long it was valid for.
3 ✓
4 ✓
5 We don't **hold out much hope**, but we are still trying to get compensation.
6 Trying to get a satisfactory answer to my queries **took up** the whole morning.
7 ✓
8 ✓

3

1 give up
2 brought up
3 fit in with
4 settled in
5 call on
6 come up against
7 build up
8 draw on

Listening

2

1 C
2 B
3 A
4 A
5 B
6 C

Recording script 2 **16**

One of the most important situations in our professional life is when we feel we have to ask for a pay rise. It can be awkward but if you aren't assertive and you don't say what's on your mind, it may lead to you feeling undervalued and having a negative attitude to your work and workplace.

A positive attitude, forward planning and perfect timing are the keys to getting a pay rise. You may be asking for a number of reasons, ranging from a bigger workload or the increased cost of living to the fact that you've found out that a colleague is getting more than you. But these arguments will be secondary to your worth to the company.

Start by taking an objective look at your career. Are you good at your job? Are you punctual and reliable? Do people know who you are, and for the right reasons? Are you worth more than you're getting paid? If so, how much?

Are there any problems that you need to address? If so, make the changes subtly, over a period of time. Bosses are not stupid, and sudden bouts of punctuality just prior to a pay negotiation will seem like the worst type of creeping.

When planning your negotiation, don't base it on your gripes. Even if you think your future in the company doesn't look too rosy, bear in mind the 'what's in it for me?' factor. You may want extra money for all those things that are on your want list, for a holiday or a car, but your boss will be more convinced by an argument based on your quality of work and dedication.

To strengthen your viewpoint, plan for potential objections. If your boss is going to resist, what points is he or she likely to bring up? You could raise some first, along with arguments in your defence. For example, the sort of line you could take is, 'I know most pay rises are linked to set grades in this company, but I believe that my job has changed sufficiently to make this an exceptional case.'

Bartering can be embarrassing, but you will need to feel and sound confident. Remember that negotiations are a normal part of business life. Never pluck a sum out of the air. Know exactly what you will ask for and what you will settle for.

The timing of your communication can be crucial. Keep an eye on the finances and politics of the company to avoid any periods of lay offs or profit dips. If your boss can be moody, get an appointment for his or her most mellow time of the day. Never approach the subject casually. Being spontaneous might make your boss nervous.

There's always the chance that you won't get what you ask for. This is often the point at which reasonable demands and negotiations can turn into conflict. Never issue ultimatums, and don't say you'll resign if you don't mean it. Boost your confidence and your argument by having a backup plan (that is, what you'll do if you don't get the pay rise you want). Plan for the future by staying positive, asking when you could next apply and what can be done in the meantime to help your case.

Exam folder 10 pages 146–147

The Speaking test

1

> 1 Students' own answers.
> 2 Examiners are looking for a range of accurate grammar and vocabulary, discourse management, clear pronunciation, and ability to display interactive communication.

Unit 24 pages 148–151

Reading

2

> 1 C
> 2 B
> 3 C

Vocabulary

1

> 1 identify
> 2 exist
> 3 prove
> 4 find
> 5 compare
> 6 develop
> 7 expose
> 8 initiate
> 9 recognise

2

> 1 identification
> 2 existence
> 3 proof
> 4 finding(s)
> 5 comparison
> 6 development
> 7 exposure
> 8 initiation
> 9 recognition

3

> 1 conducting
> 2 come to
> 3 risking
> 4 raised
> 5 find

Listening

1

1	Thursday
2	The Golden Age
3	lifestyle
4	rural
5	education
6	opinion
7	discussion
8	poverty

Recording script 2 17

I'd like to finish this week's edition of *News Weekly* by telling you a little about what's happening in next week's programme. Because of next week's sports events *News Weekly* is being broadcast on Thursday rather than Tuesday. It will be shown at its usual time of half past eight. The programme's entitled 'The Golden Age' and it's an extended programme lasting an hour rather than the usual 40 minutes. The theme is contemporary youth. *News Weekly* is conducting an investigation into modern teenagers and their lifestyles. We usually record our programmes in London but next week, we'll be focusing on young people in rural parts of the country. There are plenty of programmes about young people in urban areas – this is something different and we're sure you'll find the results fascinating.

It touches on a number of issues – modern teenagers' attitudes to work, to friendship, to leisure, among other things. It looks most deeply at how young people feel about education and it comes up with some surprising conclusions. At the end of the programme there will be an opinion poll which we're hoping that all our viewers will take part in – you'll be able to call in on the usual number.

There is also a special website dedicated to this programme. This'll host a discussion after the programme has been broadcast, dealing with issues that it raises.

News Weekly is planning to investigate a number of other controversial issues over the coming months. It will, for example, dedicate a couple of programmes to the complex relationship between crime and poverty. …

Recording script 2 18

The night sky above a Canadian mountain village lit up last night in a glowing fireworks finale of a winter games that organisers say boosted the Paralympic Games to a new level worldwide.

Sir Philip Craven, President of the International Paralympic Committee, told the closing ceremony that these Winter Games had been 'the best ever'.

Amid a glittering display of skiers bearing torches down the mountain, dance and sports demonstrations, the official flag of the games was lowered to the strain of the Paralympic theme.

'Many of you will go home as champions, you all go home as winners,' John Furlong, CEO of the Vancouver organising committee, told more than 500 athletes and hundreds more officials from 44 countries, as well as thousands of spectators before an outdoor stage.

'You have been remarkable ambassadors of the human spirit,' added Furlong.

Officials said the Paralympic Winter Games had drawn an international audience via national television broadcasts and internet viewers that set records for both winter and summer games, while a record 85 per cent of all tickets were sold for alpine skiing, biathalon and cross-country skiing, wheel chair curling and ice sledge hockey events.

4

1	Closing ceremony of the Winter Paralympic Games
2	Fireworks, skiers bearing torches down the mountain, dance and sports demonstrations.
3	Athletes, officials and spectators.
4	The size of both TV and live audiences for the games.

6

1	No
2	employing children and not paying workers the minimum wage
3	Workers are working illegally and therefore don't want to complain or they are so desperate for the work that they think it's better to have any job rather than no job at all.
4	Her boss said he would report her to the authorities and say she had lied about her age.
5	No

Recording script 2.19

Working undercover, I have discovered that many companies throughout the world are flouting the child labour laws and minimum-wage laws. And you can't pin this down to one particular part of the world or say that it only happens in big cities as opposed to country areas. I have witnessed with my own eyes child labour in cities in so-called developed nations and workers being paid well below the legal requirements in every type of work you can imagine, from agriculture to clothes factories. Unfortunately it's very difficult to get workers to complain and the reasons are numerous, from they're working illegally and therefore don't want to complain or they're so desperate for the work that they think it's better to have any job rather than no job at all. And unscrupulous employers are cashing in on this.

This overcrowded, noisy factory is in a city where outside people are eating pepper steaks in expensive restaurants, driving fast cars and earning a fortune. In here it's a different picture; it's like something from another age, rows and rows of women sewing clothes in a factory down a back alley just off a fashionable shopping street. This is what you call sweatshop labour; people working unimaginable hours, for half the minimum wage. I talked to a girl here, let's call her Janine, she's 14 and instead of going to school, she comes here to work to earn money so that she can help out with the finances at home. At first she'd intended to do it for just a couple of weeks during the holiday, but when she suggested that she might leave, her boss told her that if she left, he'd report her and tell the authorities that she'd lied to him about her age. And of course, the more school she missed, the harder it was to go back. A vicious circle.

Connecting words

1

1	as
2	because
3	Then
4	So
5	Despite
6	even
7	but
8	And what's more
9	In all
10	By then

Writing folder 10

pages 152–153

The Writing Paper: general guidance

1

Suggested answers
1 read / study
2 underline
3 plan; organise
4 choose
5 check; correct

2

It is usually sensible to pay special attention to the bullet points, the words in quotes, and the words in bold.

3

Suggested answers
1 Suzi has not completely answered the question. She is not asked to compare all the benefits, only two. More importantly, she doesn't say which benefit of young people doing voluntary work is more important. This means that she doesn't fully answer the task.
2 Marco may write very well, but again, he does not answer the question. The question does not ask for personal experiences.
3 Lisa should use her own words. She may be penalised if she just copies words from the question as this does not show her ability to write.

Unit 25 pages 154–157

Vocabulary

1

1 systematic
2 investigate
3 observe
4 involve
5 influence
6 establish
7 procedure
8 consider
9 illustrate
10 distinguish

2

1 b
2 a
3 g
4 f
5 d
6 e
7 h
8 c

4

1 A
2 A
3 C
4 B
5 C
6 A
7 D
8 B

5

1 come as (no) surprise
2 forecast a result
3 incredibly accurate / accurate prediction
4 simple procedure / follow a procedure
5 controlled experiment / scientific experiment
6 lack of evidence / concrete evidence
7 cast doubt (over)
8 learn from (your) mistakes

Complex sentences and adverbial clauses

1

Suggested answers
The adverbial clause gives more information about:
1 **how often** something happened.
2 **where** something happened.
3 **how** something happened.
4 **why** something happened.
5 a **possible situation** and its **consequence**.

2

Suggested answers
1 he could predict football results.
2 someone other than his owner asked the questions.
3 he could not see the questioner.
4 carefully observing what happened.
5 many people were suspicious of his owner and his act.
6 he could see them.

Listening

2

1 c
2 d
3 a
4 e
5 b

Recording script 2 20

Speaker 1: I was really intrigued the other day when a friend of mine told me I had good 'emotional intelligence'. EQ. Not IQ, but EQ. I'd never heard of the term so I asked her what she meant. She said that whenever she was feeling a bit down, I seemed to say exactly the right thing to cheer her up. She remembered the time she didn't get accepted on a course she'd applied for and said that I'd come up with good suggestions about what to do – and actually she did get on the course later! I think it's true that I can tell what people are thinking or feeling even before they say anything. I'm sort of 'tuned in' to people.

Speaker 2: At college, I've noticed most people, when they meet, they kiss each other on the cheek or hug each other. And, well, I mean, it makes them seem really friendly but I feel a bit awkward when they expect me to act like that too. I don't know if it's a man thing or whether it's just me but it's just not my thing to hug or kiss when I meet someone. I never know what to do anyway – kiss on both cheeks, or just one? And which one? What's the rule? Why doesn't anyone teach you this kind of thing?

Speaker 3: It's interesting, my brother, who's a doctor, can never remember my birthday. If he's smart enough to become a doctor, why does he struggle with a simple date every 12 months? Someone once told me 'there's more than one type of intelligence' which explains a lot. Some people have a visual intelligence – they need to see information to be able to understand. There are auditory learners – they can absorb information best by listening to it. And then there are kinaesthetic learners who need to physically do something in order to learn. I did a quiz once, and it turns out I'm mainly visual but also kinaesthetic. I doubt whether this would help me find the quickest way of studying anything, but we'll see.

Speaker 4: I once took an intelligence test. Lots of numbers and shapes. I gave up after ten minutes. How is that supposed to measure my IQ? Maybe if you do enough intelligence tests, you become good at them, and then you get a huge score. I'm not good at numbers anyway. My wife is. She's like a human calculator. Ask her to write something, though, and she panics. She doesn't have much confidence when it comes to writing. Maybe someone said she wasn't good at it once, and she never bothered developing it. Some people are hopeless at reading maps, my mother for example, but my dad can't understand why she can't use one. Does it mean my dad is more intelligent than my mum? I don't think so.

Speaker 5: When I hear a song, once I've heard it just a couple of times, I can remember all the words. It's like a photographic memory, but with sounds. But I don't know whether it's the actual sounds, or it's just because when I hear a song, the music communicates a certain feeling and maybe that's what I latch on to. I get caught up in it and the words get attached to that feeling. It's like when people can remember exactly what music was playing at important times, like a soundtrack to their lives.

Revision Units 21–25

pages 158–159

2

1	throw
2	trap
3	beaten
4	black
5	map
6	postcard

3

while = concession
also = listing
that's why = result
to summarise = summing up

6

1	diplomat
2	challenger
3	innovator
4	challenger
5	innovator / diplomat
6	judge
7	expert
8	expert
9	judge / diplomat

The Cambridge English Corpus

Development of this publication has made use of the Cambridge English Corpus (CEC). The CEC is a computer database of contemporary spoken and written English, which currently stands at over one billion words. It includes British English, American English and other varieties of English. It also includes the Cambridge Learner Corpus, developed in collaboration with the Cambridge English Language Assessment. Cambridge University Press has built up the CEC to provide evidence about language use that helps to produce better language teaching materials.

English Vocabulary Profile

This product is informed by the English Vocabulary Profile, built as part of English Profile, a collaborative programme designed to enhance the learning, teaching and assessment of English worldwide. Its main funding partners are Cambridge University Press and Cambridge English Language Assessment and its aim is to create a 'profile' for English linked to the Common European Framework of Reference for Languages (CEF). English Profile outcomes, such as the English Vocabulary Profile, will provide detailed information about the language that learners can be expected to demonstrate at each CEF level, offering a clear benchmark for learners' proficiency. For more information, please visit www.englishprofile.org

The Cambridge Advanced Learner's Dictionary

The Cambridge Advanced Learner's Dictionary is the world's most widely used dictionary for learners of English. Including all the words and phrases that learners are likely to come across, it also has easy-to-understand definitions and example sentences to show how the word is used in context. The Cambridge Advanced Learner's Dictionary is available online at dictionary.cambridge.org. © Cambridge University Press, fourth edition, 2013, reproduced with permission.